Virtual Politics

Politics and Culture

A Theory, Culture & Society series

Politics and Culture analyses the complex relationships between civil society, identities and contemporary states. Individual books will draw on the major theoretical paradigms in politics, international relations, history and philosophy within which citizenship, rights and social justice can be understood. The series will focus attention on the implications of globalization, the information revolution and postmodernism for the study of politics and society. It will relate these advanced theoretical issues to conventional approaches to welfare, participation and democracy.

SERIES EDITOR: Bryan S. Turner, *Deakin University*

EDITORIAL BOARD

J.M. Barbalet, *Australian National University*
Mike Featherstone, *University of Teesside*
Stephen Kalberg, *Boston University*
Carole Pateman, *University of California, Los Angeles*

Also in this series

Welfare and Citizenship
Beyond the Crisis of the Welfare State?
Ian Culpitt

Citizenship and Social Theory
edited by *Bryan S. Turner*

Citizenship and Social Rights
The Interdependence of Self and Society
Fred Twine

The Condition of Citizenship
edited by *Bart van Steenbergen*

Nation Formation
Towards a Theory of Abstract Community
Paul James

Gender and Nation
Nira Yuval-Davis

Virtual Politics

Identity and Community in Cyberspace

edited by

David Holmes

SAGE Publications
London • Thousand Oaks • New Delhi

For Vasilka

Editorial arrangement, Introduction and Chapter 1 © David Holmes 1997
Chapter 2 © Cathryn Vasseleu 1997
Chapter 3 © Nicola Green 1997
Chapter 4 © Chris Chesher 1997
Chapter 5 © Simon Cooper 1997
Chapter 6 © Paul James and Freya Carkeek 1997
Chapter 7 © Michael J. Ostwald 1997
Chapter 8 © Michele Willson 1997
Chapter 9 © Mark Nunes 1997
Chapter 10 © Patricia Wise 1997
Chapter 11 © Christopher Ziguras 1997
Chapter 12 © Mark Poster 1997

First published 1997

SAGE Publications Ltd
6 Bonhill Street
London EC2A 4PU

SAGE Publications Inc.
2455 Teller Road
Thousand Oaks, California 91320

SAGE Publications India Pvt Ltd
32, M-Block Market
Greater Kailash – I
New Delhi 110 048

British Library Cataloguing in Publication data

A catalogue record for this book is available
from the British Library

ISBN 0 7619 5609 3
ISBN 0 7619 5610 7 (pbk)

Library of Congress catalog card number 97–069197

Typeset by Mayhew Typesetting, Rhayader, Powys
Printed in Great Britain by Redwood Books, Trowbridge, Wiltshire

CONTENTS

CONTRIBUTORS

Freya Carkeek is a lawyer and a graduate of the Department of Politics, Monash University, Australia. She currently works as a legal researcher.

Chris Chesher lectures in media and communication studies at the University of New South Wales, Sydney, Australia. His PhD research is an extended analysis of how computers can be thought of as invocational media.
(Email: c.chesher@lunsw.edu.au)

Simon Cooper is a post-graduate researcher at the Centre for Comparative Literature and Cultural Studies at Monash University, Australia. He is an editor of *Arena Journal* and is currently completing a doctoral thesis on the philosophy of technology.
(Email: arena@vicnet.net.au)

Nicola Green has recently returned from researching in the Department of Sociology, University of California (Berkeley), USA. She is currently completing a doctorate in the Department of Sociology at the University of Canterbury, Christchurch, New Zealand and is interested in the multiple interfaces between technologies, feminisms, body politics and 'cultures' of all kind.
(Email: n.green@soci.canterbury.ac.nz)

David Holmes lectures in sociology at Griffith University, Gold Coast, Australia. He is also currently a Visiting Associate with the T.R. Ashworth Centre for Social Theory at Melbourne University, Australia and with the International Social Sciences, University of Edinburgh, UK.
(Email: D.Holmes@gu.edu.au)

Paul James is an editor with Arena Publications and lectures in politics at Monash University, Australia. His publications include *Critical Politics: From the Personal to the Global* (1994), *The State in Question* (1996), *Nation Formation: Towards a Theory of Abstract Community* (1996) and *Work of the Future: Global Perspectives* (1997).
(Email: Paul.James@arts.monash.edu.au)

Mark Nunes teaches in the Humanities Department at DeKalb College in Atlanta, USA. He has published articles on postmodern and poststructural thought as applied to online culture and 'virtual topographies'. He is currently working on an exploration of the social spaces produced by electronic correspondences.
(Email: mnunes@dekalb.dc.peachnet.edu)

Michael J. Ostwald is Assistant Dean in the Faculty of Architecture at the University of Newcastle, Australia. He has lectured both in Australia and internationally on architectural theory and cyberspace. His research interests revolve around the relationship between non-linear mathematics and post-structuralist philosophy.
(Email: armjo@cc.newcastle.edu.au)

Mark Poster is Professor in History at the University of California (Irvine), USA. He has published widely on the sociology of information technology, including *The Mode of Information: Poststructuralism and Social Context* (1990) and *The Second Media Age* (1995).
(Email: mposter@benfranklin.hnet.uci.edu)

Cathryn Vasseleu is a Vice-Chancellor's Research Fellow in Philosophy at the University of New South Wales, Australia. She is the author of *Textures of Light: Vision and Touch in Irigaray, Levinas and Merleau-Ponty* (1998).
(Email: C.Vasseleu@unsw.edu.au)

Michele Willson is an editor of *Arena Magazine* and *Political Expressions* and is currently undertaking a PhD in the Department of Political Science, Monash University, Australia, looking at issues of technology and community.
(Email: mawil9@student.monash.edu.au)

Patricia Wise lectures in cultural studies at Griffith University, Queensland, Australia. She has researched and published in the areas of educational pedagogy, literature, gender and cultural policy, and undertaken commissioned research on the cultural industries and new media. Current research interests include gender and technologies, youth and cultural access, cultural development issues for dispersed urban settings, and women in Australian multimedia.
(Email: P.Wise@gu.edu.au)

Christopher Ziguras is completing a doctoral thesis in the Politics Department at Monash University, Australia, on the politics of self-help approaches to health care.
(Email: cziguras@mira.net)

ACKNOWLEDGEMENTS

This book would not have been possible without the enormous enthusiasm of all its contributors, who have seen it through from concept stage to the thematic cross-referencing which punctuates the text. For providing early encouragement with the book's concept I must convey my gratitude to Bryan Turner, Robert Rojek, Grace Tarpey, and the intellectual stimulation that has come out of my association with the political and theoretical frameworks of the Melbourne-based journal *Arena*. For assisting with the book's production in a variety of ways I am indebted to Grahame Griffin, Carolyne Mason, Nicole Bourke, Jean-Marc Hero, Nerinder Virdee and Vasilka Pateras. Finally I would like to thank most especially Peter Wise, whose thoroughness and dedication in working on several drafts of the manuscript was nothing short of immense.

INTRODUCTION:
Virtual Politics – Identity and Community in Cyberspace

David Holmes

Sony should be reading Walter Benjamin

(Bingham, 1991–2)

Of the myriad technological and cultural transformations taking place today, one has emerged to provide perhaps the most tangible opportunity for understanding the political and ethical dilemmas of contemporary society. The arrival of virtual reality and virtual communities, both as metaphors for broader cultural processes and as material contexts which are beginning to enframe the human body and human communication, has attracted considerable interest from social theorists, philosophers, and cultural and historical thinkers. As an embryonic force in the production of commodities, in workplace settings (architectural, medical and military) and as a commodity itself, virtual reality is one of the first high-technologies of the science fiction mould which made its impact as a substantive reality *before* entering the popular representations of Hollywood and such like (*Total Recall, The Lawnmower Man, Virtuosity, The Net,* and so on). As popular culture, VR iconography took part in the network of new wave sci-fi films of the late 1980s where, as Fred Glass points out in the American context, 'nuclear, computer, robotics, communications and gene-splicing technologies have advanced far enough into the daily lives of large segments of the U.S. population that social and psychological issues have emerged – both for individuals and the broader society – that require narrative symbolization' (1989: 5). What is presupposed by these films, as metaphoric dramatizations and stylizations of the human–technical relationship rather than simply science fiction, is that it is possible to recognize the technosocial realities that are increasingly surrounding us as material contexts – whether these concern the technological management of the body's senses (VR) or the electronic meeting place where disembodied communication takes place (cyberspace).

Some would argue that the technosocial realities that increasingly shape our lives have a world-constituting logic to them. This logic is one of the simulation and substitution of older forms of nature and culture, a logic

which, as Ed Regis suggests, referring to technologies of biosociality, is
driven by:[1]

> *Fin-de-siècle* hubristic mania . . . for perfect knowledge and total power . . . the
> power to remake humanity, earth, the universe at large. If you're tired of the ills
> of the flesh, then *get rid of the flesh*: we can *do* that now. If the universe isn't
> good enough for you, then *remake it*, from the ground up. (1990: 7; original
> emphasis)

The ability of human beings to replace, simulate and indeed reconstitute the
world by way of technoscience, and indeed *in* the image of technoscience, is
a significant historical development since World War II, a development in
which 'the secular and scientific myth of the conquest of nature could be
fused with the logic of commodity production' (Sharp, 1985: 65). Here
postmodern technoscience can be distinguished from earlier forms of
Enlightenment science in that it transforms its object – be this natural or
cultural – into the likeness of *scientific representation*. That is to say, postmodern technoscience does not just conform or adapt to given constraints in
the physical and natural world but makes redundant what it is simulating. In
doing so, it constructs more and more abstract worlds based on intellectual
technique: the ability analytically to break down reality into very small units
and put them together again on the basis of a very abstract understanding.[2]
This is true whether speaking of the human genome project, nanotechnol-
ogy, nuclear physics or the microchip. Increasingly, the commodities we
consume presuppose the application of one or more of these technologies
based on the simulation of the represented natural world.

Postmodern technoscience also differs from Enlightenment science in that
'human needs' are no longer given, they are as much a product of the way
the world is changed as are the commodities produced to satisfy them. And
here, the significance of cyberspace crashes through to the foreground.
Because, of all of the transformations of social contexts effected by postmodern technoscience, one kind is very special – the transformation of
modes of communication and information. That is, the material transformation of social context is today most spectacularly achieved not by the
manufacture of products which satisfy cultural, subsistence and bodily
needs, but by the conversion of the communicative and informational
contexts – modes of social integration and social recognition – in which
those needs arise.[3]

While postmodern technoscience has fused with commodity production
in a bewildering array of forms relating to physical and biological needs, it
has also created, through microchip and digital technologies, the conditions
for the convergence of communicative contexts in which the constraints of
time and space on our bodies are increasingly rendered redundant. Paradoxically, digital information and communication technologies based on
the microprocessor surround us in a more visibly cultural way than do the
object-technologies which remake the natural world. The reality of the
cyborg, for example, while an entirely appropriate aesthetic for postmodern

identity, is a barely visible part of everyday life. On the other hand, cyberspace is a world where new cultural forms are being created daily by technological mediation and extension, and created in a way which is immediate and active in people's lives. But to see how this is so requires escaping the idea that cyberspace is somehow used instrumentally to achieve things and satisfy an observable need.[4] As Mark Poster observes in Chapter 12, the Internet has the presence of an environment rather than a tool. The virtual technologies and agencies discussed throughout this book cannot be viewed as instruments in the service of pre-given bodies and communities, rather they are themselves contexts which bring about new corporealities and new politics corresponding to space-worlds and time-worlds that have never before existed in human history. This shift from viewing technology as a service to viewing it as context necessarily changes the very concept of 'usefulness' or utility that originally brought about virtual technologies. For example, the so far limited 'use' of cybernetic clothing to overcome the constraints of embodiment most typically results in the abolition of the very experience in which liberation from constraint can have a cognitive meaning. Similarly, the expanding use of the Internet as an imagined means of total knowledge in a globalized world empties out the identity of its participants and, therefore, the 'social' context in which the pursuit of knowledge can be thought of as a shared goal. Information, communication and media technologies which make this simulation possible should be seen not as instruments with which we do things, but as technologies which renovate the frameworks within which we do things, including what it might mean to do them.[5]

Paradoxically, while VR worlds such as the Internet can be seen as a kind of end product of the Enlightenment, as the Interrogate the Internet Group suggests,[6] it takes on a thorough-going anti-Enlightenment 'rhizomatic quality' stemming from 'an acentred web of connections in which any point of control can be so easily by-passed that such concepts of control are displaced and outmoded' (Shields, 1996: 9). So, while the Internet's driving ideology may be the creation of a *fin-de-siècle* mania which consists of 'a sense of mastery and escape from the limits of the frailties of incarnation' (Interrogate the Internet, 1996: 125), it creates an environment in which such a drive for control becomes empty of any reasons for continuing. That is to say, the rationality disappears, but the resultant, unintended context-world remains.

Back to virtual futures

But are virtual reality and cyberspace as new as we think? In what ways has virtual culture already typified the urban and communicational social realities of twentieth-century capitalist societies? A major theme which emerges in this book is that to understand VR is to find crystallized an appreciation of the already virtual. My own treatment of this question in Chapter 1 and Michael J. Ostwald's in Chapter 7 look at how virtual realities are already embodied in particular everyday technologies such as motor cars, television and shopping malls. It is only retrospectively, as if interpretation were waiting for a historical object, that VR becomes a powerful lens for identifying almost overnight what can be called 'the already virtual'. Particularly instructive here is the fact that the scenes most commonly represented in VR computer programs and games depict the analogue experiences of space- and time-altering technologies. For example common scenes used by VR realism are simulated forms of transporting bodies such as flight simulation,[7] car travel or even walking on a walking machine rather than along a path. The televisual scene created by VR is most commonly a simulation of a technological form which is itself a simulation, rather than a pretence at simulating random spaces. Unlike the unpredictability of everyday reality, virtual experiences are clean, pre-filtered and noise-free. As Simon Cooper observes in Chapter 5, citing Pimentel and Teixeira, VR is about simplifying and managing the real by 'presenting only those details essential for enhancing a specific experience, or solving a given problem'. And this also means screening out the interference of others in instrumentally getting to the experience we need or want.

Whether we are referring to the proliferation of screens, freeways, walkmans, walking machines or shopping malls, a central feature of these sealed environments is their depreciation of face-to-face interaction and mutual presence. Furthermore, in these environments our relations to our own bodies and to other individuals (embodied or represented) in space and time tend to be standardized, routinized, instrumentalized and simulated on the basis of a more abstract space and procedure of association. But before all else, the most instructive feature of these technological forms is that they can already be considered primitive virtual realities, the significance of which is dramatically magnified by the 'comprehensiveness' of virtual reality itself.

Take cinema as an example. Usually thought of in terms of entertainment and the mediation of cultural meaning, an examination of its early development in the nineteenth century shows that its inventors shared the same kind of dream about the infinite simulation of the real that contemporary VR enthusiasts have now. André Bazin, in a remarkable essay ('The Myth of Total Cinema'), indirectly shows how VR research was already effectively being undertaken by the pioneers of cinematography and animated photography in the mechanical reproduction of an integral realism, even though its complicated visualization preceded the industrial discoveries necessary for its development (Bazin, 1974). For Bazin, the development in the last half of the nineteenth century of the phenakistoscope, the zoetrope, the kinetoscope, the phonograph and the lampascope had all taken part in the

> guiding myth, inspiring the invention of cinema . . . the accomplishment of that which dominated, in a more or less vague fashion, all the techniques of the mechanical reproduction of reality in the nineteenth century, from photography

to the phonograph, namely an integral realism, a recreation of a world in its own image, an image unburdened by the freedom of interpretation of the artist or the irreversibility of time. (1974: 21)

He documents how the entrepreneurs of this 'integral realism' regarded cinema as a total and complete representation of reality; 'they saw in a trice the reconstruction of a perfect illusion of the outside world in sound, colour and relief' (Bazin, 1974: 20). Bazin's important point is that the pursuit of an integral realism through total cinema was motivated not by aesthetic concerns but by the realization of an onto-genetic realism: the obliteration of the difference between a screen and reality itself which, if not necessarily the result, was at least the ideology.[8]

Before its recent decline as an immersive, not-quite-total world of representation, cinema, with its dominating screen and invisible audience, was probably the closest approximation to what is today marketed as virtual reality.[9] While cinema is experienced in the company of a physically present audience, it can most easily be cast as the main forerunner to a range of individuating, personalizing technologies which encourage passive consumption rather than interactivity with others. On the other hand, to examine the scope of forms of simulation in information societies is to understand the more systemic ways in which different telecommunicative and transportational forms surround our lives, recentre our corporeal experience and alter our relations to the social body.

Simulation in cyberspace occurs either by participation in media which erase the distinction between representation and reality, as with cinema, television and video games, or by technologically renewing connections between individuals in ways which produce virtual communities based on extended interactivity, as with rapid transport, telecommunications and the Internet. The idea of *extension* is accented in Paul James and Freya Carkeek's chapter on forms of abstracting the body, via social and technical agents, particularly as they relate to sexual identity. Compatibility between different forms of technological extension is also discussed in several other chapters. The discussion of Margaret Morse's work in my own chapter attempts to show how the extended interactivity available through the growth of rapid human transport mirrors, on a number of levels, the experience of 'travel' afforded by globalizing communication technologies. This is further elaborated in Mark Nunes's discussion of the travelling and spatial metaphors of the information 'superhighway' and cyber*space* used to speak of the Internet. Nunes argues that if the spatial metaphorics of the Internet were to become our most familiar mode of engaging with the world, they would also become our meta-psychological foundation for re-experiencing physical motion, speed and travel. Negotiating Cartesian space would become mediated by technological simulation. More importantly, though, negotiating Cartesian space is no longer even desirable in the face of the seduction of cyberspace.

The popularization of 'cyberspace' as a space which somehow augments the world of Cartesian space by supposedly helping us to get around it

more easily denies the fact that cyberspace redefines this world, and substitutes for it a world in which space and time are internal to the Internet's
technological capabilities. By augmenting the world in this way, the
mobility promised by the Internet amounts to an informational equivalent
to the transportation of bodies. Continuity between these forms can be
illustrated by looking at what happens to motion, speed and travel when
the computer screen replaces the windscreen of a vehicle. It is easy to
switch by distraction between both states since the 'driver' can become the
fixed point around which the image moves in high speed review, or
alternatively experiences the world as an outcome of travel, be it 'through'
informational superhighways or vehicular ones. Once the sophistication of
a simulation machine such as the Internet attains a certain comprehensiveness for the user it ultimately outdoes the reality it thinks it is
traversing, or attempting to comprehend.

   The emergence of cyberspace and virtual reality therefore allows us to
grasp anew the general forms by which the time-worlds and space-worlds of
everyday modes of life increasingly become 'lifted out' by technologically
extended modes of interchange, taking the form of successive levels of 'new
nature' for the contemporary individual.[10] Because these modes of interchange bring about new forms of social *integration* they change the
everyday cultural ground – the taken-for-granted background conditions of
contemporary social life. New technologies of simulation and communication powerfully cohere to create immersive environments which displace
our experience of monumental, architectural and corporeal social and
urban references based on presence and mutual presence.[11]

   In Chapter 7 ('Virtual Urban Futures'), Michael J. Ostwald emphasizes
the importance of architecture in the formation of generalized experience,
thereby suggesting the relevance to the emergence of VR of the view that
twentieth-century urban forms already constitute primitive virtual environments. He argues that the filling out of urban spaces by computer networks,
telecommunications links, money markets and what he calls primitive
cyberspace is visibly beginning to supplant the existence of Cartesian space.
Comparing simulated urban spaces like the shopping mall to virtual electronic spaces, Ostwald shows how architectural design is becoming informed
by virtual mapping techniques like computer-aided design at the same time
as the super-structures (such as the malls) that we increasingly live with
already take on the characteristics of virtual space.

   While primitive cyberspace and earlier forms of virtual realities could not
be considered to be as interactive as they are in their contemporary form,
they nevertheless share qualities of extending space and time, of presenting
worlds which are immersive, privatized and disembodied. Successive waves
of communications and transportation technology displace modes of interchange which were founded on temporally and spatially 'closer' boundaries
of integration.[12] As technologies of extension they characteristically attenu-
ate presence by enabling only disembodied and abstract connections
between persons, where the number of means of recognizing another person

declines. In the 'use' of these technologies, be they Internet or freeways, the autonomy of the individual is enhanced at the point of use, but the socially 'programmed' nature of the technology actually prohibits forming mutual relations of reciprocity outside the operating design of the technological environment. At the same time, individuals are typically removed from control over the structure of the technology and increasingly lack the means to form relations independent of that structure. The logic is one of embracing what channelled autonomy can be gained from technologically 'finding connection in a disconnected world', as Howard Rheingold suggests in his celebration of the Internet.

Revisiting the humanities in a cyberspace era

The 'virtual imagination' displayed by Rheingold and the utopians of the Internet for the most part celebrates the new possibilities of re-anchoring culture and identity in ways that pass over the complications of industrial society. The promise of freedom from the constraints of the flesh and of communication with others that virtual realities offer paradoxically makes redundant the intellectual and critical concerns of social and political thought about the identities and subjectivities of high modernity.

Those movements in the humanities – structuralism and poststructuralism – which sought to evoke oppositional politics by problematizing or fictionalizing the individual can now be seen as a partly exhausted development, since the technosocial reality of the present has made criticism of older forms of individuality obsolete. Instead, with the emergence of processes of disembodiment represented by virtual reality culture, we are witnessing the critique of those forms of individuality *in practice*. We can no longer speak of unified 'actors' in social and political life, not because an ideological world – 'modernism' – no longer exists, but because human agency has radically changed its spatial, temporal and technological existence.

The trend towards disembodied ways of being human, brought about by virtual ontologies, has created crises for research-based approaches in the social sciences. An awareness emerges strongly that, in pre-virtual community models of understanding, space-time relations have remained largely untheorized. For example, what once went by the name of 'behaviour' can no longer be studied as it once was. The way that cognitive psychology and social psychology constitute the individual as an object of research becomes more difficult to sustain. The altered states of the subjects of information capitalism problematize the behavioural sciences in one way, but the new understandings that VR brings about afford a realization that 'behaviour' has never existed. Social action cannot be reduced to historical space-time relations, but has always existed beyond these relations by way of various mediations. The accommodation of such a realization places the more positivistic domains of the social sciences in great difficulty, as the object of ethnographic research finds itself eclipsed by the surfaces of electronically mediated identities. Take, for example, the study of child behaviour in classrooms. The classrooms are still there, the students are still there, but because students today are more likely to be interacting with computer terminals, studying their behaviour becomes somewhat antiquated. We can look at their interaction with computers or the layout of classrooms and how this affects their relations with one another, but we cannot gauge the abstracted sense in which the *use* of computers, conventionally conceived as tools of extending institutional ends, is far less important than the fact that the students are participating in worlds of recognition whose borders radically exceed the classroom and all of the institutional norms and authority which go with it.

At the same time as research has to be reconceived in a post-cyberspace world, the traditional concerns of political theory – such as complex issues of social equality – are being comprehensively supplanted by a flight towards questions of ontology. Where once social and political analyses concerned themselves with matters of exchange, production, consumption and integration as the departure point, today there is a retreat, which is also an advance, towards understanding those primary ontologies, or domains of existence – language, the body, time and space – which social thought had always worked with but had not included in its analysis. A forerunner to this was the attention given to language during the period that became known as the linguistic turn. The great model of language became a new referential setting for considering questions of power, subjectivity, otherness and identity, and, through this consideration, critical upheavals of traditional models of social and cultural life. More recently, the turn to categories of space, time and the body, and historicity (including speculations concerning 'the end of history') have followed at an astonishing pace.

Just as questions of social formation and individuality could not be addressed without examining the constructive role of language in the making of culture and cultural difference, today the new ontologies of space, time and corporeality are increasingly given a pre-sociological status. There are different responses to the demand this produces. On the one hand, there is the possibility of a return to first philosophies – reviewing, for example, Kant's theory of internal body sense (proprioception), which Cathryn Vasseleu examines in Chapter 2. On the other, accounts can be developed of how social life is already composed of various microworlds in which technology is only a random element in the determination of behaviour, which Simon Cooper explores in Chapter 5. The architectural theory that Michael J. Ostwald puts forward clearly becomes drawn into the centre of the latter concern – while the political, sexual and cybernetic investigation of the body in contemporary information societies, dealt with in most of the chapters here, also becomes an indispensable precursor to new directions in social thought.

There are, however, broader concerns carrying over from pre-virtual social theory which go a long way towards explaining the rise of technoculture and technosociality as a level of social being. While the inward-looking attention now given to 'primary' ontologies makes problematic the foundations of much sociological theory, there are strands within social theory which are able to contextualize historically the changes that have elevated the importance of ontology to an understanding of the contemporary lifeworld. The resurgence of interest in the work of Georg Simmel can be seen as an attempt to reclaim a formalized sociology adequate to the present, insofar as he has already theorized in a general way many of the spatio-temporal questions of social theory that are now becoming indispensable to its reconstruction.[13] For example, in this volume Cooper's discussion of microworlds looks at the way task-oriented consciousness places limits on our perception of our environment and generates new cognitive frames, where some elements of the physical world may acquire an extraordinary intensity and others become invisible.

Since the 1970s social geographers and urban sociologists have also been pointing to the inadequacy of one-dimensional models of social composition which produced rather prosaic investigations of the relationship between individuals, institutions and 'society' without theorizing the assumptions of corporeality underlying these. More recently, Anthony Giddens has advanced accounts of space-time distanciation which prefigure the role of pre-virtual agents such as money, travel, time clocks and writing in extending social relations (see particularly Giddens, 1990: 17–54). As Giddens points out, one of the consequences of the evolution of modernity, via such agents, is the resulting separation of time from place and space from place, which creates what he calls disembedded social systems or 'the "lifting out" of social relations from local contexts of interaction and their restructuring across indefinite spans of time-space' (1990: 21).

Through their concern for ontological questions underpinning and facilitating transformations from local to global forms of culture, these domains in social thought had already been theorizing virtual reality before it emerged as a more coherent technological form. In investigating the 'already-virtual' dimensions of modern societies, the present volume continues this trajectory of thought as a political and social theory *of* cyberspace, at the same time as it is also a revision of social theory in a post-cyberspace world. Arranged thematically, theorizations of technology, the body and the self (Part I), and community, social context and political culture (Part II) are refracted through an examination of cyberspace.

Space, a final frontier?

The insistent question of space and its relation to politics recurring throughout this volume invokes an examination of the two senses of cyberspace: as an entertainment space of consumption and as an electronic meeting place. This bifurcation corresponds to two dominant trends in information societies today – the personalization of cultural spaces and the globalization of cultural space. While the emergence of cyberspace forces us to reconsider the relationship between space and politics, the human–technical interface occurring at the personalized computer terminal and in the everyday use of personal virtual technologies also requires a reassessment of questions of human perception and the body.

Cathryn Vasseleu's chapter, 'Virtual Bodies/Virtual Worlds', is an instructive example of how virtual reality and cyberspace facilitate a re-examination of key thinkers in philosophical and social thought and, at the same time, enable a better understanding of the role of corporeality, observation and the dynamics of mind/body relations in everyday experience. In looking at the implications of virtual reality for ethics, politics and embodiment, Vasseleu suggests that the metaphysics of computer simulation was already articulated in the Copernican revolution as a theoretical paradigm of the necessity of universal illusions. For a truth-claim in which the stakes were extremely high indeed, Copernicus ventured to reject the idea of the earth as centre of the universe – in opposition to his senses – and in so doing opened up the establishment of synthetic forms of knowledge in which the subjective embodiment of observation becomes a heightened factor in epistemology. Exploring the treatment of this idea in Kant, Jonathan Crary and Paul Virilio, Vasseleu suggests that the utopian ethos of virtual reality is that it frees up the body as a factor in epistemology because the 'cognitive mastery of an objective world is indirectly realizable through an apparatus which offers a fantastic command of (cyber)space' (p. 48). By the simple existence of its technical possibility, this development has problematized *in fact* – in practice rather than in theory – the nature of representation in the contemporary world, just as it also problematizes the nature of the individual as subject of vision. Vasseleu takes up Crary's argument in *Techniques of the Observer* that, since the early nineteenth century, fabricated visual spaces (such as those deriving from optical techniques) have slowly managed to substitute for and displace corporeal space-worlds in which observation once had a meaning. Vision itself becomes transposed to a layer of cognition in which the subject is no longer opposed to an object in the traditional sense of observation and enquiry (Crary, 1990: 1). The problem for metaphysics of making the object conform to knowledge is resolved by a technology which guarantees a comprehensive control over the object's production for our senses. Vasseleu's analysis connects with a recurring theme throughout the book that virtual reality has menaced the idea that knowledge must somehow conform to the object. Instead, the objective world increasingly conforms to grids of perception because of the ways we are changing it.

VR is the only environment *other than politics* for which truth is *not* determined as the adequacy of knowledge to reality. Throughout the Western philosophical tradition, manifold theories or 'epistemologies' have been elaborated aimed at assessing how well our understandings refer to, describe or explain 'the real'. The enduring assumption in these is that 'the real' is relatively fixed and its truth revealed by seeing it adequately. However, where the real becomes highly unstable as a result of the ability to remake it over and over in a manner both comprehensive and spontaneous, we are compelled to turn our attention away from this reality and towards the logic of technoscience. This logic is one in which a fabulous reversal occurs between the fixity of the real and representation. Whereas, in modernity, science was a matter of representing the world adequately so that we might better control it, today it is as if science changes the world in a form in which our representations of it seem more and more adequate. The ideal does not conform to the real; the real conforms to the ideal. The world, once immovable and mysterious, and the object of many perspectives of understanding, no longer possesses depth, no longer resists our interrogations because it can be made redundant by simulation. The pre-virtual sensibility of working with thing-concepts whereby experience is always moving towards the real is menaced by the fact that we can bring the real to us in whatever form we so desire and, in doing so, abolish the real.

Abolishing the real, Nicola Green argues in Chapter 3, is something that occurs as a misconception by which we immerse ourselves in virtual worlds in the first place. Immersion in virtual systems is not a purely disembodied experience but demands grounding in prior forms of experience developed in social worlds of meaning and materiality. Green's distinctive contribution to understanding embodiment in virtual systems is to demonstrate that the human–technical interface necessarily draws its reference from pre-virtual social relations, even though it effaces embodiment in those relations. Green argues that recent literature theorizing the phenomenon of virtual embodiment does so from an overwhelmingly meaning-centred approach which is unable to accommodate the anthropological terrain of this reality. To account more adequately for the ways in which human bodies encounter virtual reality technologies, virtual embodiment needs to be theorized as a simultaneous state in which the subject is situated as both digitally and materially embodied, engaging in the perception and manipulation of both objects and representations across the two forms of reality at the same time. The mode of embodiment realized by immersive virtual reality technologies is situated in a kind of transitivism between the symbolic and technological realities of cyberspace.

Current debates about immersive virtual reality technologies are concerned almost exclusively with the cultural content of digital worlds and the digitally embodied experiences under construction in these human/computer systems. A perspective limited to cultural representation and meaning within digital worlds erases the construction of an embodied negotiation of the very technological systems that enable representation in first place. As such, any reflection on the phenomenological elements of material action and interpretation is effectively excluded wherever individuals construct understandings of their embodied states in encounters with digital worlds. Following the recent work of Zoë Sofia and Don Ihde, Green explores a phenomenology of virtual embodiment around four levels of human/technology relations: the extension of the senses by technology; the extension of signification and meaning by technological means; the projection of human forms onto the world of computers; and the taking-for-granted of technical systems as the background context of contemporary culture. What emerges in her analysis is that 'cyberspace' is not at all a unified space but a complex fusion of levels of realizing embodiment, a 'mutual co-constructedness of technologies and cultures'. Viewed thus, 'cyberspace' cannot simply be understood as a place of liberation from the constraints of embodiment, but as itself a culturally constructed term for the ambiguity that faces the corporeal place of the modern subject in highly informationalized cultures.

That the subject of virtual reality might be caught between intersecting ontological worlds is something Paul James and Freya Carkeek also understand as a general contradiction, one which is implicit in the way information has come to overlay forms of cultural exchange and connectedness in which the body is figured as a primary agent. They outline an anthropological approach to a genealogy of the body which historicizes it according to levels of abstraction. In specifying levels of social integration based on mediated forms of presence, James and Carkeek argue that historically the body has been a site of symbolic condensation through which community and integrative practices are filtered. They investigate this claim through illustrations of kinship and sexual relations which address forms of embodied/disembodied reciprocity from tribal to postmodern settings. What becomes the most important agent in the forms of solidarity or community is essentially recognition relations between individuals. Although only analytically distinguishable from each other, different forms of human interaction – be they embodied in face-to-face relations, extended via agents and institutions or abstracted through information – become generalized in different historical societal forms to a point where they can be said to constitute the dominant mode of social *integration*. The study of specific cultural forms is then a matter of examining which form predominates, and how the subordinate forms intersect with it. The question can be asked, for example: what is the meaning of embodiment in a society in which we are, before all else, formed and linked to others via information (so that even while we are not plugged into the Internet it still frames our lives)? James and Carkeek reveal that one consequence of informational dominance is the discarding of those aesthetics and politics that emerge from the body as a locus of integration. The instrumental and cultural aspects of information make of the body an impediment to be left behind as soon as technologically possible, at the same time ignoring the values of mutuality, continuity and co-operation that a cultural appreciation of embodiment sustains. For example, the cultural status of given names in information settings is problematized because normative Internet procedures enable and encourage pseudonyms for some kinds of communication. The possibility of appreciating the 'personal history' of a communicative agent is disavowed, with authorship removed to an anonymous pluralism of hypertextuality.

James and Carkeek's emphasis on the importance of recognition relations and their mediation by successive levels of abstraction usefully frames questions of politics and community in virtual worlds. By far the most important theme to emerge in their chapter is how the investigation of primitive and 'advanced' cyberspace brings to light not only new technological forms of interaction and 'embodiment' but also the ways in which these forms work together to reconstitute social contexts whereby we come to recognize others in our social world – the formation of community.

Raising the possibility of community in cyberspace begs a number of questions about its status as a context world. Does cyberspace constitute a public sphere? If so, can it co-exist alongside traditional public realms or is it in fact likely to supplant them? What role might the Internet play in breaking down divisions between public institutions and domestic spaces? In part, answering such questions means drawing attention to the multiple forms of cyberspace, even the multiple forms of Internet. But while the Internet is often put forward as a form of public sphere, many of the authors in this volume would disagree, arguing that the Internet constitutes an attenuation of that sphere.[14] As Mark Poster notes in his chapter,

> the notion of a public sphere suggests an arena of exchange, like the ancient Greek agora or the colonial New England town hall. If there is a public sphere on the Internet, who populates it and how? In particular one must ask what kinds of beings exchange information in this public sphere? Since there occurs no face-to-face interaction, only electronic flickers on a screen, what kind of community can there be in this space? (pp. 216–17)

Poster is asking whether or not the Internet possesses enough stability for the ongoing recognition of members of Internet communities and the stability of their own senses of self. In doing so, he echoes Steven Jones's concern in *CyberSociety* that '[i]n a near entirely ephemeral world, how does an individual, much less a community, maintain existence?' (1995: 6) To carry this further: if individuals, or even their functional substitutes, do not have substance in cyberspace, is it appropriate or even relevant to ask the cluster of questions traditionally applicable to any public sphere: does free speech, the democratic right of (electronic) assembly, political representation – indeed, does citizenship itself – exist in cyberspace? If these questions are no longer relevant, their irrelevancy becomes even more serious when we begin to read them back into settings of primitive cyberspace. For Poster, though, they are questions which remain relevant insofar as the Internet allows us finally to break with broadcast forms of media, and community thus finds possibility in the solidarity of interactivity. This interactivity is the very aspect of the Internet that has supplanted the first media-age culture industry of radiated communication.

Insofar as the electronically reified space of the Internet displaces institutional habitats, it breaks down hierarchies of race, class and particularly gender. By allowing the construction of oppositional subjectivities hitherto excluded from the public sphere, the Internet's inherently decentralized form is heralded as its most significant feature. This, Poster argues, allows the Internet to subvert political authority, which has imbued the European model of institutional life since the Middle Ages. As cyberspace identities are experienced in much more mobile and fluid forms, the public sphere enlarges in the midst of state apparatuses but, at the same time, acts to undermine statist forms of control. This tension is partly played out in those state-originating anxieties concerned as much with the encryption of information against cyber-terrorism as with the use of communications technologies in surveillance. But an examination of the architecture of cyberspace relations shows that the newer, extended electronic public sphere defies the kinds of instrumental and centralized control that have traditionally been accompanied by practices of normalization and regulation.

Compared to broadcast forms of media, the Internet indeed offers free-ranging possibilities of political expression and rights of electronic assembly which encounter far fewer constraints, whether technical, political or social. However, the economic dimensions of the Internet can often be overlooked when trading off the political virtues of cyberdemocracy against broadcast. If the Internet does enable a community of speech which transcends institutional life, is a cost attached? Though Poster and Rheingold have blamed the relative inflexibility of broadcast for producing an even more intense need for community, we might well ask with Rheingold: 'Is the human need for community going to be the next technology commodity?' (1993: 61).

It is precisely around the question of community formation that the commodification question arises. Rather than enabling virtual communities, the Internet continues the population-constituting operation that is endemic to broadcast, namely the partitioning of a mass into atomized units. The Internet can be posited as parasitic on the nuclearizing process that broadcast achieves, though it opens the possibility of commodifying cultural needs in far more comprehensive and monopolistic ways than broadcast does. Broadcast commodification involves selling the concentration spans of audiences to advertisers. The Internet exploits the dissolution of compositional and geographic community by selling lost levels of social integration to consumers in the form of time-charging for human communication. An economic analysis of the Internet therefore draws in issues of universal access, economic control and stratifications of information wealth, and information poverty, as well as the exploitation of a historically produced human condition: the loss of less mediated, and therefore less commodifiable, forms of community. As the 'next technology commodity', it is remarkable that cyberspace appeals to a need for community given its quality as a comprehensively manufactured space.

Nor does the paradox end there, because to think with a term such as space is itself problematic, as both Chris Chesher and Mark Nunes suggest in their chapters. Both engage with the empirical detail of the Internet's technical structure, not to provide guides for first-time users, but to produce critical appraisals of misconceptions about the Internet, including the misconception of it as a space. In Chapter 4, 'The Ontology of Digital Domains', Chesher charts the technical structure and conditions of the Internet by considering the computer as a projection into electronics of the modern technological project explored by Martin Heidegger in 'The Question Concerning Technology'. For Chesher, unlike a public domain, the digital domain does not pre-exist the individual but places 'the real' on call by generating a symbolic 'standing reserve' which becomes an operative resource of meaningful action. What Chesher describes as an invocational calling process forces the real to be revealed as digital representation. Just as technology in general is a mode of 'revealing' the world by way of enframing a small number of its elements, as Heidegger suggests, computer-based technologies effectively displace the real by revealing it only according to grids translatable into digital code. However, in Chesher's terms, it is important to realize that the digital domain is not a spatial reality, as suggested by the term 'cyberspace'; it inheres instead in the reality of poeisis or potentiality. Space is collapsed on the Internet because the physical location of machines is irrelevant to our connection to them. It is then necessary to think of computerized identity as related to the act of calling up information at a particular time. The real is removed from the spatial, and both are stored up and 'enframed' in the form of code.

In 'What Space is Cyberspace? The Internet and Virtuality' (Chapter 9), Mark Nunes discusses Baudrillard's account of telematics to explore the geographical metaphors of the Internet. The cultural popularizing of the Internet as an 'Information Superhighway' can be seen as driven in part by the iconography of pioneering attached to the highway grid at the moment when, paradoxically, that grid is being displaced by the rise of virtual landscapes which are somehow superior to terrestrial highways. Impelling this image of the Internet as a 'superhighway' is, according to Nunes, a certain will to power which merely continues historical ideologies of totalization. By being constructed metaphorically as a conquest of space, through an equally illusory notion that it is possible to travel in 'cyberspace', power is effectively 'transferred from the real to the hyperreal', enabling a fulfilment of a modernist drive towards mastery of the world. But this mastery is only made possible in a postmodern setting if 'the world' is effectively reduced and replaced.

Cyberspace is seductive for those pursuing the illusion of total knowledge because the Internet has no frontier – its territory has always already been exhaustively mapped in advance. Each journey is a repetition, there is no undiscovered country, no exploration of discovering, only the recovering of what is already 'there'. Nunes here agrees with Chesher's point that cyberspace is not a space at all; no 'site' exists beyond its retrieval or invocational parameters. The Internet ultimately becomes a fabulous system of self-referentiality, an illusion of totality, which is nevertheless a totality with every chance of success precisely because it never has to go beyond itself.

The analyses offered by Chesher and Nunes indicate that the Internet cannot supply the conditions for democratic speech, even if participants believe that they are in an arena of open discourse and exchange. The image of the Internet produced by both accounts is as a two-dimensional surface where electronic assemblies are programmed and conditioned by switching systems. The Internet is not capable of three-dimensional democratic assembly, nor an assembly of general will. Accordingly, there can be no protest on the Internet, no collective decision-making, no consensus or agreement which represents the will of a mass. The only consensus is a technologically congealed one whereby Internet users agree to a means of communication in which both consensus and the mass itself have been abolished. Unlike the agora or its contemporary extension – broadcast – the Internet does not enable the objectivation and consolidation of a general will: the relation of the many to the many.[15] But if the Internet is not a space in the tradition of an agora or assembly, how can the possibility of virtual communities be entertained at all?

Anyone choosing to pass over this question would still need to confront the political and ethical dilemmas of abstract communities posed by Michele Willson in Chapter 8. Willson reviews recent literature dealing with the crises of geographic communities as they are usurped by techno-sociality at the very moment that community in its virtual form is being celebrated. In considering these two very different kinds of community, the fate of the Other and otherness becomes an index of the possibility of meaningful togetherness. Willson suggests that the presence of the Other in simulated worlds is more and more being emptied out to produce a purely intellectual engagement, and possibilities of commitment to co-operative or collective projects become one-dimensional or, at best, self-referential. '"Community" is then produced as an ideal, rather than as a reality, or else it is abandoned altogether' (p. 146).

Willson approaches the issue of community by considering the relationship between computerization in public administration (as surveillance and database technology) and the Internet, noting how both kinds of digital regime manage to compartmentalize populations by homogenizing and physically isolating individuals from each other. This cellularization of the population by workstation or homepage creates the conditions in which community becomes re-valued as something that could be potentially lost. Herein lie some of the most central paradoxes of virtual community which the chapter explores. Alienation becomes a precondition of togetherness, control of the population through surveillance a condition of fraternity, the universalization of computing commodities a condition of equality. At the same time our bodies must become invisible before they can be liberated.

Willson raises the question of cyberspace community in the context of Jean-Luc Nancy's discussion of community as the recognition of difference rather than commonality. What is instructive in the work of Nancy is the sense that community cannot simply be allocated the kind of system of commonalities that the celebrants of virtual worlds promote. Community is not something to be constructed through a piece of technology, it cannot be consciously made by some collective realization that we are in danger of 'losing' it. Instead, for Nancy, it is a function of the place where individual experiences have their meeting. The suggestion that the Internet will save us from the loss of community is founded on a premise that community has to find an agent of commonality. This agent is usually transcendental and historically there have been many contenders for such a role: the Mind, God, the fatherland, Leader, Internet. To impose and presuppose community in the name of the transcendent is to disregard it since, for Nancy, community cannot be presupposed and the thinking of community as essence is the closing off of the political (Nancy, 1991: xxxviii). Individual selves are unable to find community by looking to the glory of the infinite. Rather, it is in realization of finitude that selves are able to experience being-in-common, an experience which is always negotiated and renegotiated in the never-ending perception of difference between individual selves by which ethical responsibilities and forms of respect are arrived at. In this sense we can never lose community. Instead: 'Community is made from what retreats from it' (Nancy, 1991: xxxix). It is in refusing essence that community is realized:

> By taking it as a rule of analysis and thought, we raise the question: how can the community without essence (the community that is neither 'people' nor 'nation', neither 'destiny' nor 'generic humanity,' be presented as such? That is, what might a politics be that does not stem from the will to realize an essence? (Nancy, 1991: xxxix–xl)

The import of the latter question for assessing virtual communities very much depends on what those communities consist in, and what brings them about. If it is a will to presence, or a will to power derived from transcendence, then, in Nancy's terms, the Internet, and the discourses of totality that surround it, is the latest incarnation of the infinite and the transcendent. On the other hand, the eulogizing of the Internet as a horizontal meeting place, a decentred, untotalizable medium unlike any that has existed before, suggests a place in which the realization of finitude is generalized. Resolving these two very different politics of virtual communities, the technical and social structure of the Internet, and the kinds of rationalities which promote and participate in it requires much reflection.

Further, the kinds of subjectivity that exist on the Internet may not actually possess enough substance to realize the finitude that Nancy speaks of. It is true that the Internet promises us the ability to communicate ever greater difference within the unity of a singular medium, but what is the basis for commitment to that difference? Pluralism on the Internet may be entirely generated though a play of masks in which difference does not actually have to be confronted because it can be manipulated. Raising the possibility of infinite, because ungrounded, multiplicity heralds simultaneously a kind of death to an aesthetic of difference and a closing off of the political.

Political identity in cyberspace

Given the instability of cyberspace as a public sphere or space of community in the traditional sense, what is the place of the individual within it?
And if there is a place for the individual at all, what kind of 'subject'
speaks or writes or communicates in these conditions? Although cyberspace
(albeit paradoxically) increases our experience of mobility, our ability to
map a place or social location in the world becomes problematized. In
everyday language this is evident in our increasing need to 'put back' into
our descriptions of the world the things that are otherwise given. It is now
sometimes necessary to speak of doing things in 'real time' or to refer to
our 'geographical' location rather than our location. Under these conditions, we can actually gain greater security by tying our identity to the
very objects that are fragmenting older 'Cartesian' spaces. As a substitute
for the world, the computer becomes a second self (see Turkle, 1984). We
can organize our own world on the desktop, arranging everything according to our own private sense of order and, no matter how chaotic the world
beyond the screen becomes, we can return to the safety of our terminal,
thinking of ourselves more and more in its image.[16]

Our enhanced control over the arrangement of icons on our desktops
and our ability to call up, predictably and instantly, bookmarked homepages, programs and CD-ROM information contrast sharply with our
immersion in an uneven, ever-changing and thus unmappable structure
of cyberspace. This, in turn, raises the problem of what happens to an
experience of the 'local' on the Internet, when the significance of the
computer screen transforms from a second self which is manageable to a
terminal window into diaspora. Is there such a thing as a sense of the local
on the Internet anyway, whether we are talking about Multi-User Dimensions, Usenet, Internet Relay Chat or an institutional email group, or is the
Internet more like another country? As Shields points out, the Internet is
an outcome of multiple histories and localities – and it is therefore
important to 'treat computer-mediated communications networks as *local*
phenomena, as well as global networks' (1996: 3; original emphasis). But
individual producers and consumers of content have little control over the
dissemination of material because any determined content can be repeated
outside its context of production, where it may assume an entirely different
role.[17]

When the experience of a sense of place and the possibility of producing
meaning are as decentred as they are in cyberspace, there are far fewer
prospects for co-operative political projects to develop than in other kinds
of public sphere. As Nguyen and Alexander (1996) argue, political
dialogues on the Internet are also quite transient and directionless, seldom
acquiring a substantive enough history to constitute a political movement.
We also find on the Internet less concern with expressing protest than with
expressing individual autonomy and lifestyle politics. Whether these
articulate attitudes to cyberpunk, anarchism, hacker culture, liberal rights

groups, New Age beliefs or computer utopia groups (which tend to be self-referential), all rely on ideas of global totality, or on drawing their powers from a sense of totality, while simultaneously believing that a virtual public sphere guarantees unchecked political freedom.

On the World Wide Web, radical 'groups' – which may be nothing more than websites – promote the use of the Internet as a subversive agency. Such is the case with the anarchist collective 'Bad Subjects'. Their homepage advertises itself as 'Political education for everyday life'. Since this slogan attempts to appeal to Internet participants, whose everyday is at least partly lived on the screen, the very idea of everyday life becomes problematic. It might be argued, for example, that a collective and co-operative politics against the state is impossible, and actually displaced, on the Internet. Moreover, like hacker culture, anarchist occupations of the Internet can be seen as almost exclusively reactive to the fact that the modern technocratic state has a near legitimate monopoly over the control of surveillance data. This raises the question of what kind of subversion actually goes on within the Internet if these political cultures are taken to be undermining technocratic monoliths. Do Internet anarchist movements, for example, subvert the actual authority of state apparatuses in the way power operates through them? Or does the Internet subvert only a construction of the public sphere which is invented on its behalf?

Another common form of Internet politics involves liberal concerns for citizenship. Rather than being a tool for the subversion of the state, the Internet is regarded in such formulations as a place for the continuation of citizenship – a citizenship which circulates mainly around neo-classical ideals of contracts between individual interests. The Internet is occupied by countless advocacy and liberal rights groups, each concerned with individuals' consumer and political sovereignty, thus duplicating the pressure groups found in civil society. Interestingly these Internet groups are heavily dominated by discourses which advocate rights on the net before rights in the institutional world and workplace. Again, we have to raise the question of how the political demands of these advocacy groups connect as recognition networks in which structural political agency operates in its economic, ideological and legal forms. Here, an investigation of the potential of the virtual worlds to bypass or displace institutional politics is clearly needed. At the same time, an account of the meaning of political constitution via these worlds is central to an appraisal of the status of democracy and representation in virtual communities. What, for example, is the point of extending political representation with the Internet if what is extended – political voice – is emptied out by the very process of extension?

Given the transient and one-dimensional status of political groups on the Internet, it is also useful to ask which kinds of political identity within late capitalism are most compatible with, and at home in, virtual culture. That is: how does VR express cultural trends in late capitalism, and how is it represented in popular and political consciousnesses? These are questions which Simon Cooper and Christopher Ziguras address. Cooper's chapter, 'Plenitude and Alienation: The Subject of Virtual Reality', examines virtual identity as a political subjectivity which, rather than opposing late instrumental-capitalist culture, expresses an ego-logical pre-occupation with self-autonomy and solipsistic auto-creation. Taking up Fredric Jameson's claim that the construction of private object worlds is a defining feature of reified postmodern society, Cooper attributes the utopian status of VR, in its private consumption, to the promise of tran-scending fragmented contemporary social relations. But the ideal subject of VR is less interested in 'leaving the body' to achieve this transcendence than in having unlimited control over its spontaneous reconstruction and in the experience of that construction. Cooper argues that there is a significant distance between the utopian ideology of VR and the transformations that take place in its practical use. Utopian attitudes to VR as liberating creativity are particularly problematic. Cooper asks: 'How are we to speak of creativity when the technology of VR works to reconstitute the phenomenological experiences that determine subjectivity?' (pp. 100–1). VR's claims to creativity are utterly dependent on its being cut adrift from the social and physical consequences of the processes and events it simulates. Such a separation only reaffirms VR's solipsism at the same time as producing socially referenced fantasies by allowing a VR character to act towards the world without being accountable, in a reciprocal sense, to another identity. By solipsistically dispensing with prior frames of social reference such as labour and history, VR also eliminates the conditions that generate the initial desire to be creative. As a project, VR is incapable of creativity in any sense that could be objectivated with others. Cooper reveals that, instead of constituting a movement of liberation, VR renews through new kinds of commodification the social fragmentations that it seeks to overcome.

A more direct connection between virtual reality and social movements is explored in Christopher Ziguras's examination of cyberdelia as an out-growth of New Age movements (Chapter 11). Ziguras shows how New Age constructions of the sacred are based on forms of religiosity which spiritualize high technologies such as VR. Attempts by New Age techno-physics to link thought, energy and physical form reveal less a critique of scientization than a renewal of it through the promotion of the very relations of fluidity which lie at the centre of post-industrial management processes and technical rationalities. Rather than romanticizing the systemic fluidity of the physical and natural worlds, the new spiritualism is highly solipsistic, appropriating any available technological means for the autonomous and private creation of experiential realities which are changeable at will. Ziguras notes that attaining this fluidity and inde-pendence from given relations of constraint and embodiment demands a form of autonomous subjecthood which, as a condition of its autonomy, must paradoxically deny its own construction. He is particularly critical of the New Age's inability to reflect on the social and cultural influences behind its current fetishism of cyberspace holism. As a project, the New Age advances a philosophy of self in which it is necessary to strive for the techniques that can peel away layers of socialization to reveal an authentic pre-social subjectivity. The kind of subjectivity that demands discovery, however, is one which is not confined to the constraints of being in time and space; it is a subjectivity which is 'in control' of the conditions of its experience. This particular drive for autonomy over experiential states is not something to be achieved collectively through some form of social determination. It is realized at the level of personal biography, of managing the conditions in which the private self finds itself. And it may be reached in various ways: channelling, psychic healing, miniature pyramids, perception-enhancing drugs or personal growth techniques, all of which find their nemesis in technological possibilities of managing perception such as VR.

Another political dimension broached in this volume is the gender politics of representation in and use of cyberspace. The hubristic mania of total knowledge that Cooper and Nunes uncover as driving the Internet also has consequences for a feminist politics of cyberculture, which Patricia Wise discusses in her chapter, 'Always Already Virtual: Feminist Politics in Cyberspace'. Wise suggests that the ways in which cyberspace is marketed as an imaginary place of domination to be explored and conquered achieve a 'totality' which cannot be reproduced in the real. In addition, the immersion of men in cyberculture is a continuation of the mind/body divide in Western culture in which virtual worlds are made over as an extension of male rationality. Central to this divide is the 'feminizing' of computer-generated worlds by male users according to a fantasy of uninvolved interface. Virtual spaces provide men with a totalizing illusion of control and 'interaction' with an environment where the risk provided by reciprocal embodiment is minimized. In this way, participation in any aspect of cyberspace is merely an extension of the fantasy of uninvolved sex, a generalized pornography of intellectualizing intersubjectivity as the only safe way of realizing it. Wise explores the legacy of this relation as a derivative of the Western fantasy of reason, which continues to distribute gender across the division of mind and body so that the feminine becomes, in relation to cyberspace, relegated to the virtual as an ideal: seductive in its possibilities but made safe because virtuality is also about being 'not quite there'.

Wise seeks to turn this alignment of the feminine with virtuality towards a feminist politics which recasts women as the always already virtual of cyberspace communities. Women are ideally placed for citizenship of virtual communities, not because they can be objectified there, but because cyberspace offers a territory in which the feminine is able to realize a mirror-like specularity. Female identities in cyberspace disturb more powerfully than in any other representational environment the fantasy of objectification that is at the core of patriarchal culture. As the stakes are raised by developing technological means of reproducing that fantasy, the possibilities for undermining the privileged position of the gaze also increase. The seductions of cyberspace become ultimately fatal for the male user, who must either continue to deny embodiment as a condition of perpetuating the fantasy or confront the multiple crises that result from the shock of objectification turning back on itself.

Debating whether or not cyberspace is a continuation of institutionalized 'pre-virtual' kinds of politics and inequalities or constitutes new post-institutional political sensibilities is a persistent issue throughout this volume. To the extent that virtual worlds enable the experience of freedoms which may be denied by institutional control, they may also bring about an appreciation of the 'social construction of reality' and therefore a cynicism towards authority and political dominance. Compared with the relatively 'over-regulated' contexts of non-virtual everyday life, cyberspace is typically experienced as a way of evading such control. This in turn brings up the question of the social and political value and 'effectivity' of identity in cyberspace, an issue underscored by a concern for a politics of representation. Then there is the fact that cyberspace can be seen as embryonic of a political order or electronic 'speech community' in which individual identities, however defined or recognized, are equalized. In this view, the unequal status and value of individual and collective voices in pre-virtual worlds is said to be commensurated by an acentred and seredipitous context of interactivity. Finally, there is the question of the abstract mode of integration which connectivity in cyberspace implies. What is the cost of such an abstract communion? What other levels of association might be given up in its name?

In addressing these questions, this book explores the new and paradoxical worlds that virtual realities represent, materially, culturally and politically. It explores the somatic, spatial and temporal features of these worlds and asks: given the powerfully mediating and above all constituting forms which cybernetically extended social relations engender, how are we to speak of *experience* in these relations? What sort of politics based on a lived or learned reality can be developed on the basis of this experience?

Notes

1. The distinction between biosociality and technosociality is a useful one in any discussion of cyberspace and virtual reality. Biotechnologies are said to give rise to *biosociality*, Paul Rabinow's term for 'a new order for the production of life, nature and the body through biologically based technological interventions' (Escobar, 1994: 214), while *technosociality* refers to 'the state in which technology and nature are the same thing, as when one inhabits a network as a social environment' (Stone, 1992: 610).

2. For a discussion of the role of *intellectual technique* in the transformation of cultural and material levels of social organization, see Sharp (1985). I would like to declare my indebtedness to Sharp's theoretical approach to a contemporary theory of social integration which has substantially influenced sociological understandings of cyberspace presented here. Another way of thinking about the processes of micronization is to follow Schopenhauer, for whom, according to Gaston Bachelard, the micronization of life-forms is less a means of 'managing'

the world than it is of 'possessing' it or replacing it with the imagination: 'In line with the philosophy that accepts the imagination as a basic faculty, one could say in the manner of Schopenhauer, "The world is my imagination". The cleverer I am at miniaturizing the world, the better I possess it' (1969: 150).

3 With this point the present volume concurs with Rob Shields's claim that:

> The current status of the Internet and its technologies represents a critical juncture in the development of 'virtual reality'. This is more than simply a stage in technical development or a marketing test: it is a *conjuncture* in the most profound sense of social arrangements and technological capabilities which stretches the 'lifeworld' and spills out of the computer world to refigure the conventions and routines of daily life. (1996: 6; original emphasis)

4. What also becomes important in this book is the way the appropriation of the virtual problematizes sociologies of technology which retain some idea of technology as use value.

5. Take, for example, a personal computer: it may be 'used' in a tool-like manner to type up a script, but as soon as it is connected to thousands of other computers via the Internet it becomes a terminal for a vast technoscience world which it is possible, in some sense, to inhabit.

6. For this group the Internet 'represents not only fifty years of computer design, but the scientific solution to the death of God' (Interrogate the Internet, 1996: 125).

7. The flight simulator is itself an early form of VR.

8. 'The genres in art that have always experimented with movement, the frescoes and bas-reliefs of Egypt and the *trompe-l'oeil* of eighteenth-century Europe have invariably gestured at no more than a study of movement rather than a synthesis of it. They achieve this largely by the conscious employment of illusion as the lie against which expressivism and realism are rendered problematic. '[T]he aesthetic of *trompe-l'oeil* in the eighteenth century resided more in illusion than in realism, that is to say in a lie, rather than in truth' (Bazin, 1974: 19n).

9. For the first time ever, in 1992 the profits of video game sales in America eclipsed the box office sales of Hollywood's *total* output for the year.

10. Here I am extending Jean-François Lyotard's reference to computers and databanks as 'nature' for the postmodern individual (see Lyotard, 1984: 51).

11. There are two senses of convergence here: convergence between commodity technologies which can be consumed domestically and convergence between different kinds of time- and space-altering macro-technology, namely, architecture, transport and communications.

12. For a discussion of broad processes of technization and the tendency of technological change to run ahead of the models that we employ to analyse it, see Elias (1995).

13. For a comprehensive review of Simmel's work see *Theory, Culture & Society*, Special Issue, Georg Simmel, 8(3), 1991. See particularly, Frank Lechner's essay in that collection, 'Simmel on Social Space' (pp. 195–201).

14. See for example Lajoie (1995); or in this volume Mark Poster, Chapter 12: 'Cyber-democracy: The Internet and the Public Sphere'.

15. As I argue in Chapter 1, while broadcast is an unequal relation between senders and receivers of messages, it nevertheless facilitates, as an agent of recognition, the objectivation of a general will. Institutionally, political processes and practices have always centred themselves on broadcast as the dominant mode of integrating groups and reproducing norms. The mutual assembly of a mass such as media consumers, a classroom or a readership acts as an agent by which truth-claims are scrutinized by a speech community. The many speak to the many through the agency of the one or the few.

16. More significant are the consequences of tying our identities to mobile information and communication technologies. These technologies raise the possibility that we will never again be 'lost'. In pre-colonial tribal societies, such as those of indigenous Australia, there is very little prospect of being 'lost' insofar as the individual is more or less completely enveloped by the 'we'. By contrast, in industrial societies we find ourselves in constant state of being 'lost'. We can be geographically lost, intellectually lost, or emotionally lost. We spend most of our time trying to get back to somewhere, find out how we are out of touch with ourselves, find our way, overcome being lost for words, and so on. We lack control over our physical, mental

and emotional worlds. This, of course, changes with the acquisition of a mobile communication device. The comfort of knowing that you can be contacted anywhere, any time, makes
your location, or even your anxiety about the time of day, far less relevant.

17. For an excellent discussion of the status of meaningful communication in the era of
telecommunications, see Derrida (1982). Derrida's main argument is that the notion of a
closed context is an ideological one; there is an always open possibility that any sign or written
communication may at any point and at any time be plucked out of its context only to float or
be repeated somewhere else. In fact, for Derrida this possibility is structurally determined and
is what constitutes the sign as a meaningful entity. It is 'the always open possibility of
extraction and citational grafting' (Derrida, 1982: 317) which Derrida calls essential drifting or
radical alterity, and which ensures that language or a system of making meaning can never be
totalized (Derrida, 1982: 317).

References

Bachelard, Gaston (1969) *The Poetics of Space* (trans. Marie Jolas). Boston: Beacon Press.
Bazin, André (1974) 'The Myth of Total Cinema', in André Bazin, *What is Cinema?* (trans.
Hugh Gray). London: University of California Press. pp. 17–22.
Bingham, Stephen (1991–2) 'The Key to Cybercity: Stephen Bingham, interviewed by Brian
Borgon and David Clarkson', *M5V*, Winter: 25–30.
Crary, Jonathan (1990) *Techniques of the Observer: On Vision and Modernity in the Nineteenth
Century*. Cambridge, MA: MIT Press.
Derrida, Jacques (1982) 'Signature, Event, Context', in Jacques Derrida, *Margins of
Philosophy* (trans. Alan Bass). Brighton: Harvester Press. pp. 309–30.
Elias, Norbert (1995) 'Technization and Civilization', *Theory, Culture & Society*, 12 (3): 7–42.
Escobar, Arturo (1994) 'Welcome to Cyberia', *Current Anthropology*, 35 (3), June: 211–31.
Giddens, Anthony (1990) *The Consequences of Modernity*. Cambridge: Polity.
Glass, Fred (1989) 'The "New Bad Future" Robocop and the 1980's Sci-Fi Films', *Science as
Culture*, 5: 5–70.
Interrogate the Internet (1996) 'Contradictions in Cyberspace: Collective Response' in Rob
Shields (ed.), *Cultures of the Internet: Virtual Spaces, Real Histories, Living Bodies*. London:
Sage. pp. 125–32.
Jones, Stephen G. (ed.) (1995) 'Introduction: from where to who knows?' in Steven G. Jones
(ed.), *CyberSociety: Computer-Mediated Communication and Community*. Thousand Oaks,
CA: Sage. pp. 1–9.
Lajoie, Mark (1995) 'Psychoanalysis and Cyberspace', in Steven G. Jones (ed.), *CyberSociety:
Computer-Mediated Communication and Community*. Thousand Oaks, CA: Sage. pp. 170–
83.
Lyotard, Jean-François (1984) *The Postmodern Condition: A Report on Knowledge* (trans.
Geoff Bennington and Brian Massumi). Minneapolis, MN: University of Minnesota Press.
Nancy, Jean-Luc (1991) *The Inoperative Community* (ed. Peter Connor; trans. Peter Conor,
Lisa Garbus, Michael Hilland and Simona Sawhney). Minneapolis, MN: University of
Minnesota Press.
Nguyen, Dan Thu and Alexander, Jon (1996) 'The Coming of Cyberspace Time and the End
of the Polity', in Rob Shields (ed.), *Cultures of the Internet: Virtual Spaces, Real Histories,
Living Bodies*. London: Sage. pp. 99–124.
Regis, Ed (1990) *Great Mambo Chicken and the Transhuman Condition: Science Slightly over
the Edge*. London: Viking Press.
Rheingold, Howard (1993) 'A Slice of Life in My Virtual Community' in L. Harasim (ed.),
Global Networks: Computers and International Communication. Cambridge, MA: MIT
Press.
Sharp, Geoff (1985) 'Constitutive Abstraction and Social Practice', *Arena*, 70: 48–82.

Shields, Rob (1996) 'Introduction: Virtual Spaces, Real Histories and Living Bodies', in Rob Shields (ed.), *Cultures of the Internet: Virtual Spaces, Real Histories, Living Bodies*. London: Sage. pp. 1–10.

Stone, Allucquere Rosanne (1992) 'Virtual Systems', in Jonathan Crary and Sanford Kwinter (eds), *Incorporations: Zone 6*. New York: Zone. pp. 609–21.

Turkle, Sherry (1984) *The Second Self: Computers and the Human Spirit*. New York: Simon and Schuster.

PART I

THE SELF, IDENTITY AND BODY IN THE AGE OF THE VIRTUAL

1

VIRTUAL IDENTITY:
Communities of Broadcast, Communities of Interactivity

David Holmes

During the 1980s theorists of information capitalism pointed to the decline of geographical settings of community and attachment as opening onto a period of profound crisis for experiences of a sense of place and a sense of history. Several analyses explored the rise in information form and trans-national culture as reasons for the decline of geographical community.[1] Increasing migration and tourism, and the spread of global media culture across nation-states, as well as the creation of open-ended practices of communication via unevenly developing means of telecommunication, were said to contribute to a less grounded experience of culture and subjectivity. At the same time, the fusion of the market with information form extended the reach of commodity culture in ways that began more comprehensively to subsume national and ethnic boundaries. The geographical, economic and cultural movements that produced the canonizing of 'globalization' as a discourse in its own right opened up an array of substantive ethical and political questions about power relations, the status of emancipation, identity and historical experience. Whatever answers might have been offered to such questions, it became a general understanding that the newer political and social agencies were to be cut adrift from community as a lived reality. In recent times, however, there has been a significant revival of the idea of community in terms which have seemingly bypassed the confrontation with technologically extended alienation. We are increasingly witnessing accounts of the possibility of liberated and emancipated 'virtual communities' on a scale which is somehow adequate to the globalization of information.

But what, exactly, is a 'virtual community'? How can it be that, in the face of the acknowledged dissolution of so much of the solidity of traditional social forms, technological utopians and social thinkers alike are speaking the language of community? In this chapter, these questions will be examined by looking at the social, political and technical conditions of community in contemporary information societies in order to explain the current celebration of cyberspace communities. My primary focus is on the Internet as an example of a comprehensive technoscience world which has historically revealed how extended forms of the social have remade traditional forms of association.[2] Of these 'traditional forms', I argue, the most immediate and valuable contrast available for an understanding of community on the Internet is provided by mass broadcast media as a form of social integration and association.

In discussing the Internet as a 'carrier' of a form of social integration which can be distinguished from other modes of social integration, I will not be concerned with the various histories and multiple conditions that are currently addressed in cyberspace literature, nor with providing an introduction to the technical use and operation of the Internet or computer-mediated communication.[3] Rather, I am primarily discussing the Internet, as it exists today (and in the form of its becoming), in its most general characteristics as a mode of assembly whereby human association is increasingly becoming abstract as part of a general societal trend: the formation of abstract communities.[4] The processes of abstraction that presuppose virtual communities can be seen manifested individually in architecture and multimedia; cultures of transportation, tourism, migration and international commodity exchange; commodity design and urban design, the re-urbanization of cities by information technology; and collectively in the physical and cultural ways that all these activities converge. Abstract communities coincide with the processes of globalization and the mobility that space- and time-altering technologies afford. This logic of convergence is mostly dialectical. For example, the increase in global communication results in an increase in the need for face-to-face meetings, conferences and exchanges on an international scale. Conversely, an increase in global travel increases internationally serendipitous face-to-face meetings in ways that frequently need to be renewed through global telecommunications. The aggregation of such individual events results in global community systems, the abstractness of which may be gauged by the fact that the encounter of difference within them – different identities, different places, different traditions – increasingly confronts the self as entirely unremarkable. Television is, of course, put forward by many as the most spectacular agent of processes of globalization and abstraction because of its broadcast-based reach and its power of simulation. Its ability to convey complexity, the power of the image and satellite reach makes it a primary memory machine for universal culture. In a sense, it possesses more gravity than any other communication form at present, and thus more capacity to homogenize cultural references through the imperialism of advertising and popular-culture genres.

The interactive networks and technologies that are said to make virtual communities possible share with broadcast in general, and television in particular, a reach and potential for the same kinds of imperialism of representation – commercial World Wide Web sites can duplicate all the advertising icons of television. But as agents of connection between selves, rather than machines of representation, they also share with broadcast the possibility of producing electronic environments which are not merely simulations of the real but are substantively their own environments. Assuming, of course, that we understand computer-mediated communication (CMC) networks and virtual realities as environments rather than as technologies used to carry on older forms of social relationships in a new, more 'helpful' medium. This latter view is one which can be characterized as a purely informational view of communication, in which communication becomes either a means of control or a means of expressing individuality.[5] Surprisingly, it is a view which is able to find a place in one-dimensional accounts of community formation circulating in CMC literature. By these accounts, CMC is an instrument of the communication event rather than a contextual network giving the event meaning. Community, conceived thus, is premised on an interest-based definition of contractual relations.[6] Such a definition argues that individuals, or a functional substitute such as a computer identity, come together to pursue and realize common interests; which tends to privilege the instrumental nature of particular interests and needs, needs that can be met abstractly without the present-at-hand. The interest-centred view also tends to define needs according to what can be achieved via CMC, so that computerization and its connectivity are continuations of the social contract by other – if more efficient – means. It also defines the idea of community according to purely intellectual cognitive concerns.

A second view of community in the age of computer networks is developed through a reliance on depicting geographic or compositional community. Computerization thereby reduces the 'place-centred' functions of cities by limiting accidental contact among strangers. As it becomes possible to conduct economic and other affairs without entering into the company of strangers, we lose both cross-cutting ties and one of the bases of democratic public life – the possibility of mutual assembly. In other words, the cellularization of public life via the computer workstation is a disruption, or a dissipation, of community (see, for example, Calhoun, 1986).

These definitions of community are very much grounded in an unproblematized view of place. It is a kind of place where, as Steven Jones remarks, 'social scientists can observe, visit, stay, and go' (1995b: 19). As a communication technology, the Internet is seen as a means of bringing close what is far away. The physical composition of the world is the first reference here, and the Internet is tool-like. This approach assumes that identity exists only in the physical world and that individuals are able to use technologies which simulate presence and overcome absence as ways of facilitating the culture of the physical world. The individual presupposed here exists prior to its experience of the world, is unified and is able to make conscious choices about whom to communicate with and how.

An alternative view of virtual and abstract communities accepts that extended forms of interaction are not simply supplementary to existing forms of face-to-face communication but constitute, at the level of social dynamics, their own sealed realities. They are self-contained, self-referential and constitute within themselves the substance of the social relationship, with declining reference to the social event that they simulate at the level of relation and form. Extended communication technologies and agencies cannot be viewed as instruments serving pre-given bodies and communities; they are instead contexts which bring about new ways of being, new chains of values and new sensibilities about time and the events of culture. As Carolyn Marvin suggests, new communication technologies 'intended to streamline, simplify, or otherwise enhance the conduct of familiar social routines may so reorganise them that they become new events' (1988: 4). One example of Marvin's point is a recent study of telecommuting in Australia that investigated the extent to which information and the exchange of personal communication take place in one telephone conversation. Taking a sample of older adults, the study 'I Can Tell You a Remedy for Migraines' (Williamson, 1994) concluded that, rather than most people 'using' the telephone for the purpose of information, perhaps to arrange where to meet later or update their last face-to-face communication, the telephone conversation is the meeting place itself. The study noted that most research into telecommunications treat conversations and interactions as if they have a single purpose. Together with an earlier study, 'Drinks on the Phone at Five O'Clock' (Williamson, 1992), 'Migraines' pointed to the increased dependence of those interviewed on telecommuting as an agent of bonding and association. This was particularly revealed in the high number of unsolicited concerns raised about the introduction of timed local calls, which for many 'would mean that the phone could be used only for essentials or emergencies and that long, intimate calls with family and friends would be sacrificed' (Williamson, 1994: 29).

The conclusion put by both of Williamson's studies is also consistent with a ritual view of communication (see Jones, 1995b: 12) which argues that individuals exchange understandings not out of self-interest nor for the accumulation of information but from a need for communion, commonality and fraternity. 'Migraines' and 'Drinks on the Phone' reveal a continuation of social interaction which expresses a level of community – a community system – and which does not need to draw its meaning from the face-to-face exchange that it partly emulates. Indeed, it is easy to see how, when telecommuting becomes a primary mode of interaction, the communicational form (face-to-face) that it takes its reference from no longer remains the socialized norm. For example, the anthropological difficulty that individuals experience with answering machines is overcome once telecommuting establishes itself as an environment of ontological security.

The model of social integration which James and Carkeek deploy in this volume is instructive here. They distinguish between three levels of communicative integration: 'face-to-face integration', 'agency-extended integration' and 'disembodied-extended integration'. 'Face-to-face integration' is defined as that level where the modalities of being in the 'presence' of others constitute the ontological meaning of interrelations, communications and exchanges, even when the self and the other are not always engaged in face-to-face *interaction*. 'Agency-extended integration' involves the extension of possibilities of interrelation through persons acting in the capacity of representatives, intermediaries or agents. 'Disembodied-extended integration' occurs where the constraints of embodiment, such as being in one place at one time, can be overcome by means of technological extension – broadcasting, networking or telephoning to name only a few. Each level is more abstract than the one 'prior' to it, and each is implicated quite differently in how we live the relationship between nature and culture, and how we live our bodies and the presence of others. The important thing about these 'levels' is that they are ideal types which may co-exist within different temporal-spatial-embodied configurations. It is just that, within actually existing historical forms, one of them may be dominant.

James and Carkeek believe that informational form predominates in late capitalist societies to the point where other forms of interaction become low in relevance and social bonding. But this is, for them, more of an anthropological description than an empirical one. That is, to use an example, it is not by direct observation of the number of Internet interactions against the number of face-to-face exchanges that we might gauge which level is dominant. Rather, the dominant level is the one from which the general incidence of social bonding and ontological security is derived. This in turn multiplies through practices of representation and what is valued by such representation. So we may never have watched television or 'surfed' the net, but in information societies these forms nevertheless frame our lives.

A key understanding which this position offers us is that particular technologies, in this case communicative technology, cannot be reduced to markers of cultural change (it is not as if, for example, the printing press gives us one form of society and computerization gives us another form), but are interrelated elements of the trend toward communicative abstraction. For example, in their framework, television can be identified as a social form belonging to a level of integration by agents as much as by technology. Whilst television is, on the one hand, an example of broadcast as the 'one speaking to the many', it is also a means by which, culturally, the many speak to the many, via the filter of a third party. The evening news or a game show, might prescribe cultural values for audiences, but it is also an agent for re-presenting the actually existing values which are adhered to by television audiences. At the same time, however, television participates in a level of disembodied extension insofar as it removes the cultural necessity of face-to-face relations in favour of much more abstract identifications with others. Yet the flight towards abstraction in no way indicates a loss of community or sociality. James and Carkeek would agree with Rob Shields:

> Keeping a division between online and life outside of the Net requires that one maintains a distinction between social interaction in Net groups and face-to-face social interaction. . . . These divisions are clear, but to label one activity anti-social, as some journalists have done, is an over-hasty and stereotyped conclusion. Both forms of communication are types of social interaction. (Shields, 1996: 6–7)

What is problematic, however, is whether or not the individual, the sense of self which occupies face-to-face-worlds, can be equated with one occupying virtual worlds. From a technosocial point of view, the individual who occupies this extended world is not the same as the one formed in face-to-face interaction. Nostalgic communitarians point to this latter self as experiencing a loss of comprehensiveness of interaction. At the other extreme, cyberspace enthusiasts herald the enhanced autonomy which is supposedly enabled by virtual mobility. But the opposition between face-to-face and extended interactivity is, arguably, too simplistic to help us adequately understand the rise of virtual communities in cyberspace. The extension of interactivity by technological means is indeed more abstract than the face-to-face, and guarantees the continuation of reciprocity between selves; but it is unable to simulate mutual presence. On the other hand broadcast – the relation of the one to the many – as a technological medium existing long before discussion of virtual communities arose, is able to simulate mutual presence (in a number of ways discussed below) even though it lacks the qualities of mutual interactivity and reciprocity between individuals.

Broadcast, as a mode of social integration, has been an indispensable precursor to the formation of virtual communities such as the Internet. As carriers of integration, broadcast and the Internet can broadly be described in terms of the predominance of either mediated forms of recognition or reciprocity. Both processes, collective recognition and extended reciprocity, carry with them modes of integration of persons. But I would suggest that the predominant features of the Internet can never constitute the mass recognition of community in the same way that broadcast can.[7]

As is suggested in Figure 1.1, broadcast facilitates mass recognition (in the form of meaning integration) with little reciprocity while the Internet facilitates reciprocity with little or no recognition. The important point to accent here is that it is not the technologies themselves which bring about these properties in a pure one-to-one correspondence, since clearly reciprocity is inherent in a range of technological forms, from the telephone to writing. Conversely the simulation of presence is just as available to computerization as it is to cinema and television. The particular way a technology extends social interaction determines which level of community (the level of abstractness and the kind of abstractness) it contributes to. On this point, there is much confusion surrounding the heralding of a second media age which the Internet represents after television. The Internet

Communities of Broadcast	Communities of Interactivity
The many 'speak' to the many by way of the agent of message producers ('media workers', the culture industry, etc.)	The many speak to the many by way of the computer-mediated simulation of presence
Centred	Decentred
Influences consciousness	Influences individual experience of space and time
High level of recognition/identification between individuals	Low level of recognition/identification between individuals
Very low level of reciprocity	Very high level of reciprocity
Individual experiences strong identity/ identification with figures of authority, charisma or cult movements	Individual experiences weak identification with others as figures of authority or charisma
Concentration spans of audiences are sold to advertisers	The need to communicate in highly urbanized settings is sold to individuals
Primary basis of the cellularization of social interaction in information societies	An extension of the cellularization of social interaction via the workstation as well as household

Figure 1.1

definitely embodies a specific mode of social tie; but it is also, and just as significantly, an intensification of the main logics of broadcast media and their structuring of social relations. Where the Internet differs from television is in generating the seductive illusion that the mass is able to participate in cultural production.

Beyond this difference, the Internet can be seen as another agent, albeit a powerful one, of that dual process of globalization and individuation in which, as Gerry Gill describes it, '[t]here has been a shrinking of the centre of the life-world from the community to the nuclear family, with a simultaneous expansion of the setting of that centre from the parochial boundaries of the community to a more universal national and international culture' (1991: 42). What is more, for Gill, the dissolving of older communal contexts, in which 'signs and meanings seemed fixed and stable', thereby making one's self-identity more secure, has meant that individuals must now 'reach out through the media for information, models, norms and signs in order to get the cultural material with which to construct their lives' (1991: 42). Gill's argument applies to broadcast media, and indeed to all those communication and information technologies that facilitate the process by which individuals have become dependent on a global system of the circulation of signs and meanings with which to 'locate' themselves and procure a sense of identity.

Through an appreciation of the extended quality of both broadcast and the Internet, it is possible to see that, while the addition of interactivity means that they might integrate persons in qualitatively different ways (yet to be demonstrated), they both feed off one common operation – the partitioning of a mass into atomized units, the individuation of populations. The two forms of integration are in fact co-dependent – in a way that I will outline more fully – and this needs to be considered when heralding the arrival of a second media age. To this extent, the arrival of the Internet signals little change in the 'individuating' aspect of the technological mediation of embodied presence. Instead, the commodification of such modes of presencing has changed its form in a way that is far more comprehensive and monopolistic. The celebrated decentred nature of the Internet is, as we shall see, inversely related to its commodifying potential to become centralized.

Broadcast, interactivity, community

Taken together, broadcast and interactive communication apparatuses have constituted the dominant mode of commodifying cultural needs since the World War II, firstly through the production of mass or popular culture as a form of privatizing the making of meaning, and secondly through the creation of seemingly irreversible forms of dependence on high-tech systems of communication. Theorists of the Internet like Mark Poster (1995) or George Gilder (1994) suggest that culturally television is in decline, while the Internet as a specifically interactive form of engagement is growing at an enormous rate.[8] In contrast, I want to argue that rather than being a displacement of TV, the Internet is actually parasitic on it, and what is described as a second media age could more appropriately be termed a second media layer, something overlaid on TV or broadcast.

The major reason the Internet is claimed to herald a new era of community is that its supposed decentredness provides the opportunity for universal access and participation in the public sphere or, in poststructuralist positions, for oppositional subjectivities. TV, on the other hand, is a function of the programmed society, a function of a system of concentrated interests and power. Certainly in terms of content this is true.[9] The production of meaning through the media not only results in the production of a common culture, but also enables media corporations to commodify the concentration spans of audiences and sell them to advertisers. It is our consciousnesses that have a use value for media corporations, a use value which is measured by ratings and surveys. For decades media studies has examined ownership and control, advertising and the semiotic content of media texts. With the exception of a few cases, this massive body of theory has all but excluded from analysis an understanding of medium as form. That is to say, what has been largely ignored is an appreciation of the property of broadcast's power of individuation (or metro-nucleation) of the population. The extended reach of broadcast, its ability to cross the compositional borders of given communities and nations, while at the same time consolidating the nuclear, privatized household, has the effect of reindividuating citizenship and individuality. Its logic is one in which individuals become remapped for a global landscape while they are also made dependent on television as that place where the modern consumer acquires the cultural materials with which to build a lifestyle of personal object-meanings. Such dependence comes about when the forms of inter-activity present in the public sphere by which individuals reaffirm a conscience collective (Durkheim) are displaced. The logic is dialectical: the greater the dependence of the individual on television, the less dependent s/he becomes on the public sphere which is being displaced in practice; and the more such a public sphere, particularly in its architectural/compositional aspects, withers away. Of course, what television cannot supply in the face of the withering away of the public sphere is its quality as an interactive context. This is where the dialectic emerges. When tele-vision and other forms of broadcast have all but saturated global culture and the media corporations have exhausted the franchising of their recycled family serials, the Internet appears just in time to save us from the tyranny of broadcast that is said to have subjugated us for so long.

Celebrants of the Internet eulogize the virtues of being able to re-establish lost communities through interactivity. In one of his more sociological moments, Howard Rheingold asserts that virtual communities are 'in part a response to the hunger for community that has followed the disintegration of traditional communities around the world' (1993: 62). To a large extent, but not necessarily for nostalgic reasons, the ascendancy of the Internet can be explained precisely by a new kind of commodification: the sale of lost levels of community back to the consumer. Importantly though, this is only possible because of the cultural ground already prepared by broadcast. Broadcast effects a dual movement of separating and uniting a given population mass, which divides the reciprocal cohesion of subjects and reconstitutes this cohesion on a more abstract space and basis of association.[10] As Scott McQuire suggests, broadcast facilitates 'a mode of social organisation and an architecture of urban living in which the individual becomes a primary social unit' (1995: 226). This fact is exemplified in the United States where, between 1960 and 1981, the number of people living alone doubled to one in four (McQuire, 1995: 226n).

In reducing the individual to a comprehensive solipsism and the primary social unit of late capitalism, television singularly creates the cellular con-ditions for individuals to have sold back to them the very realization of community that broadcast, in its ideology, was supposed to enhance. Such an exploitation of a new dependence has always been available to television through state appropriation of television licence fees or corporate provision of time-charged services. Historically that relationship has never been prominent, though, because of the importance of the image in advertising and because making profits from selling consciousness-spans has tradi-tionally been at odds with the time-charging of human capital. This mutual exclusivity has led to the marketing of cable TV as advertisement-free consumption, while at the same time cinema advertising is often considered offensive to the consumer who has already paid for the kinds of gratification left uncommodified on free-to-air-television. On the other side of the technological coin we are dealing with, the difficulties that advertisers are experiencing on the Internet should be mentioned: at first rushing in to capture projected audiences, they find complete uncertainty about who, where and how many can be targeted.

Broadcast is an integrative layer of social organization because it facilitates the solidarity of a conscience collective by working primarily through the identification of the image. But, as mentioned previously, its regulating borders are delimited by, on the one hand, the need to sell products to consumers and, on the other, the need to sell consumer consciousnesses to advertisers. The historical production of social atomization wrought by television, combined with the globalization of information, also brings about – paradoxically – the opportunity to commodify more intensively and thoroughly than ever before communicative action itself. The paradox lies in the now universalized freedom of speech resulting in the very collective dissolution of modes of integration that new communications technologies, in their individual use, are supposed to overcome. In this process, the Internet represents little change from the technological mediation of embodied presence that the extended aspect of broadcast entails, except that it is far more comprehensive in its exploitation of solipsism.

What all this means in terms of commodification is that broadcast can be seen as having erected the honeycomb walls while the Internet arrives, announcing: 'I can see you're having trouble speaking to the person in the next cubicle. I can also see that neither of you is going to get out of that cubicle easily.' The Internet offers to the dispossessed the ability to remove some of the walls for brief periods of time in return for a time-charged fee, selling a new kind of community to those who have been disconnected from geographical communities by the very processes that the Internet itself continues. The considerably fewer vertical relationships between broadcaster and mass, which has historically been exploited by the consciousness industry, is henceforth even further flattened out to a plane of interaction where the number of relationships that can be commodified is exploded, this time according to the time-charging of communication.[11]

Anomalies of digital reciprocity

If broadcast integration provides the socio-spatial as well as the ideological preconditions of virtual communities, the promotion of any such community can only be successful to the extent that the Internet provides what broadcast lacks: connectivity and reciprocity. So far I have been discussing the Internet as a pseudonym for interactivity which, in theoretical terms, can be contrasted with the process of broadcast. Inasmuch as we can perceive such a contrast, it is not one which takes a mutually exclusive form. Examining the actual technological capabilities of the Internet reveals how it embodies and assembles a spectacular number of features which can be found across a range of technologically extended forms. As already mentioned, however, the manner of association of persons is more important than the actual technologies which achieve this. In paradoxical ways, the Internet achieves its status as a comprehensive 'environment' or technoscience world because within the one technologically born medium it manages to combine a range of possibilities, including information storage, interactivity and broadcast.[12]

It is perhaps appropriate to break down the main features of techno- logical extension here. The idea of extension, and subsequently any sense of what it is that communicative technologies do, takes as its base reference the condition of mutual presence in which embodiment in the flesh is the only prerequisite for communicative interaction. The possibility of inter- action beyond this condition requires the technologically mediated substi- tution of direct presence and mutual interaction (the archetypal example is the telephone, which, in singling out voice as a minimum condition of interaction without mutual presence, enables disembodied reciprocity). At the same time, technological extension, which can never reproduce the fact of embodiment, nonetheless facilitates a great number of possibilities which mutual presence cannot fulfil. Technological extension can modify the symmetry of a communication process (as with broadcast) or the temporal mode of presence of a communication process (as with delayed interactivity versus real-time communication and storage retrieval). Broadcast here can be in real time, as in television or radio; in stored time, as in a daily newspaper or the latest novel; or it can be embodied, as in a conference paper which might require the amplification of the speaker's voice. The temporal mode of presence of a communication process can also vary according to systems of storage and the retrieval of information (writing, computer databases). Extension via the objectivation of communication dispenses with mutual presence in the sense that the production and consumption of information are separated in context and in time. Indeed the degree of abstractness of this separation is unlimited.

What is common to both broadcast and interactive media is their cross- contextuality and their reach. One has the real-time reach of a network, the other a reach over space and time. The Internet participates in both these kinds of reach. It exhibits the dual quality of being a carrier or register of information and a means of communication. That is to say, it is itself a storage network as well as an interactive environment. The Internet is thus unique in its ability to combine possibilities of engagement – hitherto spread across technologies – by extending the properties of speech, writing and the image. As an interactive environment the Internet facilitates electronic mail (dyadic reciprocity), as well as participation in many kinds of discussion groups. But it is also capable of broadcasting information, with any particular user transmitting to the many. It facilitates powerful search processes to retrieve information stored and collated in data-banks.

And, we can add, Internet service providers and software companies are attempting to develop technologies for the real-time simulation of face-to-face, mutual embodiment – such as video-conferencing – extending the embodied/disembodied contradiction to it technosocial limit.

The consolidation of all these powerful modes of engagement into technological context-worlds has profound and contradictory implications for the formation of identity and relations with others within virtual worlds. The central dilemma for self-identity is that disembodiment within these worlds occurs not because we are mainly using our intellect when seated at a computer terminal, but because the users, consumers and players within this world are disembodied to the extent that their author-ship and identity are not capable of multiple legitimation.[13] The production of information on the Internet becomes divorced from all possible local sites, and a historical or cultural mapping of the origin or context of a communication is not feasible. This is made most transparent in reading the amazing array of statistics offered by the Internet Index.[14] In particular, the first edition of the Index, which dates back to 1993, begins by outlining the extraordinary growth of Internet users and registrations of use. This includes everything from the number of Internet hosts in Norway to the number of countries reachable by electronic mail. These figures present themselves as accurate and earnest until the final entry, which reads: 'Number of people on the Internet that know you're a dog: . . . 0.'[15] Of course, this statistic is perhaps the most important entry of all in capturing perfectly the paradox that while the Internet grows at an exponential rate the solidarity of recognition that it facilitates declines.

Returning to my earlier observation about the tension between the broadcast and interactive features of extension, I would suggest that broad-cast facilitates recognition without mutual reciprocity while the Internet facilitates reciprocity with very low levels of recognition. Recognition of socially shared meanings entails the acknowledgement of contexts of production which add something to the message beyond its repetition. The experience of a text which has no context other than its technological reproduction shifts the function of recognition of meaning to a fetishism (mystification) of the means by which it can be reproduced in such a decontextualized way.[16] The message re-establishes itself by the novelty of being able to defy the context dependence of its production. It is a novelty which can be compared to the excitement of sending or receiving a message in a bottle across the oceans. The anonymity of the process is exciting because a worldly connection can be made with unknown others, while no responsibility has to be taken for its consequences. In the same way, the meaning of an Internet message may have no more significance than a note in a bottle floating between continents.

The message floats without destination. Perhaps it will never be dis-covered. If washed ashore, someone oblivious to the world of the author and the context of the message's production may read it and feel the novelty of its singularity. But would a community be constituted by a society of bottled messages, even if there were thousands of them afloat and awaiting discovery? Of course, the Internet is different because it is faster than throwing a bottle into the ocean and arrivals ashore are more frequent. But an Internet message is not read in the sure knowledge that many others are simultaneously sharing in its communication. In other words, the Internet and the messages in the bottle are never able to constitute themselves as an event, where there can be a relationship between the many and the many. The reason there are so many Internet users is not because of the need to reconstitute community but because, while the use of empty bottles is not an outcome of commodity fetishism, the use of computers is.

Community through personalization and simulation

Having contrasted key features of broadcast as a mode of social integration with those of extended interactive forms, I now want to turn to the dual process of globalization and personalization raised earlier. Gerry Gill's argument that postmodern identity is encouraged to withdraw to the nuclear family, while at the same time being required to reach out to a global level of consumption, is an important departure point for understanding how new informational and communication technologies are re-urbanizing community in technologically extended ways. Through such extension, the connection between the individual and the social whole becomes increasingly personalized according to the use of commodities and devices which facilitate this connection. Social integration and the formation of community occur abstractly when connectivity and segregation increase at the same time. The possibility of being connected to others increasingly comes down to technologies which presuppose a single user, with the personal computer and video-game machines that demand 'face-to-face' interaction with a screen representing the most widespread precursors to personalization. Broadcast technologies, which are able to be shared in group, family and institutional situations, come to be eclipsed by technologies which physically and technically inhibit shared contexts of consumption.[17] On the Internet this process of individuation, the atomization of the population by workstation or homepage, is easily generalizable from the growth of World Wide Web traffic. With the Internet we are witnessing, on the one hand, the extraordinary reach of interactive networks and, on the other, a shrinking of geo-spatial worlds to computer screen culture.

This movement in two directions, towards the global and the personal, is magnified even further by the increased take up of personalized information technologies. Such technologies represent an extraordinary contradiction in contemporary social life. On one level they are extremely social in allowing connectivity to a global arena, whether this be real-time connection to another person, listening to globally sourced music on a personal music device, personal digital assistants (PDAs) or connecting to the Internet remotely; but at the same time they are anti-social insofar as face-to-face communication becomes an attenuated level of human association and no longer valued in cultural representation. Neither the global nor the face-to-face is more social, it is just that one mode of human interaction – direct interchange – is annulled by the predominance of the other. The technologies are, in other words, highly solipsistic. VR research is perhaps the most obvious case, being driven primarily by the construction of electronic worlds which are exclusively experienced in isolation, with the five senses cut off from socially shared worlds. But the degree of bodily isolation and solipsism varies between technologies. The walkman seals off hearing, the VR helmet seals off vision and sound, and prototypes of cybernetic clothing aim at the ultimate VR case of sealing off all five senses. By removing the number of senses involved in our direct relationship with others and the dimensions of responsibility and accountability that this might entail, we are able to relate to worlds of representation which are high in predictability for the individual user. In the case of the stereo walkman, the personalized sound space it creates sets up an arbitrary relation between 'a performance' and the environment within which it is consumed. And no-one outside this enclosed space can relate to the personal association of two senses of place, nor can they communicate even their interest in what space it is.

The personalization of space is an extension of a central principle of consumerism, the idea that autonomy and freedom can be obtained by consuming something – a commodity – which enhances our identity. In this sense, personalization refers to the way we may now consume cultural commodities with such a degree of flexibility and choice that we experience the illusion of complete autonomy over those commodities. In being able to call up any kind of information at will and no longer having to conform to programmed information, the contemporary consumer experiences the radical autonomy to remake his/her experiences in an instantaneous manner. At the very moment the individual obtains this autonomy, connections with others become, inversely, empty because of the solipsism of immersion in VR.

To the extent that it electronically simulates a socially meaningful object-world VR is a useful metaphor for understanding social relations and social contexts in which it becomes difficult, if not meaningless, to map our place, or social location, in the world. In this sense, virtual reality manifested in commodities which extend our sense of place is the most visible expression of globalization. More radically than the other agents of globalization – telecommunication, transportation and commodity exchange – VR allows us to overcome the limits of being in one location at one time. To the extent that the presence of each individual is somehow incapable of fully 'living' the global character of social life, VR offers us the option of experiencing space in perhaps the most social way we can, which is paradoxically a retreat to individuality.

qually paradoxical is the way that collective uses of personalization
gies result in the very fragmentation we momentarily overcome in
individual use of them. The logic is seductive. Geographic forms of
association, integration and solidarity are both weakened and strengthened
by technological and communicational extension. They are weakened
because our lifeworld no longer involves negotiating physical spaces with
the same proximity that occurred before the rise of technological extension.
And they are strengthened in that we can simulate the properties of those
spaces with ever greater control. But because the tendency for fragmentation always outruns the opposing tendency, we are forever seduced into
greater and greater dependence on technologies of extension. This becomes
expressed aesthetically in the dominance of screen culture within information culture. Aesthetically, screens are fetishized in the public sphere,
discouraging face-to-face recognition of others (as occurs in the case of
video-cafés, cyber-cafés and automatic tellers), and become the familiar
reference points of everyday life.[18] The sheer extent of circulation of
screens, generally as computers, televisions and video-terminals, increasingly displaces the social object world from matter-based towards light-
based mediations. As Stephen Bingham has suggested:

> Architecture is collapsing into 'screens' and electronics are collapsing into our
> bodies. We can imagine a world now in which there will be multiple screens –
> screens for everything – some of them audio screens, some of them visual. Every
> object will have a screen. We'll flow through those objects and we'll be the
> electro-object of sensitivity. passing through an architecture of screens. Such an
> environment sounds exotic and bewildering but it isn't; it will just be made up of
> the next six gadgets you buy, all of them screen activated, audio activated,
> predictive and programmed to your common behavior. You will be the cursor of
> your screen. (1991–2: 26)

Virtual convergence

While the rise of personalization is more visible than the global processes
that are contiguous with it, some analyses (including Michael J. Ostwald's
in this volume) are beginning to chart the macro processes by which urban
and information systems are converging. This convergence is said to be
responsible for the emergence of 'virtual urban space' (Ostwald) as a
context in which the experience of virtual technologies and urban spaces
tends to become homogeneous. Globally too, the application of virtual
mapping techniques, the standardization of architectural styles, and the
continuous wiring up of urban landscapes for Internet, cable television and
mobile telephone networks are flattening out the visual and cultural
differences between the urban settings of information societies. The
predictability that the individual experiences with personal information
technologies increasingly becomes matched by the predictability of urban
environments. Where our identity in cyberspace can become equated with
the cursor, our experience of self in urban space increasingly becomes

programmed according to spatial logics which cross-reference each other and converge in physical, metaphorical and cultural ways.

In an important article analysing urban cultural spaces Margaret Morse (1991) explores the relationship between the shopping mall, the freeway and television, technological forms which are increasingly linking up in ways that constitute context-worlds rather than realms of personal utility. She looks at the convergence between television, freeways and shopping malls as post-geographical spaces which displace by distraction the space-worlds and time-worlds of local community. Morse argues that today, 'on the freeway as well as the airplane, a new and paradoxical experience of motion has evolved: on one hand, the relative motion of an enclosed space beyond which the world passes in high-speed review; or inversely, the dynamic sensation of movement itself experienced by a relatively inert body traversing the world at high speed' (1991: 205). Similarly, she depicts the mobility experienced with television, whose second-order relation to VR is originary, as a travelling along vectors in many dimensions:

> Of course any mobility, experienced by the television viewer is virtual, a 'range' or displaced realm constituted by vectors, a transportation of the mind in two dimensions. Our idyll, or self-sufficient and bounded place, is the space in front of the TV set . . . [where] . . . couch bodies are also travellers, responding in a checked, kinetic way to the virtual experiences of motion we are as subjects or view in objects passing our screens. (1991: 205)

A further ontology of distraction which Morse pursues is the shopping mall, a privately practised place in which 'the shops passed in review are themselves a kind of high speed transport, the displacement of goods produced in mass quantities in unknown elsewheres into temporal simul-taneity and spatial condensation' (1991: 204). The shopping mall is the 'TV you walk around in', as William Kowinski puts it in his book *The Malling of America*: '[T]he mall is television, [in terms of] people's perception of space and reality, the elements that persuade people to suspend their disbelief' (cited in Morse, 1991: 197). Morse's sites of 'mobile privatisation' (1991: 194) are extremely interesting, especially when we notice how their closures are more easily taken up by virtual representation. They are simply the most institutionalized sites of virtual experience in advanced capitalist societies. We could list many others which are more specialized in their consumption – the gymnasium, a shooting gallery, rollerskating, the theme park: all those 'artificial' worlds that are usually institutionalized under the name of leisure but which demand that the consumer submit to closed technical and architectural tracks of means–ends grids and circuits.

Morse's analysis points towards 'the convertibility between these various systems of communication and exchange [in which] freeways, malls and television are not merely similar in form, they are systems constructed to interact in mutually reinforcing ways' (1991: 210). Her approach should not be confused with a typical conception that cars and televisions are con-sumption technologies providing the means to re-establish or sustain community, culture and nation. Instead, if we conceive of television and the freeway (be it for automobiles or optical fibre) as circuits of exchange rather than spaces or tools, we begin to find forms of subjectivity, identification, interchange and integration which are totally dislocated from that old institutionally composed sense of integration. The television, the freeway and the shopping mall cannot be reduced to service functions, either of 'culture' or of a society which has become too large and detailed in its division of consumption and production to sustain 'culture' except with the help of technological extension. They are in themselves new spaces of consumption which are constitutive of subjective forms completely displaced from the cultural worlds they are supposed to support. Rather than being occupied as a necessary function which stands in between the daily round of production and consumption, these spaces are constitutive of their own increasingly enclosed systems of culture. They are 'service functions' which have totally outgrown the imaginary communities they were built to serve.

Taken individually, the urban and technological forms which are associated with 'virtualization' may indeed be seen to be fragmenting and breaking up our experience of geographic community. However, in understanding the 'convertibility' between these forms, as Morse suggests, it is possible to see how virtual worlds actually produce a standardization of experience.

Such standardization, I would argue, tends toward the universalization of a self which finds comfort and belonging in a world of predictable and manageable cyberspaces. At the same time, citizenship for cybersubjectivity is far less problematic than for those negotiating cultural, gender and class differences in institutional life. Instead, communication and exchange in virtual worlds typically results in an androgynization of sense of self. Paradoxically, such a citizen does not have to negotiate his or her citizenship or endure various rites of passage as such citizenship is implicit to the membership of a technosocial world. The crises that various social thinkers of postmodernism spoke of in the 1980s is averted by the intensification of the global–personal relation for which virtual worlds provide a bridge. At the level of language, image and representation, which accompany broadcast kinds of media, we may well live with fields of 'stylistic heterogeniety' without norms, as Fredric Jameson (1992) described as an outcome of 'the cultural logic of late capitalism', but at the level of social connection such heteronomy becomes flattened out in the forms in which it is consumed. Virtual communities are ones which embrace these new forms of consumption – based on very abstract but quite homogeneous and secure kinds of ritual. At the level of the personal, the individual's sense of place can be seen to achieve a new sense of security when control over 'simulated' environments becomes more attractive than negotiating inflexible institutional worlds, whether this be as everyday as the experience of freedom on a freeway, rather than public transport, or of changing channels by remote control compared to 'live' entertainment. As technologies of mobile privatization remove the contraints of having to be in one place at the one time and our sense of place becomes post-geographical, we become attached to the culture and technologies of extension that displace the worlds in which we had former attachments.

What these new attachments might mean for the future of community and political representation is an evolving concern. Part of the answer lies in understanding the ways in which agents of virtualization discussed in this book, from urban to information and communication technologies, are converging towards the making of an abstract social landscape very different from an institutional one. These convergence processes, both within single commodity forms and between networks of commodities and technosocial infrastructure, are dynamic ones which require ongoing investigation if an understanding of virtual futures is to be achieved. Just as we are interested in questions of social integration, we are also interested in contextualizing VR and cyberspace in the cultural and technical worlds from which they have emerged. It is as important to stress continuities between past and present virtual worlds as it is to delineate what is new in the convergence of virtual cultures and the politics possible within them. It may be a matter of comprehensiveness – where once primitive virtual technologies were object-like appendages to social life, today virtual worlds link up to form a meaningful world of action in which social life is re-presented to us. But more importantly, it may be that our fascination with this re-presentation has distracted us from a politics which is able to act towards it.

Notes

1. Primary dissertations on postmodernism are a case in point here. See, for example, David Harvey's discussion of time-space compression (Harvey, 1989: 240–2, 284–307) and Fredric Jameson's discussion of the 'omnipresence of pastiche' as 'a whole historically original consumer's appetite for a world transformed into sheer images of itself and for pseudo-events and "spectacles" produced by informational and media technologies as technologies of pure reproduction rather than production' (see Jameson, 1992: 18).

2. The Internet is taken up here as an archetypal model of broadband telecommunications structures and as a digital environment which, as Rob Shields suggests, represents the first 'true' cyberspace (1996: 1).

3. For a guide to technical details regarding the Internet, an excellent listing is provided in *CyberSociety: Computer-Mediated Communication and Community* (see Jones, 1995a: 8).

4. While, as discussed in this chapter, the Internet's 'superstructure' is a carrier of a range of informational forms and relations including Web browsing, information retrieval programs, Usenet, Multi-User Dimensions, broadcasting programs and point-to-point email, its most significant quality which will be explored here is its interactive, point-to-point, network structure.

5. A useful definition of the transmission view of communication is given by the philosopher Jacques Derrida as 'a *transmission charged with making pass, from one subject to another, the identity of a signified object*' (1981: 23; original emphasis).

6. A definition which echoes many of the terms found in micro-economic theory.

7. By way of the recycling of a relatively finite set of celebrities, genres and conventions, the culture industry facilitates the maintenance of stable values and regulates identification with a continuous cycle of known personalities and symbolic forms. Consumers of broadcast are able

to find community in the fact that individual programmes or columns have a widely recognized history that provides continuity in the otherwise transient and relatively fragmented events of one's lifeworld. The marking of births and deaths, for example, and the rights of passage of Hollywood celebrities become more important and more familiar than the uneven appreciation of these in kinship networks. Global news networks have a ready-made news reel on the life of most celebrities to be played upon the announcement of their death. Between songs a radio station will remind you of the celebrities born on this day. Meanwhile, consumers of broadcast quickly form soap communities based on the heavily marketed serialization of a particular night in their week. For a useful discussion of the formation of community with broadcast environments see Rosen, 1986.

8. Of course, materially the *use* of the Internet is growing exponentially. According to *Byte* magazine, the number of Internet hosts has grown from four in 1970 to 100,000 in 1989 to 4,000,000 in 1995. Sourced from 'Internet and Beyond' in *Byte* (July 1995, pp. 69–86).

9. Although, as the sociologist Émile Durkheim would tell us, the conscience collective is based more profoundly in the mass than in the managers.

10. The units that are 'separated' and 'united' are not at all commensurate with individuality.

11. This is true whether the sale occurs through an Internet provider or through a tele-communications company, particularly in the case of timed local calls and their consequences for access to a 'local' server.

12. These qualities of computer-mediated communication are, I would argue, generic to nearly all the sub-media of the Internet, whether we are speaking of Internet Relay Chat, Usenet, Multi-User Dimensions, point-to-point email, or World Wide Web browsing. For a useful discussion of the temporal and structural aspects of Internet sub-media see Baym, 1995.

13. This point can be read as a continuation of the claims of recent literary theorists concerning the nature of texts in media societies. In particular, Jacques Derrida who argues in 'Signature, Event, Context' (1982) that the presence of authorship in texts becomes harder to sustain in the era of telecommunication because of the breaking down of local contexts of meaning. For deconstruction, authorship is in an 'effect' (the author-effect) of the experience of the illusion of homogeneous contexts.

14. See HREF 1. The Internet Index comprises 14 editions between 1993 and the present.

15. This particular edition is at http://www.openmarket.com/intindex/93-2.htm.

16. Hence the fascination which promoters of the Internet have with its randomness, its scale and its power.

17. Television's ambiguous character as furniture and screen consumed at a distance allows the equally ambiguous consumer/observer to 'switch' by distraction between 'observation' and consumption. Rather than consummating the integral realism of the 'myth of total cinema' (see my Introduction), television's capacity for closure is not an obvious quality of its commodity-like appearance.

18. A reality which the sociologist Jean Baudrillard has documented only too well.

References

Baym, Nancy K. (1995) 'The Emergence of Community in Computer-Mediated Communication', in Steven G. Jones (ed.), *CyberSociety: Computer-Mediated Communication and Community*. London: Sage. pp. 138–63.

Bingham, Stephen (1991–2) 'The Key to Cybercity: Stephen Bingham'. Interviewed by Brian Boigon and David Clarkson, *M5V*, Winter: 25–30.

Calhoun, C (1986) 'Computer Technology, Large-Scale Social Integration and the Local Community', *Urban Affairs Quarterly*, 22 (2): 329–49.

Derrida, Jacques (1981) *Positions* (trans. Alan Bass). London: Athlone Press.

Derrida, Jacques (1982) 'Signature, Event, Context', in *Margins of Philosophy* (trans. Alan Bass). Brighton: Harvester Press. pp. 309–30.

Gilder, George (1994) *Life After Television*. New York: Norton.

Gill, Gerry (1991) 'The Social Origins of Postmodernism', in Stephen Alomes and Dirk den Hartog (eds), *Post Pop: Popular Culture, Nationalism and Postmodernism*. Melbourne: Footprint. pp. 38–45.

Harvey, David (1989) *The Condition of Postmodernity*. Oxford: Basil Blackwell.

HREF 1: The Internet Index, compiled by Win Treese (treese@crl.dec.com): http://www.openmarket.com/intindex/.

Jameson, Fredric (1992) *Postmodernism, Or, the Cultural Logic of Late Capitalism*. London: Verso.

Jones, Steven G. (1995a) 'Introduction: From Where to Who Knows?', in Steven G. Jones (ed.), *CyberSociety: Computer-Mediated Communication and Community*. London: Sage. pp. 1–9.

Jones, Steven G. (1995b) 'Understanding Community in the Information Age', in Steven G. Jones (ed.), *CyberSociety: Computer-Mediated Communication and Community*. London: Sage. pp. 10–35.

McQuire, S. (1995) 'The Go-for Broke Game of History', *Arena Journal: New Series*, 4: 201–27.

Marvin, Carolyn (1988) *When Old Technologies Were New: Thinking about Electric Communication in the Late Nineteenth Century*. New York: Oxford University Press.

Morse, Margaret (1991) 'Ontologies of Everyday Distraction', in Patricia Mellencamp (ed.), *Logics of Television*. Bloomington, IN: Indiana University Press. pp. 193–221.

Poster, Mark (1995) *The Second Media Age*. Cambridge: Polity.

Rheingold, Howard (1993) 'A Slice of Life in My Virtual Community', in L Harasim (ed.), *Global Networks: Computers and International Communication*. Cambridge, MA: MIT Press. pp. 57–80.

Rosen, Ruth (1986) 'Search for Yesterday', in Todd Gitlin (ed.), *Watching Television*. New York: Pantheon.

Shields, Rob (1996) 'Introduction: Virtual Spaces, Real Histories and Living Bodies', in Rob Shields (ed.), *Cultures of the Internet: Virtual Spaces, Real Histories, Living Bodies*. London: Sage. pp. 1–10.

Williamson, Kirsty (1992) 'Drinks on the Phone at Five O'Clock: Telecommunication and the Information Needs of Older Adults'. Melbourne: RMIT Telecommunications Needs Research Group.

Williamson, Kirsty (1992) 'I Can Tell You a Remedy for Migraines: Telecommunications and the Information and Communication Needs of Older Adults'. Melbourne: RMIT Telecommunications Needs Research Group.

2

VIRTUAL BODIES/VIRTUAL WORLDS

Cathryn Vasseleu

. . . we always make love with worlds.

(Deleuze and Guattari, 1983: 294)

[Man] does not even remember the fact that his body is the threshold, the portal for the construction of his universe, or universes.

(Irigaray, 1993: 100)

I'm going to begin by giving some broad definitions of the cybernetic world of virtual reality (and let me add that I claim no expertise in doing so). *Cyberspace* is the space within the electronic network of computers from which virtual realities, among other things, can be made. *Virtual realities* are computer-generated systems which use cyberspace to simulate various aspects of interactive space (that is, they are inhabitable computer systems of space). Cyberspace is the space in software, which in turn exists in hardware, which exists in so-called real space, as do the human participants in virtual realities. So we can say that cyberspace is also a *medium* of participatory orientation between bodies and objects in different spaces – 'cyber' means to steer. Cyberspace is often characterized as a transparent electronic medium, or informational interface. However, equally, *a participant's body* is the medium in this interface. In fact, virtual reality is not entirely unfamiliar territory. The intelligibility of bodies has always been conditioned by their ability to form intersections with, and live their reality as, multiple culturally determined spaces.

Considerable tension exists between those who argue that virtual reality is a liberating technological revolution and those who experience the effects of this technological 'revolution' with an all too familiar despair. For example, David Tomas, one of the participants in a recent interdisciplinary workshop/symposium on virtual technologies, summarized the proceedings as follows:[1]

> After two days of presentations, discussions and behind the scenes ruminations and arguments, including the articulation of frustration and despair on the part of a large portion of women artists and theorists, there seems to be only one conclusion available for retrospective contemplation: While the majority of artists appear to have been theoretically and practically ill-equipped to deal with this new technology at the level of its technical organization, those involved in developing its hardware and software are equally ill-equipped to deal with its social and cultural dimensions as well as its political implications. (1991: 117)

Although I use this quote to illustrate differences of investment in virtual technologies, I do not agree that inadequate critical or technical facility is the only conclusion to be drawn from the forum's inability to establish a mutually satisfactory critical interface. The domains from which virtual technologies have emerged and parted company are not the cohesive canons which they are so often assumed to be. Rather, many of the paradoxes and ethical concerns which appear to have been generated by virtual technologies are themselves a kind of 'emergent behaviour' – unprogrammed effects generated within the tensions of more familiar systems of representation which have supposedly been disrupted and displaced.

The event of virtual technologies has inspired calls both for new articulations of the observer, and for alternative models and strategies for evaluating the effect of these technologies on 'everyday life' (Easton, 1991: 90). What I would like to do in this chapter is consider, first, a mode of subjectivity – dis/embodiment – supposedly being 'fabricated' within a particular type of virtual reality technology – the virtual environment suit – and, second, why some women might be despairing of such a concept. The material consequences of perspectives which disavow the corporeal basis of virtual technologies is the ultimate trajectory of the chapter. In particular, the extent to which such perspectives reproduce modes of embodiment with which many women are already familiar will be addressed. These include the reduction of their bodies to abstract and colonizable spaces – perpetuated in some virtual interactions with computer-generated images of women, and the elimination of the material conditions of embodiment, perpetuated in analogies between bodies and algorithmically created universes which can be infinitely manipulated and reproduced. In discussing these issues, links will be made with Sofia's analysis of the computer as an imaginary second self, Grosz's analogy between virtual sex and pornography, and Irigaray's critique of women's bodies as abstract space. The chapter is not intended as an indictment of virtual technology, but rather is provoked by a desire for alternative engagements and interpretations of the virtual interface. To that end, it is an attempt to unseat the perspective of a disembodied, transcendental subject in some accounts of one piece of virtual technology – the virtual environment suit.

The virtual environment helmet

I would like to begin by addressing accounts of virtual disembodiment in the domain of popular science. There, the insistence is that virtual technologies represent the possibility of both worlds and subjective figurations which somehow transcend the context of their fabrication. Let me turn to some contemporary claims about the scientific value of virtual or artificial reality:

> The ultimate objective of artificial reality research is to develop a simulated environment that seems as 'real' as the reality it depicts. The profound strength of

the interfaces, however, may lie in their ability to go beyond reality itself, by modelling in concrete form abstract entities such as mathematical equations and by enabling users to surmount problems of scale in manipulating atoms and galaxies alike. (Foley, 1987: 84)

Other examples appear in the first chapter of Howard Rheingold's popular book *Virtual Reality*, which is titled 'Grasping Reality through Illusion' (1991). Two prefatory quotations from pioneers in the field reiterate the extent to which computer simulation secures the legitimacy of an unverifiable truth of the cosmos: '[T]he computer, with its ability to manage enormous amounts of data and to simulate reality, provides a new window on [the reductionist] view of nature', and '[A] display connected to a digital computer gives us a chance to gain familiarity with concepts not realizable in the physical world' (cited in Rheingold, 1991: 13).[2]

Interestingly, Rheingold's report of his first experience as a virtual reality 'infonaut' at NASA's Ames research centre includes a description of his imagined corporeal exclusion from this new universe:

A headpiece that looked and felt like an aluminium SCUBA mask covered my face, and a three-dimensional binocular television filled my field of view with electronic mirages, no matter which direction I swivelled my head. My body wasn't in the computer world I could see around me, but one of my hands had accompanied my point of view onto the vast electronic plain that seemed to surround me, replacing the crowded laboratory I had left behind, where my body groped and probed. (1991: 15–16)

There have been a variety of different interpretations of the body in cyberspace. Postmodern cultural analyses of cyberspace characterize it as a site of fragmentation and excess connection. Another interpretation of the desire invested in this experience is that in consciously transcending the physical limitations of perception it reconstitutes the grounds for a humanist concept of agency. We already labour under a modernist legacy of fragmentation and mutilation as effects of institutionalized desire and consumption-gone-wrong. However, the rhetoric of virtual reality suggests that the cognitive mastery of an objective world is indirectly realizable through an apparatus which offers a fantastic command of (cyber)space.

In his book *Techniques of the Observer*, Jonathan Crary includes the virtual environment helmet among the many optical techniques which are currently sweeping aside established meanings of the terms 'observer' and 'representation'. He argues that as fabricated visual spaces replace terrains which once corresponded to the so-called 'real space' of perspective, vision is being relocated to a plane severed from a human observer (1990: 1).[3] Paul Virilio also describes the *loss* of an undisclosed anthropocentrism – man as the measure of all things – in the determination of dimension, now exploited, for example, in measurement revolutions such as fractal geometry, where the length of a coastline will vary depending on whether a man or an ant is doing the measuring. Virilio argues that today seeing that which is *not really* seen has become an activity which exists for itself.

Virilio calls this activity '*endotic*' (originating within) 'because it renews the very conditions of perception, which is necessary to physical reality' (1991: 83). Paradoxically, it seems, vision is simultaneously both disembodied and re-embodied in the virtual environment apparatus. Synthetic vision is then the technological synthesis, or reconstitution, of these disparate modes of vision.

It is no mere coincidence that at the same time as objects have become information and Paul Virilio is documenting the lost dimension of referentiality, technology such as the virtual environment helmet has found its most enthusiastic research funding and application in architectural, medical and military practices, and in the arcade game industry. A common constituent of each of these technologies is the creation and commandment of occupiable spaces.[4] As the possession of an occupiable dimension has become the most urgent agenda of the agent/observer, the significance of simulation lies in its *subjective* legitimation of new imagined universal territories. The 'room' for this space is emptied by applying a blindfold and blocking the ears, that is, donning a stereoscopic headset with earphones and linked to tiny video monitors. The ground of one's mastery is secured in this 'space', or void of sensation in the corporeal manifold. The 'room' of virtual reality is not a camera obscura, a darkroom in the skull admitting images from the exterior into the vanishing point of the soul. In virtual reality, consciousness explores the parameters of its own space, a world which it discovers to be infinite when algorithmically cleared of material obstacles. The accepted limitation is that from a stereoscopic perspective, objectivity is restricted to a world of appearance. Provided you do not bump into a wall, the origin of experience is diverted from the obscurity of matter to an intelligible circuitry of programmed algorithms. The authority of algorithms presupposes the authority of reason (O'Neill, 1989: 59n). The computer world, unlike the physical world, is part of the self-contained universe of the rational subject. The sensuous reality of the virtual world resides uniquely 'within' the physiological observer, who is also the autonomous producer of his or her own experience.[5] Virtual reality is not like dreaming (in the Freudian sense); in a dream there is no agency, you do not know at the time that you are dreaming. It is in the full appreciation of being 'taken in' (by an illusion) that one gets a thrill from commanding cyberspace.

Among other things, the scientific veracity of computer simulation has its origin in the Copernican revolution. Most of us will be familiar with the *second* part or conclusion of the Copernican proposition – that is, that the earth is not the centre of the cosmos, and in fact revolves around the sun. The *first* part of the Copernican proposition is that it is the spectator who revolves, not the heavenly bodies. The significance of this *first* part of the proposition is what interested the Enlightenment philosopher, Kant, who referred to the Copernican revolution as a theoretical paradigm for the production of a universal illusion (in this instance, the revolution of the heavenly bodies) (Blumenberg, 1987: 97). Kant understood that, in proposing that it was not the heavenly bodies but the spectator who revolved, Copernicus dared, in contradiction to his senses, to stake that the truth was a hypothesis which could not be proven. The force of this proposition transformed the scientific model. No longer did the model represent knowledge conforming to an actual object, but instead offered the topography by means of which the unverifiable could be inferred.

In other words, the lawfulness of appearances lay in the *negativity* of their realization. The model was a source of inference, not a resemblance (not a copy). Kant's excitement in the Copernican model was that it proposed and tapped the inaccessible grounds of illusion. What Copernicus had given Kant was a 'window' to frame the universe. With a determination to colonize the infinite terrain inside this frame, Kant proposed a new cosmology for metaphysics. The origin of observed movement was within the spectator's own synthetic activity. For Kant, the body rather than a disembodied optical mechanism such as the Cartesian 'mind's eye' becomes the locus of the observer (Crary, 1990: 69). The experience reiterates the *subjective* nature of the evaluation and not the nature of the object, which is 'known' in the process to be of consciousness's own making. To be legitimate, the objective world must conform to our knowledge, not the reverse (knowledge doesn't conform to the object – because we cannot be sure of the object itself).

However, if an effect of virtual reality is a sense of disembodied agency, this consciousness is secondary to the delineation of a physical body as the (excluded) matrix of experience. Any conscious mediation of the experience is dependent on a disavowal of this body/consciousness division. The effects of virtual reality are reported by Howard Rheingold as though a body is already given, when in fact the production of this body as the jettisoned possession, or apprehensible ground, of a *disembodied consciousness* is an unacknowledged agenda.

The virtual environment glove

The virtual environment helmet has undergone many developments since its early application in aeronautical flight simulation. One of these developments has been that it has become a progressively more wearable technology. The main addition to the stereoscopic headset has been a movement-sensitive glove. This glove records spatially the flexion of hand-joint movements using, for example, the distortion which occurs in embedded fibre-optic bundles. Tracking devices linked to a computer allow hand–computer interactions through gestures which have been transformed into disarticulated spatial coordinates. From one perspective, digitization establishes the means for translating and reintegrating the senses. However, the glove covering the hand reconstitutes touch into the capacity to control what is seen, making it an adjunct to vision. With the addition of visual and other tracking devices the spatial effects of hand, eye and head motions are reproduced before one's eyes. Incentive and action are expressed in the same movement. You are free; you are in your own hands; every move you observe is your own. Reach out and touch your data.[6]

Although on first consideration there appears to be a general emphasis on touch in virtual reality, priority is given to proprioceptive sensibility. Other dimensions of tactility are regarded as passive 'feedback' in the cybernetic compartmentalization of the faculty of touch. Where the distinction is not established, the process is disrupted – for example, the technology does not encompass the irritation of a sneeze.[7] Proprioception is the body's so-called 'internal sense' of its own position, both spatially and in the relation of parts to each other. It is a sensibility delineated subsequent to Muller's doctrine of *specific nerve energies*, which transformed sensation into a collection of physiologically distinct senses. In broad terms, the doctrine of 'specific nerve energies' proposed that the same stimulus, for example electricity, would elicit different sensations (such as visual or tactile) in different nerves. Muller also demonstrated the reverse: that different stimuli would produce identical sensations. The same visual sensation could be elicited by electricity, mechanical stimulation or light. So the perception of light had no necessary association with the presence of light. This discovery basically eliminated the referential value of light as a classically undoubted source of mediation, and opened the doors of perception to everything from neuro/computer interfaces to promiscuous means of psychedelia (anything from sound and electricity to chemicals and light). Sensation was no longer interiorized, but associated with sensitized surfaces. Stimuli replaced objects of cognitive association. The senses no longer functioned as a differentiating manifold between self and world, but as a derangeable and manipulable mechanism.

In dissected isolation, proprioception encompasses the sensory apparatus of spatial mastery. Dancers and performers of precision manual tasks are described by physiologists as its disparate but exemplary exponents. However, a body's sense of its spatiality defies simple proprioceptive reduction. Dancers define space with their bodies, and the performance of precision manual tasks takes place in a space which is at hand. More importantly, lived spatiality includes the phenomena of imaginary anatomies such as phantom limb, hysteria and psychotic spatial disorientation, all of which indicate the symbolic dimensions of any corporeal schema (Grosz, 1992). Furthermore, the work of Merleau-Ponty has emphasized the extent to which the concept of spatial mastery is undermined by one's physical installation in, or rendering by, space:

> ... the initiation to and the opening upon a tactile world ... can happen only if my hand, while it is felt from within, is also accessible from without, itself tangible, for my other hand, for example, if it takes its place among the things it touches, is in sense one of them, opens finally upon a tangible being of what it is also a part. ... Through this criss-crossing within it of the touching and the tangible, its own movements incorporate themselves into the universe they interrogate, are recorded on the same map of it. (1968: 133)

The inclusion of an image, or double, of the subject's hand in virtual reality is described as providing a means of incorporating the participant's point of view in the representation of space. To quote Myron Krueger: '[I]n any artificial-reality technology, the participant needs to see an image of her hand in order to touch objects in the graphic world' (1991: 127). Described in these terms, the virtual environment glove is a logical adjunct to stereoscopic vision. Stereoscopy was analysed by its nineteenth-century developers in terms of the resolution of simulated binocular disparity. The effect of apparent tangibility was created in the sensory confounding of image and solid object (Charles Wheatstone; cited in Crary, 1990: 122). The application of stereoscopes in nineteenth-century pornography extends the view of stereoscopy into an obscene form of unmediated ocular possession (Crary, 1990: 122–7). However, the emphasis in these analyses is on mechanisms of convergence. This does not explain the significance of the illusion of perspective, which incorporates the perpetual negotiation of a point of view in the lure of layers of stereoscopic space. If pornography has capitalized on the implied tangibility of stereoscopic images, scientific optical technologies – from stereoscopic microscopes to virtual space simulators – have capitalized on its infinitely manipulable objectifying effects and shifting points of view. Thematically, the effect of stereoscopy suggests something more constitutive of disjunction than unmediated tangibility; a means of touching without being touched. If anything it is oscillating between a lawless and an uncontaminated optical contiguity, displacing flesh as the medium of touch. (I will take up this theme in the final section, in relation to virtual sex.)

However, the illusion of masterful integration with this complex, shifting stereoscopic space, rather than dispossession by it, is dependent on something prior to an image which allows the subject to see herself or himself in the field of vision. This is a disavowed corporeal reference which is *both* a limitation to experience *and* a means of experiencing the virtual world. Returning to Kant, it is salutary to note that although Kant regards space as an a priori intuition (that is, you cannot conceptualize an object without it), a subject is unable to relate to this space without appeal to an exclusive *corporeally* defined space. In his paper 'What is Orientation in Thinking?', Kant actually spells out his reliance on a body's uniquely defined spatiality as the subjective ground of all empirical, abstract or conceptual determinations:

> To orient one's self in the strict sense of the word means to find, from one given direction in the world . . . the others. . . . In the dark I orient myself in a familiar room when I can seize on a single object whose position I remember. Here nothing helps me except the capacity of determining positions by a subjective ground of distinction. . . . I soon orient myself through the mere feeling of a difference between my right and left sides. . . . I can broaden this concept even more, since it consists in the ability to orient myself not merely in space (i.e., mathematically) but in thought as such (i.e., logically). (1949: 294–5)

Orientation in the otherwise hypothetical objective world is predetermined by a 'fleshed out' differentiation of that world. The pleasure of being blindfolded and transported through virtual space with every reconstitution of one's own point of view also depends on an exclusive corporeal reference – the body groping around in the 'outside' space. Kant is only able to account for difference spatially, in terms of an object's definition by/within a posited all-inclusive space. (It is not possible to think here of a priori incommensurable spaces.)

A modern-day physiologist might be quick to reduce Kant's subjective grounds of distinction to the body's proprioceptive parameters. As has been discussed already, this is clearly a limited conceptualization of a body's 'internal sense'. The issue which is of importance here is Kant's unaccounted-for reliance on a corporeally differentiated dimensionality which is separate from, but somehow conditions the differentiation of entities in, his a priori space (Irigaray, 1985: 203–13). In other words, the difference in the feeling of the body relies on an intuitive constitutive schema. but this spatiality is independent of a priori space. The parameters of this schema are established by the morphological spacing of flesh, not a body as an object conditioned by a priori space. This marks a break between objective space and an undisclosed vitality of dimension; of flesh defined by flesh; of a subjectless/objectless difference in the flesh. In contrast to attempts in much of the current rhetoric surrounding virtual technology to obliterate differences in spatiality, the exploration of this vitality and incommensurability of dimension is something that, as I discuss in the next section, virtual technologies may have much to offer to theorists of the body.

The virtual environment suit

The current way to inhabit virtual environments most completely is by putting on a full body data suit; 'Smart Skin'™ is the commercial name for one such prototype (Rheingold, 1991: 347). If the body has previously been described as being left out of virtual reality, it assumes an essential but paradoxical interiority to a disembodied consciousness within the virtual 'birthday suit'. In the pursuit of a shared consciousness, the fold of consciousness is reversed. It turns from being contained in the body to becoming a container or skin conveying the body in cyberspace (de Kerckhove, 1991: 100). Among the rewards of assuming this shared consciousness is the 'ecstasy' of a communal exchange of virtual sex:

> Picture yourself a couple of decades hence, dressing for a hot night in the virtual village. Before you climb into a suitably padded chamber and put on your 3D glasses, you slip into a lightweight (eventually, one would hope, diaphanous) bodysuit, something like a body stocking, but with the kind of intimate snugness of a condom. Embedded in the inner surface of the suit, using a technology that does not yet exist, is an array of intelligent sensor-effectors – a mesh of tiny tactile detectors coupled to vibrators of varying degrees of hardness, hundreds of them per square inch, that can receive and transmit a realistic sense of tactile presence. (Rheingold, 1991: 346)

The term 'teledildonics' has been coined for this technology. Despite the overdetermined reference to a phallic imaginary, teledildonics has been hailed by its enthusiasts as the ultimate eradicator of corporeal limitations to sexual experience. In other words, teledildonics avoids the issue of negotiating sexuality as a corporeally mediated exchange. Instead of messy and tenuous interpretations, the expression of sexuality becomes an intelligible exchange of information, the erotogenic effects of which depend on where your anatomy 'interfaces' with the tactile s(t)imulator.

While much of this technology does not yet exist, the disposability of significant corporeal specificity in virtual reality has been exalted by Randal Walser as follows:

> In cyberspace, there is no need to move about in a body like the one you possess in physical reality. You may feel more comfortable, at first, with a body like your 'own' but as you conduct more of your life and affairs in cyberspace your conditioned notion of a unique and immutable body will give way to a far more liberated notion of 'body' as something quite disposable and, generally, limiting. (cited in Rheingold, 1991: 191)

Mikey Halliday expresses his faith in the technology as a way of confronting the libidinal limitations of sexual stereotyping, as it is represented by some gay politics: 'In Virtual Reality, you could create a true Queer Nation and girls, imagination could be the only limitation in re-creating evolution without patriarchy. With it, we can create the ultimate Pleasure Dome' (1991: 28).

It has been said that teledildonics, or 'interactive tactile telepresence', as it is more soberly described, is a 'thought experiment' that got out of control (Rheingold, 1991: 348). Quantum physicists have used such techniques to imagine themselves within mental models, but there is an earlier precedent for such a tactic. Far from being a thought experiment that got out of control, virtual sex has implications which extend the significance of Kant's Copernican 'thought experiment' into virtual relations with sexual objects. But this is a consciousness that defies not only matter, time and distance, but responsibility, vulnerability and accountability. Elizabeth Grosz draws an analogy between accounts which emphasize the psychotic fantasy of disembodied sexual pleasure in virtual reality and more traditional accounts of masculine – both hetero- and homosexual – consumption of commodified sex, such as pornography and prostitution:

> . . . the common fantasy of a laborless pleasure, a pleasure or desire which has no responsibilities, a work of consumption with no trace, no effect, no cost of labor. . . . To have sex, but to suffer no consequences, to pay no price (bar financial), to bear no responsibility. Something for nothing. (Grosz, 1992: 8)

A fantasy of the virtual environment prosthesis lies in the belief that, inasmuch as one is dispossessed of one's habitual spatiality in interactive cyberspace, differences between objects and bodies are formally reproducible in an abstract algorithmic space. The apparent 'deterritorialization' of matter is what simultaneously conditions an object's constitution in the computer matrix. Cybernetic interaction replaces and excludes the incommensurability of materially constituted spaces. Represented in visualized space, the material has no claim to the space of its own definition, while its vacant patency is a matter for free negotiation and manipulation in the electronic matrix of virtual space. The freedom of play with simulation is coincidental with this displacement of the material in its algorithmic reduction. Ignoring all that is displaced and recovered or reconstituted in this spatial coordination, formal differences will merely proliferate in the play of an infinitely reorganizable unified interface. The sex of a participant, technicians suggest, will be taken into account where appropriate as a concavity or convexity in spatial form.

A coextensivity of electrical currents with biological currents has been proposed as the principal factor in establishing an interface between virtual technology and human bodies (de Kerckhove, 1991: 100). The common currency of this hybrid apparatus is electricity, suggesting that virtual experience is a closed circuit between neurones and computer parts. However, an effect of this association which is overlooked is that in also characterizing the *technology* in corporeal terms it establishes the means by which intimacy with virtual environment technology can be substituted for relations with a different body. Is this not also the equation which generates the mobilization of flows and mechanization of passions in the coupling of desiring machines? As Deleuze and Guattari say, there is always something statistical in this love, and something belonging to the laws of large numbers. Cyberspace in these terms is thus an ideal love object – infinite, reiterative, excessively recombinant: 'we always make love with worlds. And our love addresses itself to this libidinal property of our lover, to either close himself off or to open up to more spacious worlds, to masses and larger aggregates' (1983: 294).

Perhaps there is more to be gained from considering the imaginary relations with virtual technologies in different corporeal terms than hybrid formations or tool-like extensions of one's own body. In the first place, the technology has a face. Cyberspace is not a transparent medium. It is an orientating and originating interface. There is an ethical moment to be addressed in its difference from the alterity of the face-to-face. Whose body or body-image is one interacting with in tactile telepresence? I am arguing here not for an ethical relation to this technological self but, rather, for regard to be given to the representation of its imaginary. The way one represents this self will affect what one does and becomes with it. In her feminist analysis of virtual reality, Zoë Sofia considers the effects of regarding the computer as a second self and its attendant sexualization of cyberspace (1992: 16). For example Sofia describes a computer hacker's imagination of this space as something to be penetrated, manipulated, cut up and appropriated, and compares this to some women artists' dialogical negotiation of the space as though it was another semiotic actor in the world.

Secondly, in virtual reality the site of reproduction is relocated from the maternal body to the matrix of cyberspace. Women have been accused of being opposed to various virtual technologies which will render them obsolete because the technologies can reproduce themselves.[8] Apart from the elision of reproduction and representation, virtual technologies have corporeal origins not only metaphorically, but, as Ingrid Bachmann notes, in the mainly young female workers whose participation in the production of technologies that can reproduce themselves is represented on the labels 'made in Hong Kong, Taiwan, Korea, the Dominican Republic, Mexico, Philippines' (1991: 53).

Thirdly, cyberspace has already lent its form to a new kind of body politic. For example, using the work of Foucault and Deleuze (among others), D.N. Rodowick (1990) makes a distinction between notions of mass culture and an atomized collective or a culture of the mass. Dominated by statistical and demographic models, the mass is no longer considered as a subject capable of expression; rather, it is an anonymous serialized mass that is 'randomly sampled', and governed by 'popular opinion'. To quote Rodowick:

> Rather than a collectivity of individuals, broadcasters increasingly conceive their audience as a virtual, mathematical space. In their currently developed forms, statistical and demographic research proliferate strategies that deprive the body politic of agency by converting it into a virtual – and therefore quantifiable, measurable, and 'manipulable' – space. (1990: 36)

Finally, to return to bodies as worlds, Irigaray gives an account of the sexual specificity of the concept of formal or empty space, which is unable to resist its penetration, inhabitation and enjoyment by the subject. While some may take experiences in this controllable coordinate form as a serious sexual pleasure, the unwelcome reduction of their bodies to such abstract space is the more familiar experience of many women confronted by issues such as sexual consent and abortion. The determination of one's body as a negotiable *territory* is an attempt to address this conceptualization. It is advocated by Irigaray as one political means for women to establish the rights to refuse entry to, or dwelling in, what they are determined to claim as the space of their own bodies – room of their own in the *flesh* – rather than a time spent by others in an abstract space.[9]

The concept of a sexual encounter as something which can be plugged into and turned off is consistent with an imagined freedom to move between a world of technology and a place where you turn back into your physical self. The effect of this spacing is the illusion that there is a way of being in possession of something without being reduced to matter oneself. This is a form of telepresence which absents itself from the vulnerability of 'being there' in the flesh. The ultimate trajectory of such a desire is 'reality without risk': a de-realizing displacement of spectacular violence demonstrated, for example, instant by instant in the American Gulf War operation.

Effects such as these, which are inescapably real to some, cannot be figured in the unconstrained joy of the virtual 'infonaut' who enters by inference into relations with objects of an unreal nature. The aims of many who are investing in virtual environments are being directed towards the legitimation of fantasies of disembodied mastery and eradicated corporeal limits in the shared imaginative universes of their creation. But this fantasy is bound to the bodies it excludes. The paradoxical fold in the body of disembodied consciousness suggests opportunities for redeploying space by exploring differences in the spatiality of bodies, or considering their differences in a suit.

Notes

This paper was presented at the Hybrid Connections Conference, University of Technology, Sydney, July 1992, and originally published in *Australian Feminist Studies*, 19, Autumn, 1994: 155–68.

1. I am grateful to Gary Warner for introducing me to this collection of documents relating to the seminars and artists' residencies addressing the theme of *Bioapparatus*, which occurred at the Banff Centre for the Arts between October and December 1991.
2. The citations are from Heniz Pagels, *The Dreams of Reason*, and Ivan Sutherland, 'The Ultimate Display'.
3. W.J.T. Mitchell comments that this severance has been going on since at least the 1820s (1992: 94).
4. For a discussion of simulation and occupiable space see Andy Darley (1990: 50–1).
5. See Jonathan Crary for a discussion of Goethe's post-Kantian subjectivist vision (1990: 69).
6. This is the name of an article on the data glove, which also features sub-headings that make puns on (g)love. See Eglowstein (1990: 283–6).
7. James D. Foley makes the incidental comment that sneezing disrupts the cybernetic feedback mechanism (1987: 86).
8. In his discussion of concerns about superintelligences and machine–human symbiosis Paul Brown, for example, refers to the artist Stelarc's suggestion that self-replicating machine intelligences and human symbions won't need mothers (1990: 237).
9. Irigaray's intervention into the sexualization of space is discussed by Margaret Whitford (1991: 160).

References

Bachmann, Ingrid (1991) Untitled contribution in Mary Anne Moser (ed.), *The Bioapparatus: Reflections Beyond the Interface of Theory and Practice*. Canada: Banff Centre for the Arts.

Blumenberg, Hans (1987) *The Genesis of the Copernican World* (trans. Robert M. Wallace). Cambridge, MA: MIT Press.

Brown, Paul (1990) 'Metamedia and Cyberspace', in Philip Hayward (ed.), *Culture, Technology and Creativity*. London: John Libbey. pp. 227–41.

Crary, Jonathan (1990) *Techniques of the Observer: On Vision and Modernity in the Nineteenth Century*. Cambridge, MA: MIT Press.

Darley, Andy (1990) 'Abstraction to Simulation', in Philip Hayward (ed.), *Culture, Technology and Creativity*. London: John Libbey. pp. 39–64.

de Kerckhove, Derrick (1991) 'Bioapparatustalk', in Mary Anne Moser (ed.), *The Bioapparatus*. Canada: Banff Centre for the Arts.

Deleuze, Gilles, and Guattari, Félix (1983) *Anti-Oedipus: Capitalism and Schizophrenia* (trans. Robert Hurky, Mark Seem and Helen R. Lane). Minneapolis, MN: University of Minnesota Press.

Easton, William (1991) Untitled contribution in Mary Anne Moser (ed.), *The Bioapparatus*. Canada: Banff Centre for the Arts. p. 90.

Eglowstein, Howard (1990) 'Reach Out and Touch Your Data', *Byte*, July: 283–6.

Foley, James D. (1987) 'Interfaces for Advanced Computing', *Scientific American*, October: 83–90.

Grosz, Elizabeth (1992) 'Lived Spatiality: Insect Space/Virtual Sex', *Agenda*, 26/7: 5–8.

Halliday, Mikey (1991) 'Virtual Reality', *Hell Bent*, 2: 28–9.

Irigaray, Luce (1985) *Speculum of the Other Woman* (trans. Gillian C. Gill). Ithaca, NY: Cornell University Press.

Irigaray, Luce (1993) *An Ethics of Sexual Difference* (trans. Carolyn Burke and Gillian C. Gill). Ithaca, NY: Cornell University Press.

Kant, Immanuel (1949) *Critique of Practical Reason and Other Writings in Moral Philosophy* (trans. Lewis White Beck). Chicago: University of Illinois Press.

Krueger, Myron W. (1991) *Artificial Reality II*. Reading, MA: Addison-Wesley.

Merleau-Ponty, Maurice (1968) *The Visible and the Invisible* (trans. Alphonso Lingis). Evanston, IL: Northwestern University Press.

Mitchell, W.J.T. (1992) 'The Pictorial Turn', *Artforum*, March: 89–94.

O'Neill, Onora (1989) *Constructions of Reason*. Cambridge: Cambridge University Press.

Pagels, Heinz (1988) *The Dreams of Reason*. New York: Simon and Schuster.

Rheingold, Howard (1991) *Virtual Reality*. London: Secker and Warburg.

Rodowick, D.N. (1990) 'Reading the Figural', *camera obscura*, 24, September: 11–44.

Sofia, Zoë (1992) 'Virtual Corporeality: A Feminist View', *Australian Feminist Studies*, 15, Autumn: 11–24.

Sutherland, Ivan (1965) 'The Ultimate Display', in *Proceedings of the IFIP Congress*. pp. 506–8.

Tomas, David (1991) 'Technicity and the Future of Their Bodies', in Mary Anne Moser (ed.), *The Bioapparatus: Reflections Beyond the Interface of Theory and Practice*. Canada: Banff Centre for the Arts. pp. 117–20.

Virilio, Paul (1991) *The Lost Dimension* (trans. Daniel Moshenberg). Brooklyn, NY: Autonomedia.

Whitford, Margaret (1991) *Luce Irigaray: Philosophy in the Feminine*. London: Routledge.

3

BEYOND BEING DIGITAL:
Representation and Virtual Corporeality

Nicola Green

If Virtual Reality is already a battleground for control of the cyborg as metaphor and as moneymaker, its battle lines are multiple and fractured, and the contending forces are characterised by shifting alliances and conflicting investments.

(Markley, 1996: 9)

So far, debates on virtual systems have been framed through questions about the form and representation of digital bodies. Such a frame invites problematizing. Critical attention needs to be paid not only to how bodies are signified in digital worlds, but also to the *social* constitution of virtual embodiment. That is, to the ways in which bodies exist – as both digital and non-digital, both cultural and technological – at the same time and across the spaces of embodied practices within a number of social worlds. This entails examining how digital representations of bodies are conceived, not only in their 'production' but also in the ways they are taken up and their meanings negotiated and renegotiated by those who use the technologies. I argue that individuals construct understandings of their embodied states in encounters with the physical elements of virtual reality systems. In other words, the virtual bodies produced through engagements with virtual reality technologies are embedded in 'pre-virtual' material social relations and, as such, necessarily incorporate social practices which categorize and standardize bodies, and also assume relations of difference and inequality between bodies. Virtual reality technologies therefore offer a site for the explicit negotiation of embodiment because virtual systems make the construction and simulation of bodies obvious. The contradictions between different aspects of bodily activity and representation in virtual reality technologies are created through the interaction of human and machine systems. This meeting of bodies and computer systems provides opportunities to explore the form, limits, abilities and expression of bodies in ways unavailable in other social contexts.

I want to explore both the representational content of embodiment in a specific digital microworld and how that world is achieved through the simulation of embodied social interaction and the negotiation of bodies in commodified human/technological systems. These concerns are articulated through an investigation of a specific kind of virtual reality 'experience': Dactyl Nightmare™, a widely distributed game played on a Virtuality® Ltd 1000CS Cyberspace unit (an experience sometimes designated by distributors and retailers of such games as 'body-based' virtual reality). Dactyl Nightmare™ provides a model through which to ask questions about converging layers of 'virtual corporeality'; in particular, about how different aspects of human/technological systems generate and negotiate the forms, activities and boundaries of embodiment across programmed and non-programmed worlds. Recognizing how virtual embodiment is created, taken up and negotiated in specific social locations, as well as the contradictions in these processes, can lead us towards some understanding of the networks of social practices that constitute 'virtual corporeality'. As such, we may be able to begin to 'transform the despised metaphors of both organic and technological vision to foreground specific positioning, multiple mediation, partial perspective' (Haraway, 1991: 21).

Accounting for virtual embodiment involves a specifically new kind of politics, one concerned with the crafting of virtual systems in particular locations and with the identification of how those located practices are embedded in relations of power and knowledge in material cultures. Theorizing this specificity involves moving between the concrete and phenomenological relationships between people, objects and signs, and exploring the ways these relationships are located in heterogeneous and sometimes contradictory domains of practice. How virtual reality technologies produce gendered, raced and sexualized bodies (and vice versa) needs to be addressed by analytical strategies which begin from a consideration of difference and heterogeneity (Star, 1991). Understanding virtual embodiment therefore entails looking at how virtual bodies are negotiated from these multiple and already stratified locations of action and reaction, rather than assuming a homogeneous VR 'user'.

Effacing physicality in digital worlds

> Because 'Virtual Reality' seeks to mimic the complexity of proprioceptive experience, it becomes an imperialist metaphor, a textual black hole. . . . Ironically. . . . Virtual Reality remains a semiotic fiction.
>
> (Markley, 1996: 7)

Advocates and critics of virtual reality technologies tend to impose a distinction between how bodies are said to work 'outside' and 'inside' the programmed worlds enabled by virtual reality systems. This distinction arises in debates about the kinds of embodied experience that are represented in digital worlds and their delimitation by technical conditions of immersive virtual reality systems. The focus on what is (or is not) represented in digital worlds accordingly obscures how bodily engagements with the technical object-components of virtual systems also contribute to the negotiation of bodily boundaries across worlds.

A number of narratives circulate about how 'embodiment' and 'disembodiment' are achieved through immersive virtual reality technologies. Jaron Lanier – who not only coined the term 'virtual reality' as a programmer in the field, but is also widely recognized throughout the 'cyberpunk' movement as a subcultural icon, a media event[1] – is one of many who talk explicitly about the materiality of human bodies, their relationships with immersive virtual reality technologies,[2] and differences between embodiment in virtual realities and 'everyday' embodiment (Lanier and Biocca, 1992). Lanier speculates on possibilities for transcending what are perceived as limitations in physical human forms:

> There's a sort of – let's say – technology as . . . an experience of infinity, as a route to a sort of social communion, and an ability to be free of physical constraints on the sources of experience. I think the direction of being interested in those things is universally human – a natural result of the human condition and the limitations of the body, and the frustrations associated with that. (Lanier and Biocca, 1992: 156)

The pliancy of embodied form that Lanier associates with a freedom from physical constraint is a product of the mind and the imagination unencumbered by embodiment in the 'real' world. For him, 'Virtual Reality is the Ultimate lack of race or class distinctions or any other form of pretense, since all form is variable' (cited in Boddy, 1994: 118). Digital embodiment transcends physical embodiment. The physicality of human bodies is effaced, people are 'disembodied' by an infinitely mutable play of digital signs and codes which represent a subjective consciousness prised from its necessary location in an organic body. Virtual reality technologies become the ultimate mind machines and encourage a social communion limited only by the extent of people's imaginative powers without reference to their physical location in time, space, and social and cultural relations.

The implication is that the physical body 'left behind' is the body marked by social life. The digital body is 'outside' and opposite to social and cultural relationships. By extension, the technological artefacts that produce digital bodies are no longer part of that embodiment. They become invisible. Their involvement, and physical and cognitive interactions with them, can be conveniently ignored along with the physical bodies of the participants. 'Technology' becomes purely digital, and can thus be rendered a-social and a-cultural. A circular and self-fulfilling argument can only result: the digital bodies represented in digital worlds are created through technologies which are already outside social relations, and will therefore transcend those relations. This serves to reinforce an assumption held by many of those who produce virtual reality technologies that the development of technological embodiment, through the digitization of the world, will *determine* cultural changes in both general and specific ways. Such an assumption about digital worlds is 'ideational'. Technological artefacts are neutralized and 'imagination' becomes the driving force in the production and consumption of digital worlds. Virtual reality systems can be ignored by concentrating on the representations of bodies and worlds in digital environments. Technologies become a device to free imagination rather than a set of artefacts and knowledges located in socially produced relationships of power.

Other writers have recognized that scenes represented in digital worlds are locations for the continuation and negotiation of dominant power relationships. They are accordingly critical of positions which assume the neutral, progressive and determining nature of technological forms. Cheris Kramerae (1995), for example, holds that the nature and function of technologies are directly determined by the institutional power relationships in which they are developed and built, and therefore maintain already established relations of gender dominance. Just as other technologies are gendered in their development and use (Wajcman, 1991, 1994), so virtual reality technologies have evolved as specifically gendered kinds of artefacts. While Kramerae acknowledges that there is potential in virtual reality technologies to disrupt dualisms between mind and body (1995: 40), she also argues that

> all-too-familiar knowledges, stories, adventures and stereotypes operate in virtual reality. The creativity doesn't come in the form of new legends. We can expect many more medieval imaginations, cops-and-robbers, sex, and other mayhem from the creators of VR. . . . VR, like all other imaginative situations, has the potential for dangers in gender stereotypes, but while, as in other kinds of play-acting, women and men can temporarily change their gender, there is little to suggest major overhauls of those so-called sex-roles in VR programming. (1995: 40)

For Kramerae, then, dominant social and cultural ideas about gendered human bodies will simply be transposed and re-enacted – re-presented in much the same form in these new technologies.

While Lanier's and Kramerae's versions of technologically mediated worlds seem diametrically opposed, their characterizations of virtual embodiment share problematic assumptions. First, they both accept that it is imagination, ideas and consciousness which determine the social form of immersive virtual reality technologies. For Lanier, 'from a virtual reality perspective, the definition of the body is that part which you can move as fast as you think' (Lanier and Biocca, 1992: 162–3). And Kramerae responds to ideals of disembodied consciousness by noting:

> Many of the people writing about VR say that its potential is only limited by the imagination of those working on the programmes. That's my worry. I'm concerned about the limited imagination of those working on and using the programs. And I think we all need to be concerned. (1995: 41)

A second assumption is that both accounts define individuals as meaning-takers rather than meaning-makers. People are characterized as accepting a singular meaning transmitted in the representational images and objects of digital worlds, a meaning which is not only singular, but also transparent. This utilizes a 'conduit metaphor' of communication in which information is unambiguously transmitted by a 'sender' which is then communicated to a 'receiver', whose understanding of that message is singular, and only reliant on relative amounts of 'noise' or interference in the message medium (Lakoff and Boal, 1995: 116). In the end both Lanier and Kramerae ignore the interpretive capacities of individuals to identify and utilize ambiguities and contradictions in fields of meaning. They ignore, too, the fact that relationships between digital and non-digital embodiments are simultaneously and mutually enacted.

To situate the making of meaning in the purely imaginary realm is to decontextualize a 'cyberspace' or digital 'space' from the material processes of technological production. Digital spaces are undoubtedly created through the imaginative interpretation of software by a human being. But the process of meaning-making is embedded in corporeal interaction between human bodies and computer hardware and software. Attending only to digital spaces ignores the physicality of technological production and consumption in everyday processes of interaction, and the negotiation of meaning that occurs during such encounters. Disregarding this is precisely what has allowed the discourse of disembodiment to become so prevalent in both popular and academic discussions of cyberspace (Benedikt, 1991; Hamit, 1993; Heim, 1993; Rheingold, 1991). It also allows the effacing of the body even in critical analyses of virtual reality technologies (Kendrick, 1996; Markley, 1996). Both Lanier and Kramerae rely exclusively on an interpretation of the digital representations generated by virtual reality technologies as independent spaces bounded by technological artefacts. They thereby tend to marginalize the ways in which human/technical artefactual systems operate *as* spaces which institute embodiment in 'virtual' locations; that is, in worlds which overlap, and which are *simultaneously* digital and non-digital.

Analysing digital bodies

If we are to analyse 'virtual' embodiment, we need to consider what kinds of bodies do and do not appear in digital worlds. At the same time, understandings of digital embodiment have to be taken apart and problematized. In doing so, we can move towards an analysis of digital embodiment which recognizes ambiguity and contradiction in cultural processes of making meaning from signs and symbols of both digital bodies and embodiment. But we need to look at digital embodiment as only one aspect of a virtual corporeality and to demonstrate the ways that the meanings attached to digital embodiment extend into the signs and symbols outside programmed spaces, where meaning is also negotiated rather than taken as given. This is to foreground an analytics which 'accounts for the articulation of the mental and the exo-semiotic, the articulation between the material context of daily life and the signifying processes within a social context' (Gottdiener, 1995: 26).

The political valencies of any human/technological system are difficult to identify in abstract terms (Balsamo, 1993: 694). Accordingly, it seems useful to concentrate on one specific site of signification and interaction that foregrounds issues of embodiment and material culture. The Dactyl Nightmare™ games systems have been distributed for at least six years and is found in many, predominantly Western, nations.[3] Dactyl Nightmare™ has as its objective the accumulation of as many points as possible by shooting at and hitting other characters in the game. The game is played across a series of game boards suspended in space and connected via flights of stairs. Both the player and his/her 'opposition' are represented by digital bodies. One opposing character is cast as 'human'. When played in networked pairs, the body of the human opponent is the representation of another player. When played alone, the opponent's body is a simulation generated by the computer. The other opposing character is cast as 'non-human'. This recurrent threat is a pterodactyl which attempts to pick up and then drop (thereby 'killing') the players in the game. How is corporeality achieved in this digital world? What social processes contribute to its construction? What practices in these technical systems indicate that issues other than representation are at stake?

While the current reliance on the ideal of a body freed from physical constraints and constructed through the powers of imagination might provide an opening onto the question of corporeality, we will soon find ourselves going well beyond that. In Dactyl Nightmare™, the digitally generated signs of bodies are the central images which generate meanings about embodiment within the digital environment. In terms of signification, it is therefore important to consider the manifestations of digital representation – the objects, including digitally rendered bodies – that the player perceptually encounters when the game begins. The most important considerations here concern how meanings about embodiment and disembodiment are negotiated through assigning a digital body to a player in the game, and how the player experiences and takes up the representation of his/her body and those of others. But meaning only resides in the material world – in materially and culturally inscribed objects – insofar as the human subjects who are the creators and interpreters of cultural and social interaction are concerned (Gottdiener, 1995: 172).[4] Meaning emerges from representation, but is not limited to it.

Mark Gottdiener's approach to the study of signs usefully teases out the interaction between sign value and material social and cultural relations. For Gottdiener, the 'expression' is the appearance or shape of objects. The expression of a sign refers to 'objects themselves . . . which exist materially, even if that materiality is simply a text' (Gottdiener, 1995: 28). The 'content' refers to both generalized sets of ideas and cultural mores, and more specific sets of ideological relations that are coded in particular ways in specific modes of social interaction (such as discourses within institutional or organizational settings). In the digital bodies of Dactyl Nightmare™ the 'substance of the expression' is the material form of the representation encountered, the means through which the representation occurs, the objects and texts with which individuals engage. The material form of these object-bodies is as digital 'texts', 'formalizations' or perhaps, more properly, layers of formalization, from binary code to programming and graphics languages. Here, '[t]he primary kinds of work involved in creating formal representations are: abstracting (removing specific properties) quantifying, making hierarchies, classifying and standardizing, and simplifying' (Star, 1995: 90).[5] The representations are digital and their substance is etheric, so the 'disembodiment' of these bodies is articulated through their 'immateriality' in juxtaposition with and opposition to the material substances of organic bodies. They can be digitally reproduced infinitely in the same form, and the evidence of this 'immateriality' is in the reproduction of the same form for all the human bodies in the game. Their materiality is as simulations.

The 'disembodiment' of digital bodies is also achieved through the 'form of the expression' – the 'shape' of the sign – that is drawn from specific ideologies. The digital character of the objects is reinforced through their immediate appearance, which is derived from a range of more general discursive positionings of 'the body'. Then there is the morphology of the digital body, its contours and its surfaces, its shapes and textures; a general and abstract idea of 'the human body' which formalizes and simplifies the parameters of shape and texture attributed to a 'normal' body.[6] In Dactyl Nightmare™, the digitized bodies that players are assigned take the form of a 'generic' human figure, a chunky body with the barest outlines of arms and legs, and represented as having blue legs, a white torso, and a dark upper head (culturally inscribed with jeans, T-shirt and short dark hair).

The degree to which this form is taken as a representation of a human figure depends on how the shape and substance of the sign work with ideologies that create meaning though reference to shared conceptual categories. The shape of the sign corresponds to the 'form of the content', the particular and institutionalized ideological understandings on which the appearance of these particular signs rely. The formalized, abstract and 'generic' digital bodies encode discursively produced understandings about the forms and activities of human bodies when interacting with computer technologies – especially virtual technologies. In Dactyl Nightmare™, ideologies of digital embodiment can be identified in how digital bodies are made and how they can act in digital spaces. Dactyl Nightmare™ presents specific modes of interaction in digital space through which players can understand their 'disembodiment'. One game scenario is a 'hit' on another player, a second is receiving a hit on your own body from other players, another is being picked up by the pterodactyl, taken to a great height and then dropped. In each instance, the digital body flies apart in polyhedral pieces, and is more or less immediately reconstituted in a different location. Another device is a change of point-of-view. When picked up by the pterodactyl the player's view suddenly switches from the digitally embodied to one high above the field of play, watching the pterodactyl fly high with his/her virtual body. The point of view changes again when a body is 'dropped', the visuals suddenly tumbling around until the body hits the game board, when it is reconstituted once more in a different location. These devices code disembodiment and an opposition to more everyday material embodiments by representing bodily impossibilities and under-scoring the otherness of digitally embodied experiences. The 'form of the content' codes the 'substance of the content' and enacts more generalized social discourses. The transcendental and 'over-determined' digital body finds easy compatibility with dominant accounts of embodiment offered by Western thought and its mediation of the world through technological artefacts.

Technologies take humans beyond the boundaries and limitations of their organic physicality, extending their senses and enabling activities otherwise impossible.[7] Feminist philosophers and social theorists have explicitly examined this ideal as masculinist; that is, the imagined bodies of scientific and technological rationality are constructed around the assump-tion of a masculine embodiment (Traweek, 1988: 41). From this point of view, virtual realities are imaginaries in which individuals can act from a point of disembodied consciousness, leaving their bodies behind (Foster, 1993).

Mapping the production of 'disembodiment' in digital representation can demonstrate how digital bodies institute powerful fictions in the experience of 'being digital'. The negotiation of any representation, however, involves extensive positioning and repositioning among those who do the work of crafting and reading such signs. There may be several signs for any given object, and meanings for each sign can be generated from a range of cultural sign systems. A different critical reading of, for example, the discourses of 'disembodiment' can look to the ways in which digital bodies reproduce familiar conceptual schemes of spatiality and embodiment in material worlds. Such an embodiment is produced by being assigned a body which is oriented in three-dimensional space according to notions of up/down, forward/back, inside/outside, self/other. In one sense, the reinsti-tution of these bodily orientations is congruent with the notion of 'disem-bodiment' as outlined above, the separation of 'mind' and 'body', with the body as a 'vehicle' for the explorations of an individuated, coherent, autonomous and above all rational self. In another sense, the reimposition of three-dimensional spatiality refers participants back to the far more messy and everyday constitution of embodiment – and the 'undecidability' of boundaries between mind and body in those modes of embodiment. How digital bodies produce notions of space and time therefore makes sense only insofar as it relates to other objects and surfaces positioned in relation to them. The surfaces of each digital object in a programmable world provide points for the formation of discernible objects and spaces in thoroughly 'organic' ways.

Digital bodies are positioned in systems of signification within digital worlds which place each sign in fields of other signs: fields which frame the flow of meaning through relations of correspondence and difference between many signs and referents. The social practices that create ideological relations of meaning are always already built into the object world. The meanings attributed to digital bodies in Dactyl Nightmare™ only make sense insofar as they are associated with formalized objects, which are positioned within a range of other objects. This sign system is not, however, restricted to the objects within the digital world. Understanding about digital embodiment is created with reference to fields of representation outside the digital world, in more everyday contexts.

The kind of complexity that emerges from multiple, layered and sometimes contradictory representation is simultaneously in tension with social practice. Not only wider representations but also wider social practices create meaning in both programmed and non-programmed worlds. Interpretation, action and reaction are each positioned through the particularities of code and context. The experience of digital embodiment only makes sense with reference to the practice of human embodiment simultaneously 'outside' the digital world; and in non-programmed worlds, embodiment is already constructed and negotiated. The bodies in Dactyl Nightmare™ are read not as generic figures, but as specifically gendered; and overwhelmingly these bodies are gendered masculine by those who retail and play the games. When playing the game for the first time I assumed that my generically shaped opponent, generated by the computer, was male. Gendered and racialized bodies emerge – partially and ironically – from the notion of casting off the culturally inscribed markers of difference. These 'generic' digital representations of bodies are situated in a field of signs, referents and meanings which are formulated in contexts of phallogocentric and Eurocentric representations. Such representations code dominant understandings of bodies. As Kramerae (1995) argues, the representations of some material bodies are privileged at the expense of others.

At the same time, however, gender emerges from the biographies, histories and bodily activities, and from the performances of players in Dactyl Nightmare™. Digital bodies are only referenced as male when the player is acting against a digital body generated randomly by the computer. In a networked game, the generic bodies take on the more 'everyday' and performative genders that the subjects construct and negotiate around their organic embodiment. For example, women can and do experience the digital representation of their own body as female. This contradiction indicates potential disruptions in meaning and understanding between the representation of bodies within exclusively digitized contexts, and virtual embodiment across both digital and organic modes of interpretation and action. It offers the possibility of performing gender and making it explicit rather than assumed. Examining the activities taking place at the sites where virtual reality technologies are used draws attention to the inevitability of material and organic embodiment in virtual systems (Stone, 1991, 1996). And considering the material activities associated with creating virtual embodiment identifies the importance of human/technological networks of practice which enable virtual worlds (Kendrick, 1996; Markely, 1996). Signs translate the meeting points between material worlds and fields of meaning.[8] The material world intrudes in fields of meaning, continually reasserting its existence in a phenomenology of everyday embodiment. While meanings are structured through the achievement of power and knowledge, they are nevertheless negotiated on the basis of a 'pragmatic understanding which is based in the reflexive experience of everyday life' (Gottdiener, 1995: 26). Bodies are produced through both processes of signification in social contexts, and the simultaneous physical engagement with a material milieu in which any particular body is situated at any one time. Human practices in social worlds of meaning and materiality both give rise to and reproduce relations of power. Social interaction is the sphere where meaning is articulated, deconstructed and negotiated in specific institutional and organizational contexts.

A phenomenology of virtuality

> Technoculture . . . is located as much in the work of everyday fantasies and actions as at the level of corporate or military decision-making.
>
> (Penley and Ross, 1991: xiii)

By way of outlining a much needed phenomenology of virtual culture, Zoë Sofia (1992, 1995) conceptualizes different levels of phenomenological human/technology relations, of which the interpretation of representations in systems of signification is only one. Drawing on the work of Don Ihde (1990), Sofia proposes four categories of relations between human bodies and technological systems. Embodiment relations are cases where technology is a tool or technique which extends organs or senses in mediated ways. Hermeneutic relations are the significatory or textual relations of technology where instances of tools and techniques are interpretive vehicles for comprehending the world. Alterity relations (also addressed by Turkle, 1984) refers to relations between human beings and technical systems where those systems and the objects constituting them are things-in-themselves with 'quasi-human' properties. And background relations are social processes where technical objects or systems become an assumed element in the world or form the world, at least temporarily.

Virtual reality technologies can be seen as 'horizontal instances' of technologies which push the boundaries of what Sofia calls technology/body relations to the point where the limits of each become indistinct.[9] The feedback mechanisms through which virtual reality technologies operate make digital realities strong in embodiment relations. The prosthetics become the body, and the boundaries between a notion of an individuated organic body and a set of technical artefacts becomes blurred. Because of disjunctures between digital and material spaces, however, the illusion of digital body enhancements or freedoms tends to be shattered when one is suddenly halted in mid-movement by a large plastic bar which 'isn't there'. As a prosthetic extension which transparently 'frees' the organic body from physical limitations, digital realities remain vulnerable to the intrusions of the physical world.

As representational systems, digital worlds, in Sofia's terms, are thoroughly hermeneutic technologies. Digital objects provide a 'map' for understanding the exploration of digital frontiers and their differences from more everyday embodiment. Furthermore, the components of VR systems, especially those built for entertainment, are 'high-tech' forms – they embody what advanced technology is supposed to look and feel like. Sleek surfaces, industrial plastic casings in black, computer cables and wires in obvious places. The visibility of the non-human elements of the techno- logical system forms meaning around the experience at the same time as generating an attempted escape from human connection with those objects when in the digital world.

Because the technological system enables those very worlds, however, the boundaries between what counts as subject and world become blurred. On the one hand, the head-mounted display connects referentially with other science fiction texts such as the Borg in *Star Trek: The Next Generation* (Fuchs, 1995), signifying infinite technological progress and expansion, and the frontiers of human/computer relations where human/machine hybrids are created. On the other hand, the form of the material object is not always consistent in its attempts at a seamless high-tech fantasy of human/ computer hybrid systems. I have known staff in retail outlets to 'fix' the objects when they are not working properly by smacking one in a pre- determined spot, much as one would an old and recalcitrant radio or television set. This activity intervenes in the interpretation of virtual systems as representing a new and progressive technological era.

Alterity relations, as theorized in the work of Sherry Turkle, are invoked when objects are seen as things in themselves. On the one hand, the 'magic' of the black boxed computer process that conjures a world might suggest that one is dealing with another quasi-intelligence which has the power to create worlds. Alterity relations, the construction of the computer and its activities as another 'self', tend to become established in the digital world in its less sociable instances. When a player is competing against a figure randomly generated by the software program, the computer becomes the 'opponent', another human 'self'. On the other hand, the humans behind the computer are more visible in VR in ways that are not so obvious in, for example, the programming languages of personal computers. If graphics in virtual realities are meaningful to their participants, and recognizably represent dominant assumptions about embodiment, the humans behind the computer become more 'present' than they are in representations like the code of computer languages, which may make no meaningful sense to 'non- expert' participants.

Digital worlds also excel in pushing the boundaries of background rela- tions, but then again only within those worlds. To create a microcosmic world is arguably the most extreme of background relations. On the other hand, the systems themselves are not yet common enough to become part of the generalized material landscape. The places where they are used are generally highly specialized, and they are not yet as 'background' as, say, television sets or even door closers (Latour, 1992).

Dactyl Nightmare™ reveals how the phenomenological interaction of subjects with the machine intrudes on digital spaces and constructs a virtual embodiment which is both material and digital. The boundaries and modes of action of human subjects in the game are partial, and doubled. The experience of playing is not bounded by the moments when the digital action begins and ends, but is constituted through the process of participating in material, as well as digital, spaces. To achieve this positioning, individuals must physically engage with artefacts, which may or may not fit their particular physical bodies, in order to achieve an experience of a virtual body and a virtual environment. There are pragmatic activities associated with 'fitting' a particular human body to a particular technological system and, when fitted, the player continues to interact with a system of objects in the material world at the same time as interacting with different kinds of objects in the digital world. Players must position their heads in distinctive ways inside the headset for the three-dimensional effect to work; they are attached to the framework of the 'pod' via a retractable cord which they must be careful not to get tangled in when they move from side to side or turn around; and they must manipulate a handset, with one button as the trigger for a 'gun' in the digital world, while another allows them to move forward in the digital world. The requirements for action in digital spaces are not always compatible with those of the material spaces that the organic bodies simultaneously inhabit. Advertising images of the activities available in virtual systems and the bodily activities of individuals using those systems are worlds apart. In the advertising, individuals are portrayed as active, their bodies moving around swiftly, aggressively shooting opponents and ducking in the return fire. Playing the game was very different for me: I could feel myself shuffling around and tangling the cord; and I have seen others who were just as unsure of themselves becoming awkwardly slow or even brought to a complete halt by their confusion at new ways of moving. The interfaces of digital realities are not at all 'intuitive'. They require significant learning and, even when repeat players master the skills required to move in these worlds, the 'interactivity' they provide is limited.

The production of virtual bodies is thus a phenomenologically partial process in this virtual reality system. Digital bodies are not only put together through multiple interpretations of relational signs at the level of conscious and unconscious cognitive processes; they are also subject to further negotiation through the possible forms of action and interaction between digital bodies in digital spaces. Moreover, the enactment of embodiment – the ongoing negotiation of corporeal boundaries – is subject also to the organic body's pragmatic encounters with technological systems. Virtual bodies are created through contradictions arising between locations across both material and digital – that is, virtual – worlds. But the pragmatics of these activities extend further than the micrological spaces of the virtual system. The pragmatics of exchange values in capitalist systems of commodification also contextualize the phenomenologies of these particular technics:

> . . . signs circulate . . . between the level of lived experience, their creation through use values in everyday life, and their expropriation by the hierarchical systems of power including their use for exchange value in the marketing of commodities. Thus signs are not only symbolic expressions but also expressive symbols that are utilized as *tools* to facilitate social process. Signs are really sign vehicles that constitute the media of social interaction. (Gottdiener, 1995: 27)

The virtual system as a sign acquires exchange value through the context of its commodified location as an 'experience' among others in entertainment markets. It also acquires material value through the positioning of the technical artefact in markets of production, distribution and consumption. The digital experiences available to a consuming public are initially produced through the impulses of capital accumulation and profit motives (Brook and Boal, 1995). The whole point of making digital experiences available to a consuming public is to gain some profit through their consumption. Marketing and advertising are important parts of this process. The generalization of representations and the production of digital embodiment in games like Dactyl Nightmare™ are carried out with this aim in mind. In this context, the 'experience' of virtual embodiment must be differentiated from the everyday, and specifically tailored for particular locations of use. The virtual experience accordingly includes the interpretation of a number of advertising and marketing images and texts which frame that experience before the player even engages with the machine. This can be achieved in different ways. Billboards outside retail spaces evoke the experience – the outline of an individual wearing a head-mounted display articulating with more generalized popular media texts to denote the crossing of boundaries to another world. Inside, posters position digital worlds as other. One such poster, headed 'Because Reality Sucks', continues: 'Here's the deal. Reality has toxic waste spills, transmission overhauls, and bad hair days. Virtual Reality, on the other hand, has nothing but totally fun games played in strange yet stylish headgear. Which would you prefer?'[10] The machines also stand as advertisements themselves in their physical manifestation: in their size and their more or less prominent location in specific spaces. And, most forcefully, playing the game advertises the experience. Potential consumers can watch the bodies of other players as they negotiate the vagaries of virtual embodiment. Banks of television screens – more familiar media – allow anyone nearby to watch and assess what is happening 'inside' the digital world. At the same time, other consumers can watch and learn from the human bodies, enclosed by the machine but also on display, about negotiating the artefact that they, too, may choose to meet.

There are people who consume enthusiastically many times over. But not everyone 'buys' – and not everyone who buys an experience 'buys' any particular ideology about embodiment. Many simply consume by watching rather than directly entering into the exchange relations of capitalist economies. Game vendors provide many reasons for this. Some argue that it is a fear of the 'other', a fear of what the technologies might do to someone's sense of embodiment and being in the world. Other accounts describe an explicit resistance to spending money in this particular way. Exchange value is always relative, and its relativity is influenced by the strategic positioning of individuals who assess their desires for consumption in relation to their perception of how, and whether, those desires will be gratified, and by the possibility of a refusal to be complicit in the production of these desires for their bodies. The games can also be rejected outright in a refusal to engage with the content and the representational activities within the digital world. Predominantly cited is the violence – either implicitly or explicitly acknowledging the powers of crossover between digital and material/organic worlds.[11]

And not everyone comes back. Again, sales people produce different theories as to why. Some people cannot play the game without becoming violently ill. Not only do bodies need certain attributes such as vision and limbs to play these games, they must also have attributes more usually 'hidden'. An inner ear imbalance, for example, can produce violent nausea while playing. Other consumers try it but find their desires unfulfilled, or at least find them unsustainable. Their initial curiosity satisfied, they look on the games as 'pretty neat', but fail to find them convincing enough to question the nature of their reality or their usual sense of embodied subjectivity. Other aspects of their histories and biographies, other spheres of both digitized and non-digitized embodiment, remain more compelling and interesting for them. The domination of capital, while always present and implicated, can also fracture. It is sometimes unsuccessful in its production of the desire to be digital as a new sphere of consumption, and is negotiated pragmatically and strategically by its potential participants.

Conclusion

Even in as mundane a site as a virtual reality game like Dactyl Nightmare™, played perhaps once for curiosity and an ephemeral pleasure, a precarious and largely indeterminate negotiation of embodiment emerges. Virtual embodiment is enacted in different but simultaneous social and cultural worlds, and we should take seriously the proposition that analysing virtual reality technologies foregrounds issues of multiplicity. Mapping the complexity of multiple worlds involves looking at how both representations and material activities are contested critically when embodiment is performed across programmed and non-programmed worlds. If multiplicity and heterogeneity are central themes in how virtual bodies are crafted, then it seems that recent feminist work which stresses 'multivocality' in relation to formalization, standardization and organizational complexity has much to offer an analysis of virtual corporeality.

It is tempting to look at virtual reality technologies and see oppressive power in its formalized practices of representation. A politics of formalism is based on simplification and abstraction, and choices are made in formal representations about what to retain and what to discard (Star, 1995: 113). All such choices are political, and the processes that render what remains as culturally intelligible are also at issue in the creation of digital bodies. One way to see this politics of formalism is as the possession of influence, structured in already established relations between individuals and social groups, with which one can exercise 'power' at the expense of others – 'power-over' (Law, 1991: 165–8). Analytical agendas which begin from this assumption of 'power-over' tend to talk about the reproduction in technologies and technological artefacts of oppression experienced in other fields of social life. Underrepresentation is a specific issue here. The solution to the exclusionary aspects of these power relations is strategies of inclusion: the bodies, experiences and contexts not presently represented in virtual reality technologies need to become available.

I have argued, however, that social and cultural meanings about embodiment generated by virtual reality technologies cannot be analysed solely through a generalized discussion of textual or symbolic formal representations. Despite representational practices which attempt to formalize and abstract embodiment through the creation of generic digital bodies, corporeality in virtual systems remains inevitably, and simultaneously, material. The ontological status of virtual worlds is worked though at the level of embodiment, in the ways people negotiate 'being digital' through the pragmatics of organic and physical activities. The concreteness of digital bodies as signs needs to be considered alongside the expression and context of those signs, and the ways meaning is produced – ways that are sometimes contradictory.

The signs within digitally bounded worlds are disrupted through the phenomenological experiences of participants engaging with virtual reality technologies. 'Being digital' is not an unfamiliar embodied state at the end of the twentieth century. Before individuals encounter virtual reality systems, either through media or by connecting with computer artefacts, their bodies are already produced and mediated as digital in other, now mundane spheres of social life. The digital status of economic exchange relations, of long-distance communication, of imaging techniques and of writing are just a few of the ways that produce bodies as already digital before encounters with virtual reality systems. My own fieldwork further suggests that individuals who engage with virtual reality systems are mediated not just by being rendered digital through their bodily connection with virtual reality artefacts. The experience of enacting oneself as a digital body in a digital environment is framed through many familiar forms of media, such as television drama and advertising in sites where games like Dactyl Nightmare™ are played.

Such processes mesh with the bodily experience of being connected with particular kinds of artefacts. These artefacts are material entities produced

by systems of raw materials, knowledge and technique, the sets of institutions that distribute and circulate such objects, and the people who use
the objects in particular ways in their lives. Thus, cultural objects and the
fields of symbolism and signification associated with them can only be
considered within the context of their negotiation and use. These contexts
are institutions and organizations which sustain the relations of object,
producer and consumer, and in doing so they generate meaning.[12]

The generic digital bodies of virtual reality technologies are therefore not
only simplified and abstracted as formal representations; they are also
organizationally standardized (Star, 1991) in the sense that they are the
result of networks of activity which temporarily subsume individual differences to imagined collectivities, and which produce certain forms of
embodied behaviour difficult or impossible to subvert. These processes of
standardization can also be seen as exclusionary. They institute differential
access and prompt differential effects of technologies, excluding specific
groups of people from the use of the technologies. It is easy to assume
'power-over' in practices of organizational standardization, as well as in
representation. To argue for strategies of inclusion, however, is ultimately
to run the risk of repositioning the work of artefact building and digital
representation as a technological problem which technicians can 'fix' by
modelling social life more accurately – more convincingly – and thereby
reinscribing the status of 'technology' and 'society' as separate fields.

Perhaps one way to think about power relations in virtual reality technologies is to acknowledge the boundary crossovers engendered by virtual
corporeality – that is, to think about how domains 'outside' the ostensibly
digital are themselves virtual. Virtual embodiment is one way of thinking
across multiple social worlds which are both 'inside' and 'outside' relations
of 'power-over' – virtual embodiment addresses the equally generative and
productive aspects of 'power-to' (Law, 1991). There is a need to use a
concept of virtual embodiment which accounts for the networks of relations
that institute bodies as an effect of particular technologies, at once both
materially and representationally inscribed in locations across multiple
social worlds. This certainly includes asking critical questions about how
and why particular bodies create virtual reality technologies in specific
ways, and how these ways of doing – methods and results – become
stabilized networks of standards in particular locales. Just as important,
however, is asking critical questions about disjunctures and contradictions
in virtual embodiment practices. What kinds of discourse and modes of
social action are available to negotiate collectively the interaction between
different kinds of materiality, different kinds of inscription, different kinds
of embodiment?

Processes of standardization (Star, 1991) can intersect with individuals'
histories, biographies and contexts in a number of ways. Individuals
confronting the technologies that embody and produce standardization can
be located within the frame of reference for the standards, and can participate in the community generated through those standards. Alternatively,

individuals may be located outside the frame of reference for the standards – and although flexibility can incorporate a number of differences between people, its scope of reference cannot be too flexible, or the products will not be standardized. In this scheme, individuals can choose to participate or choose to resist, but only in terms of the standardization that precedes their contact with the technologies. These positions constitute the 'inside' and the 'outside' of relations of standardization.

There are other locations available for social actors and, as Star argues, necessary for feminist theorizing about technologies:

> The power of feminist analysis is to move from the experience of being a non-user, an outcast or a castaway, to the analysis of the fact of . . . technologies . . . and implicitly to the fact that 'it might have been otherwise'. . . . We can bring a stranger's eye to such experiences . . . there is nothing necessary or inevitable about any such science or technology, all constructions are historically contingent, no matter how stabilized. (1991: 38)

I have attempted to indicate some of the ways in which digital bodies are represented in virtual reality technologies and to consider how individuals both participate in and resist the standardization implicit in digital embodiment. There are individuals whose bodies are outside the standards of digitized bodies by virtue of their material characteristics – bodies which cannot use the technologies, as well as bodies culturally inscribed with markers of otherness which the generic abstractions do not draw on for their formation. But to argue for the inclusion of these characteristics is not to challenge their constitution as important differentiating markers between bodies. Embodiment is negotiated across different domains of social practice every day. We cannot 'presume either unity or single membership, whether in the mingling of humans and non-humans or amongst humans. . . . We are all marginal in some regard, as more than one community of practice (social world)' (Star, 1991: 52).

Virtual embodiment presents contradictions in the work of digitized standardization, contradictions which present a range of possibilities and problems for thinking about different ways of being embodied. Being digital is one means of embodiment, virtual corporeality is another. I still think that perhaps I would like to be the pterodactyl.

Notes

1. Cyberpunk is a much-debated literary sub-genre of science fiction and a popular cultural movement, ostensibly merging the sensibilities of punk and cybernetics. Review and critique of the cyberpunk movement include: Bukatman (1993), McCaffrey (1991), Pfeil (1990) and Ross (1991).

2. When I refer to immersive virtual reality technologies I mean those human/technological systems that employ a head-mounted display to generate three-dimensional digital environments. The participant is located within the environment through sensor feedback to the computer about the body's orientation in space. As suggested by these characterizations, the human is an integral part of the system. Without the human component, virtual reality technologies are so much plastic and silicon.

3. Virtuality® Ltd is one of the longest lasting and most financially successful of the firms developing virtual reality systems for entertainment markets. According to the participants in my research who distribute and retail virtual reality experiences, Dactyl Nightmare™ is one of the most popular games played on the 1000CS Cyberspace unit (these units are 'reprogrammable' in the sense that a number of different games might be played on them). There are other games, such as Legend Quest™ (a 'medieval' adventure game with characters such as elves or dwarfs which a player can take on), but Dactyl Nightmare™ remains more popular. In some retail outlets these units are continually running the game to the exclusion of others.

4. Specific objects in material worlds can be considered 'actants' rather than 'actors'. Material objects can be bearers of meaning, 'acting' on behalf of human subjects. They thus 'participate' in human interaction insofar as they have effects on human activity – including the human interpretation of meaning and the sets of social interaction that are generated through, and influence, the making of meaning. See Rachel (1994).

5. These bodies are often formalized in specific ways because of particular technical constraints. The choices of what to simplify constitute the politics of the formalization and standardization. See Star (1991, 1995).

6. Elizabeth Grosz (1994) argues that every material body is simultaneously constituted through an imaginary social body. This imaginary body is more fully articulated in psychoanalytic thought, and also owes a debt to Maurice Merleau Ponty's work on perception (1962).

7. Many authors have argued that media technologies both draw on and feed the desire to transcend the boundaries of human bodies. McKenzie Wark (1994) details the 'virtual' experiences of Gulf War technology. The perception and experience of that war were constructed through a mediated position as audiences took on the point of view of a missile homing in on its target.

8. The ongoing intrusion of the material world into processes of signification is what halts the potentially infinite regression of meaning. Gottdeiner (1995) argues convincingly that while deconstruction made a coherent critique of Saussurian linguistics in terms of the ambiguity of meaning, it simultaneously 'textualized' the material world.

9. Sofia maintains that 'cyberspace or virtual reality forms an irreal technological cocoon with no necessary external referents' (1992: 19), with regard especially to hermeneutic and background relations. My argument is rather that virtual reality technologies can be more or less horizonal across digital and material worlds. More bluntly, the 'external referents' here cannot be effaced because these are human bodies located in organic time and space. Even when we are 'there', we are also and inescapably 'here'.

10. Cybermind Corporation Ltd. (Copyright 1995.)

11. It is a common argument that the violent or sexist cultural content of television determines a violent consciousness in individuals who unproblematically accept that violence as reality. The same kind of argument exists with regard to video games. See Provenzo (1991) and Williams (1974).

12. As much as all three aspects of commodity relations have equal theoretical importance, their importance in social practice might have different valencies at different times and places. It is certainly possible at times – such as in advertising – for the referent of the sign to be totally effaced – to slip away under the play of signs. In analysis, though, the possibility of the reining in of meaning by different users, and alternative possibilities to the play of signs, must be considered.

References

Balsamo, Anne (1993) 'Feminism for the Incurably Informed', in Mark Dery (ed.), *Flame Wars: The Discourse of Cyberculture. The South Atlantic Quarterly*, Special Issue, 92 (4): 681–712.

Benedikt, Michael (1991) 'Introduction', in Michael Benedikt (ed.), *Cyberspace: First Steps.* Cambridge, MA: MIT Press. pp. 1–25.

Boddy, William (1994) 'Archeologies of Electronic Vision and the Gendered Spectator', *Screen*, 35 (2): 105–22.

Brook, James and Boal, Iain A. (eds) (1995) *Resisting the Virtual Life: The Culture and Politics of Information*. San Francisco: City Lights.

Bukatman, Scott (1993) *Terminal Identity*. Durham, NC: Duke University Press.

Foster, Tom (1993) 'Incurably Informed: The Pleasures and Dangers of Cyberpunk', *Genders*, 18, Winter: 1–10.

Fuchs, Cynthia J. (1995) 'Death is Irrelevant: Cyborgs, Reproduction and the Future of Male Hysteria', in Chris Hables Gray (ed.), *The Cyborg Handbook*. New York: Routledge. pp. 281–300.

Gottdiener, Mark (1995) *Postmodern Semiotics: Material Culture and the Forms of Postmodern Life*. Cambridge, MA: Basil Blackwell.

Grosz, Elizabeth (1994) *Volatile Bodies: Toward a Corporeal Feminism*. Bloomington, IN: Indiana University Press.

Hamit, Francis (1993) *Virtual Reality and the Exploration of Cyberspace*. Carmel, IN: Sams Publishing.

Haraway, Donna (1991) 'The Actors are Cyborg, Nature is Coyote, and the Geography is Elsewhere: Postscript to "Cyborgs at Large"', in Constance Penley and Andrew Ross (eds), *Technoculture*. Minneapolis, MN: University of Minnesota Press. pp. 21–6.

Heim, Michael (1993) *The Metaphysics of Virtual Reality*. New York: Oxford University Press.

Ihde, Don (1990) *Technology and the Lifeworld: From Garden to Earth*. Bloomington, IN: Indiana University Press.

Kendrick, Michelle (1996) 'Cyberspace and the Technological Real', in Robert Markley (ed.), *Virtual Realities and their Discontents*. Baltimore: Johns Hopkins University Press. pp. 143–60.

Kramerae, Cheris (1995) 'A Backstage Critique of Virtual Reality', in Steven G. Jones (ed.), *CyberSociety: Computer-Mediated Communication and Community*. Thousand Oaks, CA: Sage. pp. 36–56.

Lakoff, George and Boal, Iain A. (1995) 'Body, Brain and Communication', in James Brook and Iain A. Boal (eds), *Resisting the Virtual Life: The Culture and Politics of Information*. San Francisco: City Lights. pp. 115–29.

Lanier, Jaron and Biocca, Frank (1992) 'An Insider's View of the Future of Virtual Reality', *Journal of Communication*, 42 (4): 150–72.

Latour, Bruno (1992) 'Where are the Missing Masses? The Sociology of a Few Mundane Artefacts', in Wiebe Bijker and John Law (eds), *Shaping Technology/Building Society*. Cambridge, MA: MIT Press. pp. 225–58.

Law, John (1991) 'Power, Discretion and Strategy', in John Law (ed.), *A Sociology of Monsters: Essays on Power, Technology and Domination*. London: Routledge. pp. 165–91.

McCaffrey, Larry (ed.) (1991) *Storming the Reality Studio: A Casebook of Cyberpunk and Postmodern Science Fiction*. Durham, NC: Duke University Press.

Markley, Robert (1996) 'Introduction: History Theory and Virtual Reality', in Robert Markley (ed.), *Virtual Realities and their Discontents*. Baltimore: Johns Hopkins University Press. pp. 1–10.

Merleau-Ponty, Maurice (1962) *Phenomenology of Perception* (trans. Colin Smith). London: Routledge and Kegan Paul.

Penley, Constance and Ross, Andrew (1991) 'Introduction', in Constance Penley and Andrew Ross (eds), *Technoculture*. Minneapolis, MN: University of Minnesota Press. pp. viii–xvii.

Pfeil, Fred (1990) *Another Tale to Tell: Politics and Narrative in Postmodern Culture*. New York: Verso.

Provenzo, Eugene F. (1991) *Video Kids: Making Sense of Nintendo*. Cambridge, MA: Harvard University Press.

Rachel, Janet (1994) 'Acting and Passing, Actants and Passants, Action and Passion', *American Behavioral Scientist*, 37 (6): 809–23.

Rheingold, Howard (1991) *Virtual Reality*. New York: Summit Books.

Ross, Andrew (1991) *Strange Weather: Culture, Science and Technology in the Age of Limits*. New York: Verso.

Sofia, Zoë (1992) 'Virtual Corporeality: A Feminist View', *Australian Feminist Studies*, 15, Autumn: 11–24.

Sofia, Zoë (1995) 'Of Spanners and Cyborgs: "De-homogenising" Feminist Thinking on Technology', in Barbara Caine and Rosemary Pringle (eds), *Transitions: New Australian Feminisms*. St Leonards: Allen and Unwin. pp. 147–63.

Star, Susan Leigh (1991) 'Power, Technology and the Phenomenology of Conventions: On Being Allergic to Onions', in John Law (ed.), *A Sociology of Monsters: Essays on Power, Technology and Domination*. London: Routledge. pp. 26–56.

Star, Susan Leigh (1995) 'The Politics of Formal Representations: Wizards, Gurus, and Organizational Complexity', in Susan Leigh Star (ed.), *Ecologies of Knowledge: Work and Politics in Science and Technology*. Albany, NY: State University of New York Press. pp. 88–118.

Stone, Allucquere Roseanne (1991) 'Will the Real Body Please Stand Up? Boundary Stories about Virtual Cultures', in Michael Benedikt (ed.), *Cyberspace: First Steps*. Cambridge, MA: MIT Press. pp. 81–118.

Stone, Allucquere Roseanne (1996) *The War of Desire and Technology at the Close of the Mechanical Age*. Cambridge, MA: MIT Press.

Traweek, Sharon (1988) *Beamtimes and Lifetimes: The World of High Energy Physicists*. Cambridge, MA: Harvard University Press.

Turkle, Sherry (1984) *The Second Self: Computers and the Human Spirit*. New York: Simon and Schuster.

Wajcman, Judy (1991) *Feminism Confronts Technology*. Cambridge: Polity.

Wajcman, Judy (1994) 'Technological A/Genders: Technology, Culture and Class', in Leilia Green and Roger Guinery (eds), *Framing Technology: Society, Choice and Change*. London: Allen and Unwin. pp. 3–14.

Wark, McKenzie (1994) *Virtual Geography*. Bloomington, IN: Indiana University Press.

Williams, Raymond (1974) *Television: Technology and Cultural Form*. New York: Schocken Books.

4

THE ONTOLOGY OF DIGITAL DOMAINS

Chris Chesher

Your gaze settles on a standard personal computer on a desk which might be in any middle class Western home. The camera tracks forward, smoothly descending towards the grey box. It accelerates and slips effortlessly through the floppy disk slot and into a fantastic world: cyberspace. You swoop across a terrain of glowing electronic components, buzzing with activity, fly by a pair of holographic, educational whales and then fall headlong into the imaginary tunnel of an optical fibre connection, darting through the twists of cable taking you ever towards limitless frontiers of power and knowledge. This is the now standard fantasy in computer-graphics about the new worlds opened up by computer technology: new spaces where all the old limits might be transcended.

If computers do create new worlds, these are quite unlike the cyberspace envisaged by advertising agencies with big special effects budgets. Computers create digital domains: parallel universes where events occur outside the usual physical spatial constraints. Software engineers have built vast stock markets, libraries, shopping centres and entertainment complexes only seen through small screens on desks. On-screen text has replaced physical documents. Figures in spreadsheets have substituted for banknotes. The very nature of work processes has changed (Zuboff, 1984). When performed on computer, writing, cataloguing, communicating, interpreting and controlling are now very different activities. The new practices are qualitatively different to their analogue predecessors precisely because computers are not spatial. Sending an email is a procedure quite different to typing and sending a letter. In some cases, no equivalent existed before the computer: there is no physical equivalent to chatting online with people around the world through the Internet. Technologies constitute new fields of possible action in which different logics and dynamics emerge. The effects of incorporeal network-mediated events are no less real than physical events: transactions of money, images, texts or control data are just as valid in 'cyberspace', even if they are not physically manifested by artefacts in space.

Computer domains are hard to imagine. When smokestacks and speeding trains transformed the landscape during the industrial revolution, change was undeniable, even if there was no political agreement on its social value. Some Utopians of this time celebrated while Luddites resisted, but no one could avoid seeing the change. The 'information revolution' lacks such conspicuous material manifestations. The mysterious fridges with flashing lights in 1950s movies and the grey boxes of 1990s PCs are modest artefacts which do not correlate with the scale of change that they represent. To fill a vacuum in the popular imaginary, artists and designers created spatial metaphors of the logical worlds of computers: televisual 3D spaces. The language and imagery used to describe and promote computers refer to new spaces: info-bots on surfboards shooting down superhighways across glowing hallucinatory landscapes.

The idea that computers create new spaces has subtly set the terms of debates around computer technologies. Digital domains are significant new virtual universes, but spatial metaphors do not adequately define their topology. Using a computer is closer to speaking than travelling. Digital domains make the world available on call. They make space irrelevant. Users can buy and sell commodities without going to the mine or factory. They can sell to someone without meeting them. They can refuse them credit without them asking. They can kill someone from the comfort of a cockpit. These applications share some formal properties – they make the world invocable as digital domain. This chapter explores the ontology of digital domains and their politics. First, though, is a critique of conceiving cyberspace as spatial.

Cyberspace's imagined spatial ontology

Spatial metaphors are commonplace in discourses about computers, although not universal. Some of the most common sources of a techno-spatial imaginary are science fiction, cinema and television, human–computer interface design and political rhetoric. In each case, the authors or designers were influenced by perceptions about their audience's expectations and experiences. Spatial metaphors helped make the concepts more tangible than the low-level abstractions of machine code. To make a concept tangible, though, can often enough begin to suggest that the particular implementations and configurations of the system it describes are natural, inevitable and pre-ordained.

In science fiction, parallel universes and worlds through looking glasses are commonplace, so it is no surprise that projected advanced computer systems create fantastic universes. The most famous cyberspace is the original: in Gibson's *Neuromancer* (1984). His cyberspace is more contemporary nightmare than utopian projection. The world of the novel weaves together themes of mysticism, corporate power, cyborgs, drugs and mental illness. There are similar themes in Neal Stephenson's *Snow Crash* (1992), although the Metaverse is more faithful to potential computer applications. Where, in *Neuromancer*, characters jack in with neurologically wired decks, those in *Snow Crash* put on goggles and earphones. In each case, the techno-worlds are used in the framework of hyper-capitalist dystopia. Their design – corporatized virtual spaces – reflects the alienated worlds of the novels.

Ironically, these nightmares came to inspire people proposing designs for actual systems. John Walker at Autodesk, the American software company, started a 'cyberspace initiative' in 1989 to build Gibson's vision. This is not the only paradox. The 'virtual reality' dream of creating a computer-built world which mimics the experience of space illustrates how US culture in particular values spatiality and direct, rather than mediated, experience. VR inverts the limitations of the experience of using computers – they are synthetic and aspatial – by claiming that the systems create a *better* experience and a *new kind* of space (HREF 2). The hyper-mediated worlds promise a perverse fulfilment of a high-tech nostalgia for a pre-tech world.

Even architects imagining what cyberspace might be like have been inspired by Gibson. In an early book on cyberspace, architect Michael Benedikt describes a system which aims to create a usable virtual space (1992: 119–224). He proposes principles of dimensionality, continuity, curvature, density and limits which provide virtual space with a reassuring uniformity (1992: 132). His cyberspace resembles a neon-glowing urban grid – a matrix of cells, each of which represents an institution. Users can cruise in a 'probe' over the rows of thousands of data cells. The cell reasserts property relations: 'owned and maintained in some way, it corresponds to the idea of property, of real estate' (1992: 202). The shape of this vision of cyberspace is unapologetically political: 'Just as in the real world, the size of a plot of cyberspace is itself information: about the power and size of the institution that owns and operates it' (1992: 203). This ontology is conservative, precluding the possibilities of the virtual world's escaping the constraints of the spatial world. Benedict's instinct is to impose on cyberspace a phenomenal uniformity which can be controlled, commodified and mapped.

Cinema and television have used three-dimensional computer graphics to represent the world inside computers. Both the physical computer, with circuit boards and twisted cables, and the scrolling text most common on computer screens lack televisual impact. By contrast, computer animation sequences, which often require days of production to provide seconds of screen time, have been widely used in advertising and special effects. These images have become inseparable from popular conceptions of how computers actually work. Computer companies have themselves encouraged this: one of Intel's 'Intel inside' ads, for example, features a sequence which takes the viewer on a fantasy voyage down a network cable. A seamless transition finds the virtual traveller on a journey down the canals of Venice. Films such as *TRON*, *The Lawnmower Man* and *Ghost in the Machine* have further reinforced the imagined spatial manifestations of the computer world. Shiny 3D worlds suit the narrative and aesthetic conventions of cinema but, as I will explore later, misrepresent the topology of computers' data architectures.

Computer interface design also often uses spatial illusions to help people manage files, browse through documents and use programs. Computer graphics had a long history before they became a key to using computers. Ivan Sutherland imagined computer-generated space as early as the late 1960s (Woolley, 1992: 41). From that time, games were also creating 2D and, subsequently, 3D spaces; and video games became a huge market. When software developers realized potential users went beyond the spotty-faced niche, they found there was money to be made from 'the rest of us' by making computer use more like playing games. Designers aimed for ease of use and 'intuitiveness' to expand markets, and spatial metaphors became commonplace with the interfaces for WIMPs (windows, icons, menus, pointing device). Macintosh OS and Windows use icons within windows to represent files and logical system entities. Mouse gestures can perform commands. Users suspend disbelief by accepting spatial cues such as the capacity to place items in different parts of the screen or sending things to the back. Behind the windows, though, the topology of dataspace was always non-spatial. This was betrayed by features like user scripting, search and replace functions, and automatic wizards and helpers, which transcended the spatial illusions.

The spatial metaphors chosen by West Coast American developers were heavily charged with that cultural context. The desktop and trash can are office-like spaces – out of place in other settings. Software primarily supports the goals of office workers, who are the largest group of customers. People who want to achieve other kinds of work must adapt or abandon software that is not designed for their application.

Spatial metaphors are commonly used in rhetoric about policy on computers. The Electronic Frontier Foundation, the pro-network lobby group, envisages networks as some kind of electronic equivalent of the American West. John Perry Barlow describes cyberspace as an inspiring vista of a new frontier:

> Today another frontier yawns before us, far more fog-obscured and inscrutable in its opportunities than the Yukon. It consists not of unmapped physical space in which to assert one's ambitious body, but unmappable, infinitely expansible cerebral space. Cyberspace. And we are all going there whether we want to or not. (HREF 1)

The envisaged space refers quite uncritically to a heroic history of westward American expansion. Barlow presents this as a universal good. However, the imagery is culturally specific – it is a myth for white male Americans. Far from liberating everyone, the rhetoric builds boundaries across the imaginary landscape, reminiscent of the forgotten victims of the heroic colonialism to which he alludes. The wired will colonize the new frontier; those left behind are the tired and hungry masses. But there is no space for other possibilities: it is coming, like it or not.

US Vice President Al Gore's 'Information Superhighway' vision is another example of a spatial imagining of networked computer-based communications infrastructure:

> One helpful way is to think of the national information infrastructure as a network of highways, much like the interstates of the 1950s. These are highways carrying information rather than people or goods. (HREF 3)

Gore also referred to avoiding 'bottle necks', ensuring 'public right of way' and establishing 'road rules'. The historical reference to the 1950s freeway system was a way to claim authorization for the US Federal government's involvement in building computer networks in the 1990s. Included in the National Information Infrastructure legislative program was the attempt to implement the controversial 'Clipper Chip', a standard form of encryption which aimed to ensure government agencies could tap into digital communications. The automotive metaphor cleared the rhetorical path for a virtual highway patrol. However, the attempt to introduce the Clipper Chip failed, largely because of the Electronic Frontier Foundation's resistance. Their vision of the sweeping vistas of the frontier prevailed over the government's images of concreted highways.

Invocation, not navigation

The examples drawn from architecture, cinema, interface design and public policy show how spatial metaphors tend to encourage a single, spatial ontology of cyberspace, and thereby restrict the multitude of potential configurations of digital domains. But cyberspace is misleading because the digital domain is not spatial at all. Networks do not reproduce space, they eliminate it. The essence of computer technology is that it enables instant retrieval and processing of encoded signs. It allows signs to be constructed and recovered as data irrespective of their location in space or time. The vectors of the telephone and computer network compress space and effectively make it irrelevant within their domains.

In actual space an object is *at an address* (a particular place). In digital domains, data are located *with an address* (speaking becomes invocation). By naming an entity it appears on the interface. Using a computer on the Internet demonstrates the aspatial nature of cyberspace. Connecting to other devices involves no physical movement. Just type in a command or click on a hyperlink and the data appear within a few moments. There is little difference between connecting to a machine in the same room and connecting to one in another country. There are no spatial clues about the physical location of the particular machine to which you are connected. Assuming the network is functioning properly, you invoke remote devices by *naming* the other machine. The URL (uniform resource locator) of a document is both its name and its address.

Computers are invocational media. Using a computer is related to speech more than to travel. Data are invoked by a *command*, a *call* or a *click* on

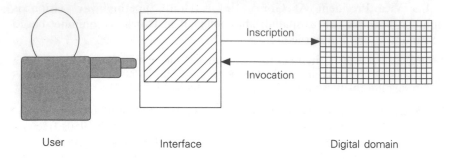

Figure 4.1

an icon. 'Invocation' is a kind of speech act by which a supplicant calls to a greater power for immediate aid. Traditionally invocation involves magic or a deity, but it is a useful metaphor for how computers allow people to 'call up' data. It is not literally magical but, as Arthur C. Clarke argued, 'any sufficiently advanced technology is indistinguishable from magic' (HREF 4). Many writers have observed that computers are reminiscent of magic (Davis, 1993). They resemble magic because users can provide simple commands to summon up complex things. Computer invocation is possible because of the way the technology is engineered: as digital domains of randomly addressable digitally encoded symbols.

The generic term 'computer' actually refers to an assembly of functionally separate devices which act in seamless combination. It is important for our purposes to distinguish these components and their relationship (see Figure 4.1). The sites of the *digital domains* are data storage devices: RAM (random access memory), which is the fastest; disk, which is slower; and remote network connections. The first computers had no storage devices, and so were not complete invocational media. They calculated only according to the configuration of physical switches and plugs. Almost all computers now incorporate some form of data storage, so they can be said to work with digital domains.

The central processing unit (CPU) is the enabler of invocation. It is the greater power which users invoke. It 'calls' storage devices to add, remove or alter data. It receives inputs from peripherals and sends outputs. The CPU adds data through inscriptive invocation. Programmers write programs, new invocations – spells that can be invoked later. Users enter data by encoding logical and physical entities as symbolic, addressable signs. The data are accessible again only with the power of the CPU, and only through interfaces.

Interfaces – input and output devices – mediated through human interface software eliminate and reconstitute space as representation. The most common input devices – analogue to digital converters, translators to the virtual – are keyboards, mice and microphones. They are the physical means by which users inscribe in the digital. At the other end of the process

– digital to analogue conversion – are the screen, speakers and other output devices. These are how the data from the digital are *located* again. They return the data to a location. What had been virtual, encoded and aspatial in digital domains is output again in a particular place at a particular time (text in certain type styles, on a screen on a computer in someone's office or home). This process is often experienced as a seamless loop of input and output, inscription and invocation, where users have a tangible sense of presence and engagement. As long as the system is working, users typing on a word processor or playing video games barely notice the detour through the digital domain.

Ontology of digital domains

Digital domains are not spatial, but universally addressable. They only exist to make invocation possible. Digital domains are plural: networks are not universally interconnected and are not equal in size, nor identical in operation. They range in size from microprocessor-controlled consumer goods to the Internet, which connects millions of people within one domain. Everything in digital domains is indexed. Within the CPU itself, data are stored in registers. In RAM, they are in memory addresses (various addressing systems are used by different operating systems). Hard disks store data on disk sectors indexed by disk directory data maps. On a network, individual machines have addresses (on the Internet this is the Internet Protocol (IP) address, which is both a name and number unique to a machine). The World Wide Web's addressing scheme (URL) can potentially address any available document on any machine connected to the Internet. In each case indexes to larger storage containers are crucial to sustaining the possibility of invocation.

Space in the physical world becomes time in the ontology of the digital domain. Distance is manifested in invocational delays of nano- or microseconds. Manufacturers have constantly shrunk the physical size of digital domain devices and increased their speed. There are two related reasons why microcomputers are small. First, military and later consumer devices (missile guidance systems and pocket calculators) needed to be small and light. Second, smaller circuits run faster and cooler. Microcircuits optimize space, access speed and weight. Although digital domains almost eliminate spatiality for the user, there is a residue of the physical in technical and economic limitations. Generally, the cost of hardware relates to the speed and size of data stores. RAM (at around 10 nanoseconds) is faster than hard disks (at around 10 milliseconds), but more expensive (currently $10–$20 per megabyte compared to approximately 30 cents per megabyte for big hard disks). As manufacturing techniques improve, more and more information is stored in smaller spaces and accessed more quickly. Ultimately, the digital domain's boundaries are the theoretical limits of physics: a bit cannot be smaller than individual atoms, and the circuits cannot operate more quickly than the speed of light.

The sacrifice made for speed is the acceptance of a rigid data topology. Computer addressing is based on Cartesian grids. Using a grid addressing system inherently prescribes all possible addresses. The Internet, for example, is based on a 32 bit addressing scheme, providing 10^{12} possible addresses. Like Borges's Library of Babel (1962) – which contains every possible book – all theoretically possible configurations of addresses are implicit in the choice of an addressing system. Grids are a modernist model of space. The ontology of the digital domain is an embodiment in electronics of the ideal of addressability that the modernist project imposed on the physical world. The grid of the nineteenth-century colonial map imposed latitude and longitude to encompass, define and therefore possess all possible places (Carter, 1987: 204). By having a potential grid reference for anywhere, everywhere was reduced to consisting of the same stuff. On a grid, 'here' and 'there' are irrelevant. In agriculture, crops were planted in monocultural rows. In the military, soldiers and vehicles paraded in columns. For the capitalist, all grid references become saleable and com-modified. The grid plan of many planned cities (especially in America, and in Adelaide and Melbourne in Australia) applied an urban planner's grid on physical space. Some grids were imposed by speculators who divided land into lots to sell them. The layout of the streets accorded with a strict Euclidean geometry of parallels and right angles, imposing a monolithic form on a diversity of places.

Spatial and lived environments resist the strict prescription to live according to grid plans. Other versions of place – memories, names, landmarks, geographic and social variation – prevail. The 'here' and 'there', and 'then' and 'now', reassert themselves in the cracks of the columns and rows. Inside the computer, though, a strict adherence to grids is possible in ways that are impossible in physical places. The digital domain is preferable to the physical world for many activities because it is not bound to place, and is relatively predictable and controllable. If people and property cannot be lined up along perfect grids in actual space, they can in the virtual.

Digital encoding frees signs from a dependence on the medium of trans-mission, and is another critical feature of the ontology of digital domains. The distinction between digital and analogue representation is philosophical before it is technical. An analogue code represents what it signifies by establishing a relationship of parallel degree. The hands of an analogue watch represent the passing of time by their position in space. The bumps in grooves of vinyl records are an analogue of vibrations in the air which are perceived as sound. The signal is analogous to what it is representing. On the other hand, a digital representation is based on a code which is originally arbitrary. Digital codes are also based on a grid, making all possible configurations finite. Where analogue involves a conversion of form, digital always involves encoding and decoding.

Computers are powerful manipulators of multiple digital representations, weaving data into multiple layers of encoding. Because there is no necessary relationship between form and meaning, the symbols can be reconfigured endlessly. An analogue television broadcast carries video and audio information in a strict order and at a strict rate. A digital data-stream, on the other hand, can carry any combination of instructions, image, sound and text. Everything is reduced to the ubiquitous binary bit: on or off. Since all signs are made of the same stuff, everything is potentially interchangeable. Any signifier that can be converted from analogue can be stored, reproduced and manipulated in the digital domain. Digital data can be copied without degradation, and remain independent of their medium. Data can be encoded several times, shuffled around, transmogrified by algorithms, and finally invoked, decoded and output.

Digital poeisis

I have described the ontology of digital domains, but have not yet explored their significance. The 'essence' of computers, in the tradition of Heidegger's essay 'The Question Concerning Technology', is not in the devices themselves (1977: 3–35). Heidegger insists that instrumental definitions describing causes and process do not address the overarching nature of the technological process. Although it is *correct* that a technology is a means to an end, this is too narrow. As society uses instrumental devices, a technological relationship to the world emerges.

Heidegger argues that the essence of technology is related to *poeisis*: a 'bringing forth' or 'revealing' of truth (1977: 10, 12). Technology's essence is in the process of potential becoming actual. By taking raw materials through a process which arranges them in a particular way, the envisioned final product is brought into presencing – revealed in a tangible and particular form. A windmill reveals the energy in the wind, brings it into presencing. What was previously not in our presence is brought forth. The technological encompasses not only the means to particular ends, but a whole relationship to the real.

Heidegger says modern technology is a more forceful and invasive kind of revealing which dramatically changes people's relationship with the world: it makes the real available as standing reserve. More than a *poeisis* (revealing), it is a 'challenging' of nature to reveal itself in a particular form on demand (1977: 14). Modern technology 'unlocks and exposes' nature (1977: 15). Coal is mined and 'challenged' to reveal the energy stored in it; it is stockpiled so that the energy is on call to produce heat in furnaces. Heidegger uses the Rhine as an example – it is dammed to store and make available hydroelectric power, and becomes something that is on call. Even as a beautiful river in the landscape, it is on call as a sight for the vacation industry. Hydroelectric systems reveal the river current as electricity. Once revealed in this way, electrical energy, whether from burning coal or spinning turbines, can be stored, switched about, transformed and distributed.

Computers store up the real in digital domains as symbolic standing reserve. Invocational technology creates ontological domains which transcend the limitations of space. The real is available on call, and digital domains provide media to transmit those calls across time and space. Software continues working indefinitely according to the will of the designer; networks distribute that will across the physical extent of the domain. A shop's inventory on database allows the shop assistant to determine instantly that a particular item is available and to make the sale without necessarily seeing or touching the object. Another database, in the credit card company, invokes the customer's credit status (and part of his or her subjectivity) to approve the transaction and debit the account. In the first example the object is invoked, and in the second the person as subject is. The digital domain provides representations of the object and the person as virtual standing reserve to allow the transaction to take place (or not to take place). These data representations can be stored up, switched about, transformed and distributed more readily than physical industrial technologies can manipulate the spatial real.

Invocational media do not stop at the interface. They require that physical and cultural machinery around computers also be rearranged. First, the culture must accept the validity of the invocational call. The very concept of information as it is now conceived, as an entity with an independent existence, is specific to our historical moment. Theodore Roszak argues that the emergence of a 'cult of information' was strongly influenced by Claude Shannon and Warren Weaver's information theory after the World War II (1986: 10). In the *Mathematical Theory of Communications*, Shannon and Weaver (1949) separated information content from the means of its carriage. While Shannon and Weaver's information theory was strictly technical and not concerned with the meaning of messages, it was applied far more broadly in describing and analysing communications processes. Information was imagined as a centre of social actions – the 'information revolution', and the 'information society'. The computer as information transferrer and processor applied the epistemological model of 'information' in this tradition. Treating communications as largely a problem of 'getting the message across', and information as autonomous and central, has become a dominant and often uncriticized premise of contemporary info-culture. The operation relies on a belief that the informational sign unproblematically stands in for the actual.

Heidegger emphasizes that modern technology's particular mode of revealing involves 'enframing', and this is certainly the case with computers. Revealing is structured and predestined by the technologically mediated relationship with the real. Everything is relegated to standing reserve at the call of the particular configurations of technology. 'Enframing' occurs because the imperative to force the real to become 'standing reserve' requires an institutionalization of the manner in which revealing occurs. The technological practice necessarily imposes monolithic form on its object.

Building data structures in the digital domain inevitably involves enframing. The 'real' is removed from the spatial and stored as digital code, spread across the grid pattern of addresses. The manner in which encoding takes place – choice of code and process by which the data are input – has a powerful influence on the later revealing through invocation. When a written text is stored in ASCII code, any markings which do not fit the 256 characters in the code disappear. A database stores only a strictly defined set of information in fields for a defined category of objects. Within the frame of the database, invocation is very fast and accurate. But anything which does not fit the categorial boundaries is effectively invisible within that domain. The process of making the data fit the categories is very much an enframing. Sometimes patterns in data can emerge which bear no relation to the actual referent. Enframed by Windows[TM], information takes on a life of its own as data, projecting unworldly visions of virtual patterns with no necessary spatial reference.

Spatial metaphors like cyberspace or the desktop are a realist imposition of a single enframing as universal. By implying that spatiality (which is only reconstituted on the interfaces) is internal to the digital domain, the nature of the enframing is hidden from sight. As noted earlier, the spatial metaphors are often very useful, making the very abstract operations of the digital domain more accessible and tangible. However, in the tradition of Brechtian theatre, the illusion should perpetually be challenged, broken down and reconstituted. The structuring of the revealing should regularly be shown up as contingent and historical. The economics of standardization and mass production of software militate against such a critical conception.

The world as peripheral

The physical world is being arranged to suit invocation and begins to resemble digital domains. Computer peripherals extend the voice and ears of invocation into the spatial world. Bar code scanners require that all products be tagged with machine-readable labels. Customers must carry credit cards. Some computer sensors read patterns in the world as though they were in digital domains. Character recognition software reads text from a page. Face recognition, fingerprint recognition and other techniques read the body of the subject. Integrated into architectures of control, such systems can automatically impel insiders to keep out those who do not look right. Invocational systems formalize and embody social codes of hierarchy and power in a technical form. Sociograms and technograms merge (Latour; see Feenberg, 1991: 82). There tends to be less scope for discretionary application of power when the authority comes from a database process rather than from a person. The particular implementation of a system reflects the interests of the institution that created the database. A police database represents people as suspects and victims. A credit card database identifies subjects as debtors and creditors. A customer database identifies people as past and prospective future consumers. In each case, the data architecture reflects and reinforces the subject positions systematically imagined and constructed by the institutions that set up the databases.

The relationship between the virtual sign in the digital domain and actual phenomena is unstable because actions in the digital do not operate in the same way as the 'real' world. Universal addressability and digital encoding separate form from content. Broken off from embodiment in the physical realm, information is conducted into the spaceless digital domains of electric speed (Virilio, 1977). *Poeisis* in digital domains is qualitatively and quantitatively different to a *becoming physical*. While the destining revealing in the physical world results in physically embodied artefacts or places, invocation to the digital domain can continue feeding back on itself to reveal further encodings. Without the ambiguities or inconveniences of physical signifieds, the virtual, the simulacra, are far better subjects than anything in the real world. A crisis of referentiality emerges when the digital ontological realm supersedes the physical. Connections between data and referent become fragile and can easily snap apart because of the difference in nature of spatial *address* and invocational *address*. Actions in digital domains start taking on their own logic. The stock market crash of 1987 occurred through the virtual geography of the market's digital domain (Wark, 1995). Subjects in the digital domain are far more readily accessible than in the physical world. Databases multiply the individual whom institutions can act upon remotely (Poster, 1990: 97). Subjects and objects in dataspace constitute additional selves.

Politics of the invocational voice

Heidegger's analysis is more limited for evaluating the politics of invocational technologies. He warns of the 'danger' of 'enframing' – that it may block 'a more original revealing' and 'more primal truth' (1977: 28). His quest for a more primal truth is echoed by other critics of technologically mediated experience like Lewis Mumford. They argue that technology blinds us to seeing some primeval truth; constructed variously as a mystical, idealized, Romantic 'nature' or spiritual knowledge. Even Baudrillard's fears about disappearing into hyperreal simulation smack of nostalgia. Heidegger's conservative viewpoint lacks a critique of social power. He romanticizes a mythical past, rejecting in one stroke all contemporary technology. Don Ihde (1993) identifies a tendency for Heidegger to privilege 'good' technologies such as the stone bridge over 'bad' ones like the steel highway bridge. He argues that Heidegger tends to be nostalgic for technologies which give an embodied relation to the world. For example, he prefers hand-writing to the typewriter. Ihde says Heiddeger's nostalgia evades examining the politics of artefacts, which has been of interest to other theorists like Langdon Winner. Tom Rockmore is more damning, saying 'there is no indication . . . Heidegger . . . has a real comprehension of the nature of society' (1995: 141).

The invocational genie is already out of the bottle. There is no retreat to innocence. We are already cyborgs. Corporate and government hierarchies use computers to control commodities and subjects. Public networks, on the other hand, might give voices to people excluded from mainstream media. The questions that remain are political, and start with paying attention to the invocational voice. Who can speak? Who is silenced? Who is commanded? Who inscribes digital domains? Who writes the spells? The world is increasingly standing reserve, but which parts are standing, and for whom are they in reserve? What remains outside? Invocational media are powerful contemporary means of creating authorized knowledge and imposing power.

The Analogue Other

As economic and social activities involve more and more use of computers, a larger and more significant cleavage appears between what is or can be encoded digitally and what resists or is outside: the Analogue Other. The fluid placelessness of the digital contrasts with the cumbersome immovability of the physical. The information stored on databanks is more accessible than the knowledge bound to physical artefacts or places. Therefore the analogue tends to be forgotten and disappears. The statistical abstractions generated automatically by the maintenance of databases systematically ignore phenomena beyond the digital. The oppositional and marginal are the most prone to becoming Other. Data entry and software development are expensive. Access to powerful computer equipment and the skills to operate it are determined by social power relations. The enframing entailed by encoding privileges some forms of knowledge and renders others invisible. All these forces systematically and institutionally construct Others.

On the other hand, as often happens, the emergence of something new casts fresh light on old phenomena. Computers are still marginal to most people's daily lives. The limitations of the physical are simultaneously its strengths. In a world where simulacra multiply indefinitely, possessing a unique individual identity, persisting over time and being tied to one location have enduring value. The huge sums paid for celebrity paraphernalia or art are extreme examples of the value of the unique. People tend to prefer narrative memory to structured grids: CD-ROM multimedia has put no dent in cinema attendances. The digital is ambivalent to scale, to space and to time. The physical world on a human scale is far more finely textured. People resist technology, or are indifferent to it. In spite of all technological fantasies, people live as physical, gendered, sexed bodies, tethered to one place at one time, with inescapable life cycles. There are politics behind engineers' dreams of the world as digital domain. In the era of invocational media you have to be careful what you wish for.

92 THE SELF, IDENTITY AND BODY

References

Baudrillard, Jean (1995) *The Gulf War Did Not Take Place*. Sydney: Power Publications.

Benedikt, Michael (ed.) (1992) *Cyberspace: First Steps*. Cambridge, MA: MIT Press.

Borges, Jorge Luis (1962) 'The Library of Babel', in *Fictions*. London: Calder. pp. 72–80.

Carter, Paul (1987) *The Road to Botany Bay: An Exploration of Landscape and History*. New York: Albert A. Knopf.

Davis, Erik (1993) 'Techgnosis: Magic, Memory and the Angels of Information', in Mark Dery (ed.), *Flame Wars: The Discourse of Cyberculture. South Atlantic Quarterly*, Special Issue, 92 (4): 584–616.

Feenberg, Andrew (1991) *Critical Theory of Technology*. New York and Oxford: Oxford University Press.

Gibson, William (1984) *Neuromancer*. New York: Ace.

Heidegger, Martin (1977) 'The Question Concerning Technology', in *The Question Concerning Technology and Other Essays* (trans. William Lovitt). New York: Harper. pp. 3–35.

HREF 1: http://www.eff.org/ftp/Publications/FAQ_RFC_FYI_IEN/GII_NII/-virtual_folder: Barlow, J.P. (1994) 'Jack In, Young Pioneer!' *Keynote Essay for the 1994 Computerworld College Edition*.

HREF 2: http://english-server.hss.cmu.edu/cultronix/Chesher/chesher. Chesher, Chris (1992) 'Colonising Virtual Reality', *Cultronix* No. 1.

HREF 3: http://www.hpcc.gov/white-house/gore.nii.html. Gore, Al (1994) Remarks by the Vice President at the National Press Club Newsmaker Luncheon. National Press Club. Washington, DC: White House. Office of the Press Secretary.

HREF 4: http://www.iti.qc.ca/iti/users/sean/bunny/b02/ess/sl-clarke.html. Lehman, Steve (1996) 'Divining Arthur C. Clarke'.

Ihde, Don (1993) *Postphenomenology: Essays in the Postmodern Context*. Evanston, IL: Northwestern University Press.

Poster, Mark (1990) *The Mode of Information: Poststructuralism and Social Context*. Oxford: Polity.

Rockmore, Tom (1995) 'Heidegger on Technology and Democracy', in Andrew Feenberg and Alistair Hannay (eds), *Technology and the Politics of Knowledge*. Bloomington, IN: Indiana University Press. pp. 128–46.

Roszak, Theodore (1986) *The Cult of Information: The Folklore of Computers and the True Art of Thinking*. New York: Pantheon Books.

Shannon, Claude and Weaver, W. (1949) *The Mathematical Theory of Communications*. Urbana, IL: University of Illinois Press.

Stephensen, Neal (1992) *Snow Crash*. New York: Bantam Spectra.

Sterling, Bruce (1992) *The Hacker Crackdown*. New York: Bantam Books.

Virilio, Paul (1977) *Speed and Politics* (trans. Mark Polizotti). New York: Semiotext(e).

Wark, McKenzie (1995) *Virtual Geography*. Bloomington, IN: Indiana University Press.

Woolley, B. (1992) *Virtual Worlds*. Oxford: Basil Blackwell.

Zuboff, Shoshana (1984) *In the Age of the Smart Machine*. New York: Basic Books.

5

PLENITUDE AND ALIENATION:
The Subject of Virtual Reality

Simon Cooper

Junior Deities, we want to be. Reality is mostly given. Virtual Reality is creatable.

(Brand, 1987: 116)

Though the technology of virtual reality has not developed to the point where, as some commentators believe,[1] it will mark a new stage in human evolution, the burgeoning claims for its potential have not subsided. This chapter examines some of those claims, in particular the suggestion that the subject becomes empowered through inhabiting the space of VR. I want to argue that VR does not constitute, as many of its proponents hope, a radical break with present modes of being. Rather, the discourse surrounding VR can be seen to foreground many of the ideologies underpinning the present social formation of late capitalism. In claiming this, I take up Robert Markley's suggestion that '[c]yberspace is already marked by competing values about reality and subjectivity, by previous political struggles to naturalize and resist particular constructions of reality' (1994a: 439). In particular, VR seems to be an ideal medium for articulating the anxieties and fantasies of the postmodern subject – especially the desire for mastery through which the subject is the absolute point of reference for, and creator of, its own experiences. How the technology of VR promotes this type of ego-logical subjecthood is my main focus.

What is particularly interesting about the literature on VR is the way many commentators emphasize the increased potential for imagination and creativity that VR allows the subject. VR is seen to contrast with the technologies that previously dominated the modern social formation, such as film, radio and television, all of which followed the pattern of a relatively small number of broadcasters and a multitude of 'passive' receivers. It allows the subject to become active once again, and to reclaim aspects of creativity, imagination and interaction which were not possible in those earlier social and technological forms. Mark Poster, for instance, claims that VR has the potential to 'allow the participant to

enter imagined worlds with convincing verisimilitude, releasing immense
potentials for fantasy, self discovery and self-construction' (1994: 88). I
want to suggest that VR will only be able to empower the subject if its
'insights' are read reflexively back into the world outside its parameters.
Implicit in this argument is a recognition of the importance of preserving
present forms of worldly involvement, modes of engagement which sustain
human life and generate creative activity, rather than limit it. Such a
recognition remains unacknowledged by many of those who write about
VR.

Unlike the apparent passivity engendered by older forms of technology,
VR allows the subject to become 'active' through interacting with the
technology itself. However, we need to recognize that not all forms of
activity are the same. In examining the notions of subjective activity
promised by VR, it is worth keeping in mind Martin Heidegger's critique of
modern technology. Heidegger lamented the meaningless activity that often
marks the technological age, claiming: 'Everything is functioning. This
exactly is what is so uncanny, that everything is functioning and that the
functioning drives us more and more to even further functioning' (1981:
53). Like Heidegger, we need to distinguish between activity and mere
functioning. Many proponents of VR claim that it will 'free' us by allowing
us to create our own environment. But will VR deliver us from the woes of
the present, as its proponents claim, or will the activity that takes place
within VR provoke us more than ever into the forms of meaningless
activity Heidegger described?

Typical of the claims made for VR is that it will constitute a 'revelation':
that it will lead to a 'release of the imagination' (Stenger, 1992: 53). But we
need to ask why the virtual subject will be more creative than its
predecessor. What are the conditions that provide this allegedly enhanced
creative activity? The enabling condition of VR is its fundamental isolation
from the world surrounding it. The hardware of VR – the helmet, the glove
or the body suit – is designed to isolate the user completely from 'outside'
interference. This isolation leads commentators to promote two contradictory trajectories of virtual subjectivity. The first, and most common, is
the 'naive' conception of the virtual subject which imagines that we can
simply enter VR and remain unchanged by the technology constructing the
virtual world. This version regards the virtual subject as autonomous, as a
subject whose creative possibilities are limited only by the imagination. It
tends to rely on the romantic notion of the creative subject and ignores the
changes that the virtual subject undergoes through the use of VR technology. The second trajectory is more sophisticated and argues that VR
may disrupt the boundaries of corporeality and identity, and thus may
enable us to transcend capitalistic and patriarchal structures of domination.
Arguably the conditions of VR could lead to the creation of a 'cyborg'-like
subjectivity allowing a more effective resistance to the hegemonic patterns
of the present social formation. Both of these trajectories will be dealt with
in turn.

VR as surrogate utopia

According to many of VR's supporters, creativity is restricted by present forms of materiality. Physical and social limitations restrict the freedom of the subject. As a consequence, it is desirable to dispense with these limitations as soon as possible. The most obvious manifestation of worldly contamination is the body, which is either jettisoned completely with Manichean contempt or radically reconstituted so that its perceptual and sensory fields can be regulated. Terence McKenna provides a typical instance of this utopianism based around a dichotomizing of the material and the spiritual. For McKenna, VR is merely the first step in 'the freeing of life from the chrysalis of matter . . . where information can detach itself from the material matrix and then look back on a cast off mode of being as it arises into a higher dimension' (cited in Rushkoff, 1994: 19–20). The capacity to isolate the user from all forms of worldly involvement becomes, then, VR's apparent virtue. For the first time in history, the subject is freed from all material constraints and given new possibilities of freedom. The virtual subject becomes more powerful than its predecessor. Michael Heim says of the profound implications of casting aside worldly limitations that

the ultimate VR experience is a philosophical experience, probably an experience of the sublime or awesome . . . the final point of a virtual world is to dissolve the constraints of the anchored world so that we can lift anchor – not to drift aimlessly without point, but so we can explore anchorage in ever new places. (1993: 7)

In a moment I will take up the implications of simply lifting anchor, but it is worth noting how the possibility of (simulated) escape from the 'anchored world' has led to the construction of VR as a surrogate utopian space. The utopian fantasies that underpin VR represent a desire to escape the conditions and problems of the present world, rather than an attempt to alter them. Those who idealize the utopian potentials of VR tend to have a rather 'thin' conception of the prior-virtual setting. The world is a locus of environmental and social problems, of disease and suffering, of physical constraints; in short, a world of oppressive limitation. VR is valorized for its redemptive possibilities. Benedikt argues that VR is

[T]he realm of pure information, filling a lake, siphoning the jangle of messages transfiguring the physical world, decontaminating the natural and urban landscapes, redeeming them, saving them . . . from the diesel smoke of courier and post office trucks . . . from all the inefficiencies, pollutions (chemical and informational), and corruptions attendant to the process of moving information attached to *things* – from paper to brains – across, over and under the vast and bumpy surface of the earth rather than letting it fly free in the soft hail of electrons that is cyberspace. (1992: 3)

While Benedikt's ecological awareness is noteworthy, his Utopian construction of VR is representative of the cybernetic dream: a purging of 'noise' in all its forms. We need to explore the investments that lie behind a wish to rid the social space of 'things'. What forms of engagement will the virtual world promote? What modes of subjectivity will emerge when we communicate without the tangible presence of the other and our identity relies primarily on our ability fleetingly to reinvent ourselves? The effect of living in a world of 'pure' information has to be examined carefully. The Utopian aspects promised by the development of VR all too easily conflate into the more baleful aspects of postmodern interaction; including the development of a form of technological solipsism, ironically proposed as a step towards a new community of equality. For example, Jaron Lanier points out that the VR experience is a radically private one, where markers of identity such as race, class and gender 'all become invention. You can be whoever or whatever you want. . . . Virtual Reality is the ultimate lack of class or race distinctions or any other form of pretence since all form is variable' (cited in Orenstein, 1991: 63). Yet this erasure of identity also comes at the cost of devaluing the rich subjective experiences that result from belonging to these 'categories'. The resolution of social imbalances must come out of these subjective experiences, not through bypassing them with a technologically mediated identity constituted on a more abstract level.

Frederic Jameson has pointed out how the construction of a private object world is a defining feature of reified postmodern society where privatized 'Utopian' spaces allow one to banish the other, as well as abandoning an appreciation of the material conditions which stand behind social life (1992: 315). It is easy to see the appeal of VR at this basic level. The self-referential environment it creates fulfils the desire to transcend the fragmentation of the contemporary social realm. The virtual space is constructed as a domain where all forms of subjective experience are offered the possibility of re-enchantment as the subject customizes his/her own relation to a new environment. As such, VR is clearly an extension of the process Jameson describes. It offers the means of healing individual and social fragmentation. However, as we shall see, the virtual integration of experience takes a specific form, and is more problematic than its proponents recognize.

The construction of VR as a redemptive, Utopian space inevitably leads to the creation of a hierarchy between virtual and non-virtual subjects and environments. The reductive framing of the physical world as a limit necessarily leads to the wish to transcend it. Such a hierarchy is perhaps most succinctly captured in William Gibson's cyberpunk trilogy (Gibson, 1984, 1988a, 1988b), where the characters who inhabit cyberspace are privileged over those who still live in the 'real' world of chaos and poverty, that is, those who still inhabit 'the prison of the flesh' (Gibson, 1984: 12). Other proponents of VR echo the sensibility found in Gibson's work and construct a similar hierarchy. For example, Nicole Stenger writes with typical abandon: 'And what if the passage to a new level of humanity actually meant abolishing indeed the natural one, or at least some part of it?' (1992: 55). Yet what are the effects of devaluing the older settings of human engagement with the world? If we dwell on Gibson's work for a moment, we can see that it is precisely the sense of disenchantment with the material and finite world that creates in his characters the desperate desire to inhabit the realm of cyberspace. Gibson's characters experience cyberspace not so much as a place of unbounded creativity, but as a drug-like addiction. The comparisons between drugs and VR abound (just think of the late Timothy Leary), but Gibson is worth citing on the relations between an amphetamine high and the experience of cyberspace:

> . . . in some weird and approximate way, it was like a run in the matrix [cyberspace]. Get just wasted enough, find yourself in some desperate but strangely arbitrary kind of trouble, and it was possible to see Ninsei as a field of data, the way the matrix had once reminded him . . . then you could throw yourself into a highspeed drift and skid, totally engaged but set apart from it all. (1984: 26)

Two points come out of the comparison. The first is that cyberspace *is* addictive, especially when it becomes the only possible vehicle for transcendence. The second involves how the cyberspace experience is described: the subject is engaged and detached at the same time. These adjectives form a recurrent motif in VR discourse, and are suggestive of the way the subject interacts in VR.[2]

While Gibson's novel is a fictional rendering, it is worth noting that the narcotic framing of cyberspace aptly conveys the hierarchy that inevitably results from mediating between virtual and non-virtual worlds. VR tends to operate not so much as an empowering creative environment, but as an addictive space of desire. If the construction of the virtual space as an area of plenitude only occurs through removing the subject from the problems of the 'real' world rather than solving these problems, how is the subject to mediate between the virtual world and the world outside? This dilemma is rendered even more acute if (as I hope to show) the claims for creative empowerment in VR are largely exaggerated and rest on self-contradictory premises. The assumption that VR is place of enhanced autonomy all too easily leads to disenchantment outside the virtual environment. Markley notes that, while 'the subject is empowered in cyberspace to mark, to create, to render her desire productive; when she steps outside of Virtual Reality, she is without ready access to the creativity that defines her existence and experiences her desire as a profound lack' (1994b: 502).

Yet the answer is not simply to inhabit the space of VR as much as possible. On the contrary the 'freedom' that results from inhabiting VR comes at an enormous cost – an impoverishment of the cultural settings that enable a far richer, wider and more heterogeneous realization of human possibilities in their manual, somatic and intellectual expressions. But it is the devaluation of such settings that leads to the promotion of VR as a Utopian space. The world existing prior to VR cannot simply be seen as a historical constraint to be shed as useless baggage. Instead, it serves as a repository for deeper human needs and actually provides the grounds

n which creativity can emerge. Before this can be shown, it is necessary
xamine more closely the type of subjectivity that operates in the virtual
environment.

The virtual subject

It is somewhat mistaken to claim that many VR proponents simply want to
'leave' the body. VR includes some form of embodiment, though one that
is profoundly altered: in effect, a reconstruction of embodiment. But this
reconstruction ultimately allows VR to be the place where corporeality is
disavowed. Of course, some proponents of VR claim that they do not want
to 'flee' the body at all. Jaron Lanier argues that 'the body is a continuity'
and goes on to say that 'the sense organs . . . [are] central to our identity
and define our whole mode of being . . . the whole notion of bypassing the
senses is sort of like throwing away the actual treasure' (cited in Rushkoff,
1994: 71). Similarly, Randall Walser argues that the essential difference and
advantage of VR over film, plays and TV is that unlike, the latter,
'cyberspace embodies' (cited in Rheingold, 1991: 286). It is because VR
provides some form of embodied experience that it is regarded as different
from earlier modes of technological interaction. Because 'cyberspace
embodies' it is able to simulate better the conditions of subjectivity that
occur in the 'real' world without any of the limitations of embodiment. In
addition, the empowering aspect of VR lies precisely in the form of
embodied experience; creative flights of fancy no longer take place merely
in the mind, but are 'felt' as well. Leaving aside the problems inherent in
such a crude opposition between mind and body, these claims fail to
recognize that bodily sensations and effects which are generated in VR take
place in a different register. The two-fold desire both to escape the body
and to 'keep the treasure' marks the place where it is possible to examine
the constitution of the virtual subject and criticize the assumptions
underlying the claims for increased creativity and activity made on its
behalf. The first of these assumptions concerns the embodied subject. I
want to compare briefly the senses of embodiment that lie inside and
outside VR. Embodiment is a complex process which underlies our relation
to the world. To reconstitute the body will result in a transformation of
subjective experience. To illustrate this, I will briefly look at the work of
Maurice Merleau-Ponty to show how the lived body generates our
understanding of ourselves and our world, and how this sense of a lived
body is radically reconstituted by VR technology.

According to Merleau-Ponty our sense of embodiment is essential to the
process of both self and world constitution. The lived body provides the
'horizon and perspectival point which places me in the world and, makes
relations between me, other objects, and other subjects possible' (cited in
Grosz, 1994: 86). Important to the sense of a lived body is the experience of
bodily mobility. Merleau-Ponty writes that

[m]obility then, is not . . . a handmaid of consciousness, transporting the body to that point in space of which we have formed a representation beforehand. In order that we may be able to move our body towards an object, the object must first exist for it, our body must not belong to the realm of the 'in-itself'. (1962: 133)

Neither the subject nor the world can simply be posited, but both are instead simultaneously generated by the sense of bodily involvement with the external world.

How is this sense of a lived body re-created in VR? Despite the continual reliance by commentators on a belief that both embodiment and mobility can be effectively simulated in a virtual environment, there are several important differences between the construction of the virtual body and the form of embodied subjectivity Merleau-Ponty describes. First, there is little sense of any boundary between the virtual subject's body and the environment. The subject can (and usually does) fly and, although one can grasp objects and thus simulate some form of resistance on the part of the object, the subject can also walk through walls and into pictures, and inhabit large or small spaces. This is seen to be an advantage, as Rushkoff points out: VR 'provide[s] access to places the human body can't go, granting new perspectives on old problems' (1994: 70). Perhaps so, but it also profoundly alters the subject who operates in these conditions. The reconfigured form of embodiment provides no sense of the subject's body as *situated* in space. There seems to be little perspective through which the subject could gain a sense of body-image – essential, according to Merleau-Ponty for the simultaneous generation of subject and environment. This is also the case in Gibson's *Neuromancer* (which has influenced so many developers of VR), where the virtual subject encounters a distinct lack of embodied perspective. Scott Bukatman points out that at no time in the novel does the virtual subject ever gain a sense of bodily situation: 'the reader of *Neuromancer* is kept in the dark regarding the form of [the] body – the subject of cyberspace never examines *himself*' (1993: 207; original emphasis).

The reconstituted form of embodiment necessarily alters the mode of subjectivity operating in VR. Without a sense of definable perspective, the boundaries between self and world are irretrievably blurred. The virtual subject encounters no resistance, the body seems not so much engaged with the world as it is a passive receptor on which technologically mediated sensations impinge. Cathryn Vasseleu has noted how the sense of tactility is reworked in VR. Tactile sensations are no longer interiorized but are registered on exterior surfaces. In VR some dimensions of tactility are emphasized, others are marginalized, being regarded as 'passive "feedback" in the cybernetic compartmentalization of the faculty of touch' (p. 51, this volume). The exteriorization of embodiment renders a different sense of self and world. The effects of this reconstitution lead to what Paul Virilio calls a 'constitutive dispersal', where perspectival boundaries collapse into 'an open system in which nobody can find any perceptible, objective limits' (1991: 72). The virtual subject becomes a prosthetic subject, its body no longer locatable in time and space as everything merges into a field of external sensations. Hayles writes of the experience of VR that 'when the technologically enhanced body is joined in a sensory feedback loop with the simulacrum that lives in RAM, it is impossible to locate an originary source for experience and sensation' (1993: 174). Given this, what type of activity can take place in VR? Let us turn to Gibson again for a fictional, but nevertheless accurate description:

> Bodiless, we swerve in Chrome's castle of ice. And we're fast, fast. It feels as if we're surfing the crest of the invading program, hanging ten above the seething glitch systems as they mutate. We're sentient patches of oil swept along corridors of shadow. (1988a: 200)

Certainly Gibson's subjects are prosthetic subjects, passive receptors for the sensations passing through them. The prosthetic effect Gibson describes remains true of most forms of mobility in VR. David Holmes points out elsewhere in this volume that 'common scenes used by VR realism are simulated forms of transporting bodies such as flight simulation, car travel or even walking on a walking machine' (p. 4). Rather than empowering the subject, the erasure of a previously lived constitutive field renders the subject victim to what Virilio calls the 'inertia of speed'. For Virilio, technological progress infinitely promotes speed, as the subject passes from a perceived freedom of movement to a tyranny of movement. Arguably, VR creates the very kind of prosthetic activity where the simulation of movement leads to a speed-inertial effect. The subject of VR tends to become, to paraphrase Baudrillard, a mere screen for the assimilation of data. The claims for enhanced freedom in VR are rendered suspicious because, as Virilio points out, 'the field of freedom shrinks with speed. And freedom needs a field. When there is no more field our lives will be a terminal, a machine with doors that open and close' (1983: 54). The simulation of embodiment creates a vastly different sense of self and world, one that allows the illusion of autonomy to become more concrete. Yet this autonomy comes at a cost. Subjective experience is now framed by technological processes in a manner previously unimaginable.

VR and creativity

Much of the discourse surrounding VR assumes that the subject will simply be able to enter VR and be free to work and play essentially unchanged. The perceived advantage of VR lies in its ability to simulate the 'real' world without any of its limitations, thus leaving the subject free to create. This type of claim all too often ignores the transformative aspects that the technology will have on the subject as it renders his/her virtual world. If, as I have argued, the conditions making a virtual environment possible radically alter the mode of subjectivity that operates there, the notion of the creative subject needs to be reconsidered. How are we to speak of creativity when the technology of VR works to reconstitute the phenomenological experiences that determine subjectivity? Instead of inhabiting a free space of the imagination, a brief look at VR technology reveals a mode of subjectivity overdetermined by the technology in which it operates. The virtual subject is, in a sense, spoken for in a way previously unimaginable. Cut off from the material settings that originally frame the desire for creativity, one can argue that any notion of creativity in VR operates in a completely different register. If we understand creative activity, in the broadest sense, to stem from some desire for transcendence, it is possible to argue that such activity is restricted in VR because the forces that produce the desire to create are, by definition, alienated. Freed from material constraints, from chaos, noise and struggle, creativity within VR might be characterized as creativity *without work*. I want to show that the creative process is bound up in the subject's engagement with the material world. Closing off, or filtering out, the less desirable aspects of this world may well lead to an impoverished practice of creativity.

In contrast to those who see the world prior to VR as one of limitation, it can be suggested that meaningful activity derives from an intimate involvement with the world. Francisco Varela argues that purposeful action emerges from perceptual breakdowns which generate 'microworlds'. Microworlds are the constellation of material forces that generate a particular mode of subject behaviour. They are historically and culturally constituted, and contribute to the enactment of the subject's environment. Action on the part of the subject involves '[embodying] a stream of recurrent microworld transitions' (Varela, 1992: 328). Perception and action are both constrained by the world and enact the world. Varela gives the example of a man out for a walk who loses his wallet. The world of this walker is constituted in a particular way – he is relaxed, enjoying the surroundings, perceiving the environment in a certain manner. Suddenly he realizes that his wallet is missing. Breakdown. A new constitutive frame emerges. He remembers leaving wallet in a shop. His pace quickens, and he takes little notice of his surroundings. His attention is directed to getting back to the shop without delay. He is concerned about losing money and documents. He visualizes the wallet sitting on the shop counter, and is concerned about whether it is still there. His mode of operation has shifted, with a corresponding shift in cognitive assessment and emotional tonality. Varela's point is that cognition emerges from the rich complexity of physical engagements with the world. Furthermore, creative activity emerges out of chance encounters which cause the subject to choose between microworlds or to develop new ones. Varela writes that

> the key to autonomy is that a living system finds its way to the next moment by acting appropriately from its own resources. And it is the breakdowns, the hinges that articulate microworlds, that are the source of the autonomous and creative side of living cognition. (1992: 329)

Reality does not pre-exist in the form of representations to be recovered by consciousness. Accordingly, microworlds cannot be calculated in advance because the chaotic elements from outside the system work to produce the generative breakdown from which new microworlds emerge. Varela compares the cognitive process to an unruly conversation, arguing that 'the very presence of this unruliness allows a cognitive moment to come into being' (1992: 336). This cannot take place within a closed system, however, because 'the very heart of this autonomy, the rapidity of the agent's behaviour selection, is forever lost to the cognitive system itself' (1992: 336). Thus 'noise' is not the restriction of creativity, but its underpinning. Here lies a crucial distinction between virtual and pre-virtual environments. For many commentators, the advantage of VR is that, unlike 'normal' reality, it creates an environment free of noise. As Pimental and Teixeira explain:

> Unlike the randomness of everyday reality, a virtual experience is a planned experience in which every sensory detail is a design decision. The usefulness of virtual environments is not that it duplicates all the details of reality (a fact technically impossible), but because it functions like our consciousness as a filter and focus, presenting only those details essential for enhancing a specific experience, or solving a given problem. (1993: 147)

Our consciousness may function like a filter, but the important difference is that the environment it engages with has not been filtered in advance. In the virtual environment, the chance operations that generate creativity are severely restricted by the design decisions needed to make VR a convincing illusion in the first place.

Given Varela's description of the cognitive process, and the contrast to the 'planned environment' of VR, what are we to make of the claim that the virtual subject will in fact become *more* creative? With the fundamental separation from the material realm that defines VR, it follows that the ability to experience a generative breakdown is drastically reduced. The sensorimotor capacities engaged with the world are largely controlled and generated by the technology that constructs the virtual environment. The experience of loss or crisis that might send the subject on a purposeful activity is denied by the technology that attempts to render a world of full presence. The significant reduction of 'noise' works to stifle rather than enhance purposeful creativity.

We could argue therefore that the nature of VR erodes the conditions that make creative activity a significant transformative experience. The space of VR cuts itself off from the very materiality that informs our experience. The fundamental alienation from the prior world of physical and social engagements invites the dream of a pure realm of self-presence, but any creative process within this realm takes place in a significantly different register. The subject operates in VR only by removing him/herself from the processes of labour, history and the social realm. The attraction of VR is its promise of renewal; the subject can reinvent him/herself and the world through endless narratives of re-creation which are, by their a priori removal from the material realm, limitless in their possibility. However, as Markley points out, such narratives do not emerge existentially but occur instcad as heavily mediated effects of the technology that produces a new mode of subjectivity (1994b: 503). While VR is seen to enhance subjective experience, it also severs any involvement with the prior frames of reference generating the initial desire to create.

The desire for a renewal of creative activity arises as the contemporary subject feels severed from meaningful relations with the world. Perhaps it is the lure of new spaces to inhabit, 'pure' unreified spaces, that forms the attraction of VR. But the perceived benefits of VR are derived from assumptions which increase rather than combat the further reification of life. Consistently in the discourse of VR there is a tendency to devalue the variety of concrete social and environmental settings that gives meaning to human activity. The assumption of autonomy, of the subject's freedom to create, comes only through removing the subject from these settings. The promise of a mode of being which takes place on this abstracted level ends up enforcing a process of reification rather than resisting or overcoming it. The fundamental alienation that VR offers severs the subject from the very possibility of experiences which might be more resistant to the process of commodification that s/he is partly trying to escape.

VR and cyborg subjects

Not all commentators on VR subscribe to what might be called a more 'naive' version of virtual subjectivity – naive in the sense that the complex manner in which we engage with the world is taken for granted. Instead of emphasizing VR as a realm of plenitude and self-presence, Mark Poster suggests that VR might work to disrupt older, more hegemonic conditions of subject formation. He argues that '[b]y directly tinkering with reality, a simulational practice is set in place which forever alters the conditions under which the identity of the self is formed' (1994: 79). Rather than promoting a surrogate freedom which comes through severing the subject from the world outside VR, Poster would see VR as providing forms of subjective experience which might work to disrupt contemporary forms of domination. Certain forms of virtual experience could work to constitute a more heterogeneous 'cyborg'-like subjectivity similar to that envisaged by Donna Haraway. Poster claims that VR helps create 'multiple realities' which fragment the subject so that s/he can no longer be formed within a modern framework. The more rigid, often hegemonic structures through which identity is formed are shattered through VR-like technologies. The corresponding multiplication of realities leads to new possibilities of freedom.

The difference between Poster and the commentators referred to earlier is that Poster is aware of the transformative capacities of VR technologies, in the sense that the subject cannot enter VR and remain unchanged. His analysis also retains a degree of reflexivity in that the experiences of VR can be read back into the world as a means of analysing structures of subject formation. Poster claims that VR's potential lies in 'interfering with the process through which subjects recognise that they are constituted and that they may, with the proper mediations of others, reconstitute themselves and their world so that subject definition becomes its desired goal and social end' (1994: 58).[3] Poster claims that VR operates to denaturalize assumptions about the givenness of identity, physicality and embodiment, and claims an emancipatory potential for VR since such destabilization can bring oppressive structures into question. How would the experience of VR promote a destabilization of identity (and is this necessarily a positive thing)? Poster may not necessarily allow us answers, but N. Katherine Hayles suggests that the mechanism of VR might contribute to an appreciation of alterity and an undermining of the monadological subject. Noting an important difference between virtual space and the Lacanian mirror, Hayles argues that the cyberspace screen problematizes the process of identification. The technologically rendered cyberspace 'puppet' promotes a sense of alterity as it provides a different locus for subjective sensations. Hayles claims that 'the putative subject is the unconscious embodied in a physical form, while the object is the puppet behind the screen. Since the flow of sensory information goes in both directions, however, the puppet can be seen as the originary point for sensations (1993: 187).

This disorientating effect has the potential to generate a radical ambiguity which challenges the 'customary construction of the bodies' boundaries, opening them to transformative configurations that always bear the trace of the other' (Hayles, 1993: 187). Many of the claims made for VR do not share Hayles' insight, which suggests that the experiential challenge of alterity encountered in VR is not a strong one. The destabilizing of the relationship between self and other that can occur in VR may only be useful as an experience which is read back to our relationships outside VR. The subject in VR remains largely autonomous and removed from more disturbing forms of otherness. The phenomenological disruption encountered in VR may provide a trace of alterity, but we can argue that it remains a *sanitized* experience, not disturbing enough to displace the fantasies of autonomous subjecthood. Certainly it has not disturbed the fantasies of many cyberspace enthusiasts.[4]

Care needs to be taken when emphasizing subject formation as a primary means of resistance to hegemonic practices. While Poster's analysis of the potential for radically new modes of subjectivity is more sophisticated than many others, we still have to emphasize the importance of preserving certain forms of engagement which are not so easily accommodated by the linguistic theory that informs his position. Certain 'depth' formations which lie outside the logic of the signifier may prove more resistant to the instrumental tendencies of the information age than a flexible subjectivity *per se* can. Poster recognizes this tension in relation to multiculturalism, in that technologies such as VR which might contribute to a more flexible process of subject formation can also contribute to the erasure of ethnic identity (1994: 90). The problem, however, may be a great deal broader than this specific issue.

Subject formation can occur in a variety of ways – it can occur through the desires of a radically autonomous 'super-subject' whose autonomy is derived from abstracting the self from concrete social settings such as home, neighbourhood and other local contexts. Or the subject can form as a result of practices which recognize the interrelationship of self and world. In other words, that there is a need to remain tied to constitutional frames which grant a degree of substance and permanence to the process of subjecthood, rather than a more universalized, abstracted range of positions which the subject can choose from and disregard at will. The lure of VR is all too often the promise of unbounded autonomy, a promise which can only lead to disenchantment.

We have seen from the work of Varela and Merleau-Ponty that subjectivity is a process embedded in the world, that subjective experience is informed by the practices engaged in by the subject. Yet the manner in which VR technology operates, and *which it is valorized for*, is precisely to remove the subject from the complexity of social practices that have previously constituted a meaningful experience of the lifeworld. To make this point is not to suggest that VR cannot contribute to the disruption of certain modes of subject formation. But the process can only lead to emancipation if it is adopted in a reflexive manner which recognizes the importance of constitutional frames occurring outside, and prior to, that provided by VR. Haraway is fully alert to the problems here and warns about dangerous misappropriations of her work: [A]ny transcendentalist move is deadly. . . . These holistic, transcendentalist moves promise a way out of history, a way of participating in the god trick. A way of denying mortality (1991: 16).

The problem with much of the discourse on VR is that it tends towards precisely the transcendentalism Haraway warns against. The danger lies in the VR experience's becoming the dominant constitutional frame through which we understand the world. To desire a renewal of creativity and meaningful activity is one thing, to gain these by denying the importance of older ways of being is quite another. The technological mediation of subjective experience that superficially allows the subject more autonomy (through more choice) can collapse all too easily into the further colonization of the lifeworld. The struggle over the cultural meanings of VR signify that now, more than ever, we need to preserve the practices which resist reification, and which allow a broad range of subjective experiences to unfold outside the sphere of mere 'functioning'.

Notes

1. J.G. Ballard's prediction on the jacket cover of Rheingold's *Virtual Reality*.

2. It is precisely this combination of detachment and 'functioning' that has led to ethical concerns over the use of VR technology in war. Needless to say such a combination also fulfils an ideological fantasy of capitalism   functioning workers without the corresponding sense of alienation that is typically produced under capitalist relations.

3. We might wish to question how VR's end can be said to be *social* at all. We could hardly suggest that it is being marketed in the interests of realizing a reflexive subjectivity.

4. See, for example, Elizabeth Grosz (1992) or Patricia Wise in this volume on how VR promotes the patriarchal fantasy of disembodied sexual relations without labour, cost or responsibility.

References

Benedikt, Michael (1992) 'Introduction', in Michael Benedikt (ed.), *Cyberspace: First Steps.* Cambridge, MA: MIT Press. pp. 1–25.

Brand, Stuart (1987) *The Media Lab: Inventing the Future at MIT.* New York: Viking.

Bukatman, Scott (1993) *Terminal Identity: The Virtual Subject in Postmodern Science Fiction.* Durham, NC: Duke University Press.

Gibson, William (1984) *Neuromancer.* London: Grafton.

Gibson, William (1988a) 'Burning Chrome', in William Gibson, *Burning Chrome.* London: Grafton. pp. 195–220.

Gibson, William (1988b) *Mona Lisa Overdrive.* New York: Bantam Books.

Grosz, Elizabeth (1992) 'Lived Spatiality: Insect Space/Virtual Sex', *Agenda*, 26/7: 5–8.

Grosz, Elizabeth (1994) *Volatile Bodies: Toward a Corporeal Feminism.* Sydney: Allen and Unwin.

Haraway, Donna (1991) with Constance Penley and Andrew Ross, 'Cyborgs at Large: An Interview with Donna Haraway', in Constance Penley and Andrew Ross (eds), *Techno-cultural.* Minneapolis, MN: University of Minnesota Press. pp. 1–20.

Hayles, N. Katherine (1993) 'The Seductions of Cyberspace', in Verena Conley (ed.), *Rethinking Technologies.* Minneapolis, MN: University of Minnesota Press. pp. 173–90.

Heidegger, Martin (1981) 'Only a God Can Save Us', in Thomas Sheehan (ed.), *Heidegger: The Man and the Thinker* (trans. William J. Richardson). Chicago: Precedent Publishing. pp. 45–67.

Heim, Michael (1993) *The Metaphysics of Virtual Reality.* Oxford: Oxford University Press.

Jameson, Frederic (1992) *Postmodernism, Or, the Cultural Logic of Late Capitalism.* Durham, NC: Duke University Press.

Markley, Robert (1994a) 'Introduction: Shreds and Patches: The Morphogenesis of Cyberspace', *Configurations*, 3: 433–9.

Markley, Robert (1994b) 'Boundaries: Mathematics' Alienation, and the Metaphysics of Cyberspace', *Configurations*, 3: 485–507.

Merleau-Ponty, Maurice (1962) *Phenomenology of Perception* (trans. Colin Smith). London: Routledge and Kegan Paul.

Orenstein, Peggy (1991) 'Get a Cyberlife', *Mother Jones*, 16 (3): 61–4.

Pimental, Ken and Teixeira, Kevin (1993) *Virtual Reality: Through the New Looking Glass.* New York: McGraw-Hill.

Poster, Mark (1994) 'A Second Media Age?', *Arena Journal*, 3: 49–92.

Rheingold, Howard (1991) *Virtual Reality.* London: Secker and Warburg.

Rushkoff, Douglas (1994) *Cyberia: Life in the Trenches of Cyberspace.* London: HarperCollins.

Stenger, Nicole (1992) 'Mind is a Leaking Rainbow', in Michael Benedikt (ed.), *Cyberspace: First Steps.* Cambridge, MA: MIT Press. pp. 49–58.

Varela, Francisco (1992) 'The Reenchantment of the Concrete', in Jonathan Crary and Sanford Kwinter (eds), *Incorporations: Zone 6.* New York: Zone Books. pp. 220–39.

Virilio, Paul (1983) *Pure War* (trans. Mark Polizotti). New York: Semiotext(e).

Virilio, Paul (1991) *The Lost Dimension* (trans. Daniel Moshenberg). New York: Semiotext(e).

6

THIS ABSTRACT BODY:
From Embodied Symbolism to Techno-Disembodiment

Paul James and Freya Carkeek

The avant-garde tends to read about it rather than do it. Nevertheless, techno-sexuality in its various guises is burgeoning. From low-grade cyber-porn to virtual-sex discussion groups, the phenomenon of technologically mediated sexual relations is taking hold. The Silicon Matchmaker Network, one of many such services, had 57,772 active users in its 1996 date-a-base. America Online, which has over five million subscribers, incorporates an extensive range of chat rooms under its People Connection Service. The homepage for Persian Kitty's Adult Links, sponsored by Naughty Neighbours Online and claiming 'A quarter million fast-downloading hardcore amateur pix', had 34,274,955 visitors between 1 January 1996 and the time when we chanced upon it, 26 September 1996. Whether it be sex without the embodied presence of another person or the technological enhancement of the sexual body, the broad range of practices from telephone-sex to cosmetic surgery illustrates an emergent but already pervasive development in these postmodern times. Such practices are part of the broader phenomenon of techno-disembodiment – an increasing abstraction of the way in which we live our bodies and a generalizing of the technological mediation of social relations.

The culture of late capitalism is overcome by an extraordinary fascination with the body. Concomitantly, our relationship to our bodies is being mediated and penetrated to its core by a myriad of technological incursions. Our relationship to others is becoming dominated by increasingly disembodied modes of social engagement. These contradictory developments – on the one hand, the reflexive fascination with taking control of our bodies and, on the other, the abstraction and disembodiment of social integration – are thoroughly bound up with each other. They reinforce each other in an intimate spiral of externalized desire and an internalized sense of incompleteness. In the face of the contradictory nature of this process, contemporary social theories, from psychoanalytic approaches to structuralist and poststructuralist accounts of the present, seem unable to take up its full complexity.

Truth may be stranger than fiction, but in this case fiction provides a good way into describing some contemporary developments in the abstraction of the body. Whether you collect your cultural cues through the variously disembodied media of print or electronics – from reading the *London Review of Books* (see Loose, 1992) to clicking onto Internet sites such as http://www.regsex.com[1] – or whether you keep your finger on the pulse of groovy street by gazing through the half-reflective windows of its *mise en scène* bookshops, you will eventually come across the new genre of writing on cyberculture. Nicholson Baker's novel *Vox* is an example of cyber-realism. It is written as one long telephone conversation between two strangers, Abbey and Jim (why are we bothering to tell you their names?). They have never met and probably never will, and they use their own names to tell stories in the third person more often than they do to address each other. Abbey and Jim happen to 'cross wires' on a phone-sex party-line. The novel renders as fictional dialogue a phenomenon which first began in the United States in the late 1980s. Along with introduction agencies, computer-to-computer introduction networks, video-dating libraries, AIDS-screening agencies, lifestyle clubs and other services for the lovelorn, lonely or 'simply too busy', phone-sex marks a new stage in the mediation (and simulation) of intimacy.[2]

Vox is such an uncritical reflection on this kind of transaction that we might say that it is much the same as the Playboy™ homepage in engendering the commodification of disembodied eroticism; the difference is that its sales are made in the avant-garde literary marketplace. *Vox* is part of a genre of social practices and image productions which are sufficiently prevalent to engender academic papers on 'Sex and Death among the Disembodied' (cited by Rheingold, 1991: 351–2 – Rheingold's book has itself received extensive popular attention). We join Abbey and Jim as they transfer to a fibre-optical, ninety-five-cents-per-half-minute 'back room' in order to find one-on-one disembodied intimacy. As the blurb says (drawing us, the readers, into a further layer of the disembodied circuit of meaning): 'we eavesdrop on them as, little by little, they talk themselves into increasing levels of self-disclosure':

> I called tonight [Abbey says] I think out of the same impulse, the idea that five to six men would hear me come, as if my voice was this thing, this disembodied body, out there . . . but then, when I actually made the call, the reality of it was that the men were so irritating, either passive, wanting me to entertain them, or full of what-are-your-measurements questions, and so I was silent for a while, and then I heard your voice and liked it. (Baker, 1992: 146–7)

The ambivalence of Abbey's response, wanting to be desired as an abstract thing but not objectified in the old-fashioned way, hints at abiding contradictions in our relationship to our bodies; to ourselves that is, and to others. There is a dense condensation of meaning at the heart of the sexual body, a condensation which at one level assumes and reinforces our sense that our bodies are integrated and coherent entities. However, it is this very condensation that, in the context of contemporary social relations, allows one of the body's senses to be separated out as a one-dimensional extension of the whole. It allows interaction to be reduced, for example, to a telephone conversation of hearing-voicing without immediately provoking an identity crisis.[3] It allows the voice to be abstracted over space – via satellite, 'out here under the stars', as Abbey says with self-consciously unromantic irony – and to be abstracted without necessarily reducing the erotic effect of 'this disembodied body'.[4] Indeed, pushing at the cultural-technical limits of the integrity–fragmentation contradiction can, in the short term, supercharge the disembodied body with 'sensual', transgressive ambiguity. Teledildonics, the projection of computer-simulated sexual arousal by wearing plugged-in bodysuits, may never become widely practised, but it certainly provokes interest as a risqué possibility. The Internet Relay Chat Services – called IRCs in cyberspace jargon – are jammed with people typing lascivious messages to each other and finding expressions of happiness in typewritten signifiers such as :-).

At this point, however, the contradiction folds back on itself. Without continuing to draw off our historically ambivalent faith in embodied relations, techno-sex quickly becomes hollow, unsatisfying, no more erotic than collecting answers to what-are-your-measurements questions. And herein lies the rub – or so we will argue. By continuing to draw off that ambivalent faith, techno-sex and the many other practices of disembodying interaction contribute to a changing and increasingly abstracted dominant ontology of disembodiment. It is not just a question of declining intensity. For a time, techno-sex can be both intense and apparently liberating. After all, it does vitiate complications of the flesh. One of the most common defences of cybersex is now the argument that techno mediation allows for safe sex, AIDS-free interaction. As Abbey implies, embodied sex is distracting, too many things happen, and it is feculent: 'I like to think *about* cocks in me, though. Also, yeah I do unfortunately tend to get yeast complications from real sex' (Baker, 1992: 122; Baker's emphasis).[5]

Nor is it simply a question of criticizing techno-sex in itself. You are right to think that we have already allowed undercurrents of sardonic depreciation to affect the tone of our description of techno-sexuality, but that does not take the critique very far. Rather, we will argue, critically understanding techno-sex and other forms of 'techno-relations with strangers' entails looking at the much broader context of forms of embodiment within contemporary social relations. It is in the context of the increasing privatization, rationalization and commodification of the lifeworld that techno-sex contributes to hollowing out the taken-for-grantedness of human corporeality. Paradoxically, though, it is on this same taken-for-granted sense of embodiment that techno-disembodiment residually depends for its erotic-romantic charge. This spiralling contradiction underpins, on the one hand, the desire to teleconference with Kathy's Dream Girls at $5.99 US per minute of interactive cyberpornography <shudder> and, on the other hand, the simple confidence to enter the newsgroup alt.irc.romance discussion on 'falling in love over the Internet' and affirm joyfully that 'I did!' (NREF 1, September 1996).[6]

Our argument is, in short, that broader processes – objectification, privatization, rationalization, commodification and technological extension and mediation[7] – are part of an increasing abstraction of the frame of social integration; and that this development, as uneven and contradictory as it is, is making our relationship to our bodies increasingly vexed. This vexation is thinly veiled by the fact that some individuals do fall in love in cyberspace and some men do get sexual pleasure from blurry collections of coloured pixels resembling the shapes of naked women. Understanding this broader context will take the chapter into the realm of comparing different social relations across history and place. Techno-sex is merely an example, some would say even a trivial one, intended to carry us into a broader realm of cross-cultural comparison.

In focusing on the body, this chapter seeks to consider two related themes. First, it examines how bodily symbolism is part of a process of connecting and defining the self and the community. The easiest way to do this is comparatively, contrasting forms of embodiment in different contexts from tribalism to postmodern capitalism. This then allows us to broach the second theme. Is the reconstitution of the lived senses of our bodies in contemporary Western society stripping the body of its capacity to enrich the social connectedness of people? The current sense of an image-dictated, 'shapable' body; the current debates over whether or not advances in medical technology are an unproblematic liberation from the constraints of our mortal bodies; and recent developments in feminist attitudes to embodiment will be considered, all the while attempting to reveal the tensions and contradictions in the textured modern/postmodern constitution of the body. Our overriding concern is to argue for an alternative framing of the current practices of social interrelation, one that attempts to bind considerations about the value or otherwise of the various modes of dis-embodied extension within a framework which, in practice, instantiates condensed and complex *limitations* on embodiment. These are the limitations entailed in the *ontology* of face-to-face relations. This is not an argument for a return to kinship-based or close-knit parochial com-munities. It is to argue for the ontological importance of relations of continuity, reciprocity and co-operation. It is to suggest that the constraints of embodiment are not simply impediments to be left behind as soon as is technologically possible.

Before proceeding, we need to define some terms and very briefly summarize our method. We draw on a position developed over many years in the pages of *Arena*.[8] For the present purposes we propose to introduce only the notion of 'levels of social integration', understood as intersecting forms of structured practices of association between people. These are analytically distinguishable levels; they obviously do not exist as pure forms. However, it is easiest to begin by describing them that way rather than in the complex intersections of lived practices where different levels of

Levels of integration	Levels of abstraction	Contradictions between nature and culture	Societal forms given the dominance of a particular level of integration
face-to-face integration	decreasing	condensing	tribal to traditional
agency-extended integration	↑ ↓	↑ ↓	traditional to modern
disembodied integration	increasing	stretching	modern to postmodern

Figure 6.1

integration may contradict, qualify, dominate or be 'thinned out' by other levels of integration. In our immediate context, we can distinguish three levels:

1. face-to-face integration;
2. agency-extended integration;
3. disembodied integration.

Face-to-face *integration* is defined as the level where the modalities of being in the 'presence' of others constitute the dominant ontological meaning of interrelations, communications and exchanges, even when the self and the other are not always engaged in immediate face-to-face interaction. Under such forms of interrelation, the absence of a significant other, even through death, does not annul his/her presence to us. Agency-extended integration involves the extension of possibilities of interrelation through persons acting in the capacity of representatives, intermediaries or agents of others.[9] Disembodied integration is the level at which the constraints of embodiment, for example being in one place at one time, can be overcome by means of technological extension – broadcasting, networking or telephoning, to name only a few. As described, each of these levels is more abstract than the level 'prior' to it, and each is implicated quite differently in the ways we live the relationship between nature and culture, and the ways we live our bodies and the 'presence' of others.

Ontological contradictions inevitably arise in the intersection of these levels, and in the intersection of the cultural practices conducted at each level with the world-as-given, the natural. It is our argument that such contradictions, including the culture–nature contradiction, are enriching as long as any one level does not come to constitute the dominating mode of living-in-the-world, and so does not thin out prior levels of human interrelation (see Figure 6.1).

Natural symbols' and the lived images of social relations

The most basic question to which the body-as-a-natural-symbol contributes is how social groups bind their members and create boundaries which reinforce the sense of communality. In contemporary Western societies, even the most gregarious individual could not be said to have meaningful and complexly textured relationships with more than a few dozen others, yet, as Benedict Anderson suggests in writing about the nation-state, there is a 'remarkable confidence of community in anonymity' (1983: 40). Our interest here is in the role played by the body as a universally shared experience and a symbolic form in creating bonds, both in the more abstract settings of anonymity and in the more concrete settings of reciprocal tribalism. Bodily symbols, images and signifiers – from the metaphors of blood, bile, semen and milk to representations of Unknown Soldiers, national heroes and religious figures – draw on the power of symbolism to make sense through linkage and 'remembrance'. Symbolism 'explains' by drawing on the creative human ability to interpret the unfamiliar through imaginative connection with the known. In one case, the intimate familiarity of the body relates citizens to the Body Politic. In another, the transubstantiation of bread and wine relates Christians to the Corpus of the Church community. Order, continuity, integration and depth of meaning are gained through symbolism's bridging of this distance (Cohen, 1974: xi). While the linkage made by a symbol is, in one sense, arbitrary (a sense emphasized by poststructuralists), it gathers meaning and thus becomes non-arbitrary when it is interpreted by an agent who lives its 'message'. A rich interweaving of practices, mores, values and sense-messages forms the background against which symbols can yield meaning. Hence, bodily symbols reveal as much about their cultural setting and the practices and perceptions which constitute attitudes to the body as they do about that which is being signified.

The 'social need' to develop and define relationships with others does not diminish as the means of societal integration become increasingly 'distantiating';[10] however, the form in which it is expressed grows increasingly abstract as it is reconstituted. This abstraction is paradoxical because, while it continues to reproduce the desire for group identification, drawing together the faces of the nation or the world in written, pictorial and, most recently, electronic images, it also seems to weaken the depth of the connection, integrating an amorphous mass of strangers. Through their diffuseness, both national and global communities 'stretch' the sense of integration found in the reciprocal, kinship network of tribal or traditional societies. This stretching, this abstracting of the social horizon, has virtues in that historically it has formed part of the basis for the enriching possibilities of a universalizing ethic, highlighting the 'needs of strangers'. However, it is this same stretching which thins out the connection that is so crucial for maintaining a depth of ontological security. The fragility of social identity in Western late capitalism already suggests a possible answer to the issue of how the constitution of persons differs across historical and social settings. But this will be considered in more detail later in relation to the image of the body in contemporary culture. We still need to say more about symbols in general, natural symbols and, more particularly, the culture of the body as a 'natural symbol' (Mary Douglas's term).

Symbols work to integrate societies and express the meaning of social relations. A society's sense of community, whether tribal, modern or post-modern, becomes personal and knowable in part through the representations made by symbols. As carriers of richly condensed networks of meaning, symbols are part of this multilayered complexity. Symbolism is capable of secreting history in its layers of possible interpretations and referents, yet can be recouped, or even culturally managed, to represent new images and relationships. Symbolic forms are powerful, energetic tools in cohering and ordering social relations, because they are expressed in richly dramatic sequences of imagery. The imagery is palpable and intense despite its inevitable representational abstraction or distance from what it portrays. All meaningful symbols are thus always caught in a meshing of cultural contradictions between (what we have analytically distinguished as) more concrete and more abstract levels of social integration.

The body can be used in integrating a community and defining its social relations as both a universalizing experience – the human body as common to all of us – and a particularizing experience – the body as a marker of difference: gendered difference, ethnic difference, differences of age, family, and so on. Paradoxically, both these relations of embodiment, we would argue, find their richest and most stable expression in contradictory intersection with each other. In other words, embodiment is most pregnant with meaning firstly, where the universalizing (more abstract) modalities qualify without annulling the differentiating, exclusionary, inward-turned and more concrete modalities of symbolically likening the community to a body; and, secondly, where the cultural infuses without technocratically rationalizing the body as biologically given. It is richest, that is, where the culture–nature contradiction is not so stretched by the possibilities of techno-science that we (our bodies) become reduced to pliable constructions, the 'soft infrastructure' of our dreams for liberation from our mortal, defective, differentiated and socially demanding flesh and blood.

Valorizing either the more abstract universalizing forms or the more concrete differentiating forms has worrying consequences. At its politically most disturbing, the heightening of a sense of external boundaries as given can be lived in terms of 'orifices' to be carefully guarded against the poisoning of foreign intrusion. Internal cohesion, allegiance and familiarity can be reduced to the harmony of the essentially bounded, fully closed, interconnected human body. The human body provides a readily available image for societies which treat their interconnectedness as if it were organic, a 'body' which functions in complex and mysterious ways relying on the cohesion of its disparate elements. The fact that treating the body as a natural symbol can be part of generating a culture of narrowly bounded exclusion should not, however, lead us to conclude that we need to be liberated from 'boundaries' and 'modes of exclusion' *per se*. Moreover, we should not be deluded by the deconstructionist creed that 'seeing through' processes of meaning formation makes one the master of it. Symbols express socially constructed practices but, in their framing of meaning, they also gain the power to structure and overdetermine processes of social formation. In Mary Douglas's words, they sometimes 'lash back at the people' who create them (1970: xiv). It is a dual and reflective process of structuring – people create the symbols which in turn define their society, social behaviour and relationships, and even their sense of body, from which the symbols derived. Bodily symbols can form an elaborate code which regulates dress, posture, etiquette, social contact, expressions of respect and an innumerable list of other social behaviours, each in themselves of limited consequence but which together, as a generalized code, define and affirm the social order. These proscriptions are particularly applicable to face-to-face relations and so are most easily identifiable in communities in which, historically, such relations have formed the dominant level of integration – tribal, kinship or close-knit parochial communities.

It is at the face-to-face level that the humanly created need for the ontological security of group association is revealed most starkly. The study of tribal societies is revealing here because even in these apparently most concrete of settings a primary level of abstraction occurs (Sharp, 1985). In tribal communities, the 'natural entity' of the body is already abstracted beyond its condition of being biologically extant through complex lines of kinship and ritual association, lines which affirm imagined and lived modalities of co-presence despite their extension across temporary absence and even across the parting death. Pierre Bourdieu's comparison of two forms of tribal kinship, official and practical, offers an example of an aspect of this move beyond the literalness of blood ties. He argues that while actual genealogical kinship organizes and legitimizes on official occasions, more often kinship relationships are cultivated, existing only through and for the practical interests they serve. Leaving aside the way in which Bourdieu reduces the distinction to the constitutive primacy of self-interest, it draws our attention to how even such primordial relations as blood ties are lived-imagined abstract relationships (Bourdieu, 1977: 34–8).[11] That is, even something as 'thick' as blood is part of a cultural rather than simply a natural relation. Bourdieu's distinction can be paralleled to Douglas's contrast between tribal rituals which are just commemorative and those in which the symbolic action is considered to be efficacious (Douglas, 1970: 8). Efficacious rites rely on the participants' receptivity to extension of 'logical' principles beyond their concrete settings so that they might be imagined to effect change on a person, occasion or environment. Tribal sorcerers rely on this abstraction of direct agency in their performance of magic.

At a very basic level the human body is always treated as an image of society – interest in its apertures reflects the social preoccupation with entrances, exits, escapes and invasions; it is impossible to consider the body as natural with no sense of its social-cultural dimension. The emergence of what we have been referring to as the nature–culture contradiction was integral to the process of hominoids becoming human. In part, this is why it is possible to say that even in a tribal setting there is a form of abstraction of the body. Victor Turner's study of the Ndembu in Zambia reveals how that people experience society as an intricate arrangement of descent groups structured by the bodily inscriptions of age, gender and genealogical hierarchy. The colours of the human body – black bile, red blood, white milk – form a vivid symbolic centre for the patterning of complex representations of male and female spheres, of nourishing and destructive powers of purity and pollution (Douglas, 1970: 10–11). However, the interpretation of this symbolic organization grows increasingly abstract as it is more inclusively extended.

The body is used in many tribal societies as the basis for a symbolic order which orients people in relation to each other, setting the limits of remoteness and nearness. This has both positive and negative implications. With the abstraction of public versus private spaces and with the development of a gendered distinction around the contradiction between nature and culture, the positive virtues of a partial separation between men's and women's cultures have in many cases hardened into public patriarchy. Women of the Baruya, a New Guinea mountain tribe, stop, turn their heads and draw a flap of their bark cloak across their faces when passed by a man journeying on the roads between villages (Godelier, 1986: 9–10). The women's subordinate public placement in relation to men in the tribe is both abstracted in the bodily gesture and made more concrete by the frequent acting out of the ritual respect.

The internal/external dichotomy is highly visible in tribal settings where there are explicit, often sacred, values placed on inner and outer parts of the body. The segregation metaphor orders social arrangements abstractly into a meticulous separation of pure from polluted, sacred from profane, male from female, or initiated from child or stranger. An example of how the body is basic to the physical structuring of place is given in a description of the Baruya family house (Godelier, 1986: 10–11). It is completely segregated by gender as though an imaginary line ran through the hearth at the centre of the house. The wife and children sleep and eat on the side closest to the door, while the husband and any other men entering take up the place on the other side, beyond the hearth. No woman may enter the male part of the house and she must avoid stepping over the central hearth lest she pollute the place where the husband's food is prepared. The hearth itself, built by men from the husband's family, is symbolic of kinship and lineage. Here our argument for a renewed politics of embodiment obviously does not entail a return to the *content* or *modalities* of gendered relations found within tribal reciprocity, the kinds of enactments that we have just been describing. Rather, it is an argument for a politics of embodiment which reasserts the form expressed by those modalities: the relevance of embodied-gendered difference; the importance of recognizing that our bodies are not just our individualistic self-creations; and the value of retaining a respect for cultural (embodied) boundaries insofar as they enhance the dialectic of difference and connection.

We will go on to suggest that the capacity for the body to be the figure of an integrating, organizing, symbolic form is greatly diminished in late-modern/postmodern societies. This should not be taken as implying an argument that embodiment becomes irrelevant to post-tribal processes of structuration, continuity or ontological security. In the private sphere, in a post-World War II working-class English home, for example, the body defines an outlay of space and it structures 'appropriate' behaviour within specifically bounded places. The back of the house contains the kitchen, bathroom and toilet (providing privacy for body functions), while the front of the house, containing the parlour, is given over to public, social relationships where the body is required to present itself with formal decorum (Douglas, 1970: 158).[12] However, the contrast with tribal forms of embodiment cannot be understated. Modernity has involved an increasingly self-conscious acculturation of the 'excesses' of the body as a natural symbol.

In the broader sphere of the contemporary nation-state, changing one's national identity still involves one's own body. It requires a ceremony of symbolic boundary-crossing, Ironically, however, it is a ceremony of 'naturalization' which self-consciously subordinates the significance of birthplace to transform an alien into a citizen. The ceremony treats the nationally 'naturalized' body in a more abstracted way than the rituals of tribal boundary-crossing or identity transformation, which call for the bodies of the initiates to be physically changed. National naturalization assumes, almost perfunctorily, an abstract overlay which has reconstituted the cultural meaning of birth. By contrast, for example, Aboriginal initiation ceremonies entail a bloody renaissance, a *rebirth* of the initiate's actual body (Myers, 1991: 228–33). The body metaphor is not irrelevant to 'naturalization' in the modern context. Any would-be citizen must attend the ceremony *in person*, swear an oath, and receive a document confirming his or her transition out of the old cultural inscription of what birth means to identity. Similarly, leaving one's homeland is still not entirely straightforward. In Australia during its Bicentenary year, expatriates like the late Peter Allen (proud recipient of the Order in Australia) and Rupert Murdoch (a little sheepish at becoming an American citizen) were confidently voicing that sentiment of postmodern nationalism, 'I still call Australia home.' Notwithstanding this layer of sentimental attachment, Rupert Murdoch is now an abstracted global citizen: the streets of New York serve as well as anywhere else for his constitutional walks.

To the body as an individualized project

We have seen how the body is already abstracted, even in the most bounded of face-to-face settings. However, the abstraction that occurs in tribal settings has a condensed depth which is rarely found in late-modern/postmodern society. Our bodily symbols and images are constituted in a very different way. More abstract modes of social interrelation have come to overlay and, very often, to change the nature of our embodied interactions. The electronic image brings impassioned faces of Chinese students pleading with each of us to support their struggle, yet most of us have never stood where they stand in Tiananmen Square nor spoken to them in person. For a time we may respond with public outrage to the inhumane way they were treated, but we cannot know these people as more than encapsulated, time-frozen images. The unnamed young man who stood in front of an oncoming tank becomes an abstracted symbol. We cannot obtain a sense of him as a complex, multi-dimensional person. The image has consumed the subject. While we can celebrate the expansive sense of humanity this creates, we should not forget that the processes of abstraction through which this is possible place our relationship with the abstracted Other under shearing strain. Unlike the tribal form, this abstraction has stretched so far beyond the more concrete face-to-face experience that it has lost the layers which texture and amplify it. As quickly as we were first drawn to empathize (although maybe the more abstract concept 'sympathize' is a more accurate term here) we become injured, bored, hardened or even resentful. The abstraction is no longer just an extension of a relation previously or potentially experienced as embodied presence. It has created a completely new form of interaction which can draw only on our sense of what a fuller relationship might be.

Similarly, our own bodies have become increasingly problematic to ourselves. The modern/postmodern body has pushed the 'I am body, yet I have a body' paradox (Turner, 1984: 7) to its limits. The body has been abstracted as a malleable form. It remains important to the constitution of identity, but more as the constructed image through which the self is presented to others than as a locus of the simultaneous connection and separation from others. The experience is one of an individualized tension – the 'disembodied embodiment' in which the body is part of the 'creative project', an objectified container for effecting appropriate style. The body has become the ultimate commodity, a packaged entity which joins the 'inner' and 'outer' worlds of selfhood in a belief that the body can and should be 'worked on' (Lynch, 1987: 128, 136, 138). The body is no longer a natural, reassuring condition from which stable metaphors can grow. Caught in the expectation that it should be constantly modified and reformed through diets, aerobics, plastic surgery and fashion, the body becomes an immediate but abstracted 'experience'. The fetishism of breast enlargement is only the most controversial and latest example of those listed in books with titles such as *Cosmetic Surgery: A Consumer Guide*. The symbolic significance of the body has thus been changed by capitalist developments grounded in personalized consumption. The body becomes an industry, with mass consumerism ascribing the signs of appropriate identity (Balsamo, 1996; Turner, 1984: 30, 109).[13] It also becomes a science, with medicine ascribing the frame for viewing our corporeal defects: baboon organs have been transplanted into people in over 30 operations since 1905; by 1988, two million people in the United States, 87 per cent of them female, had undergone cosmetic surgery.

Just as George Bernard Shaw's heroine in *Pygmalion* has her identity synthetically built by mastering the appropriate insignia of the upper class, so, in George Mead's terms, the contemporary body 'internalizes the external' (see Burke, 1957: 96–7). And we become objects not just of the gaze of another but also of ourselves. Rosalind Coward identifies the sense of fragmentation which develops when different parts of the body are referred to in the third person as 'problem areas':

> If the ideal shape has been pared down to a lean outline, bits are bound to stick out or hang down and these become problem areas. The result is that it becomes possible, indeed likely for [people] to think about their bodies in terms of parts, separate areas, as if these parts had some separate life of their own. (1984: 43–4)

The contemporary image of the body would seem to have lost its capacity to offer deep ontological grounding. Along the way modern body metaphors such as 'the body politic', 'body corporate' or 'body of people' have become shallow or procedural senses of group or association. The complex analogue the body once provided for an intricately structured social system has been 'hollowed out' as it has been segmented and commodified. The symbolism which in tribal settings provided a knowledge of structure and consonance inscribed in the body's natural patterning is being increasingly lost to late-modern/postmodern society.

The status of the body in late capitalism reflects a paradox characteristic of the disembodied level of integration. While there has been the consolidation and generalization of a universalized perspective of the Other, witnessed in the extension into globalism, there is also a heightening of the sense of the particular and local. A parallel tension constitutes the body as an abstract homogenized form: the changing but universalized standard to be attained, yet also the physical space into which one can retreat to experience the inner, more real self. New Age meditation, yoga and similar mind/body communion experiences use the body as a capsule into which the weary postmodern body can crawl to be rejuvenated. Yet even this intimate retreat has become thoroughly commodified, individualized and privatized. The example of Tokyo's night-life district offering Brain Mind Gymnasiums full of machines which, according to their promoters, 'help you find yourself' may seem bizarre, but it is only a step beyond the now-naturalized. walkman. The strategy behind the Japanese manufacturer's design of the walkman was to produce insulated space for people by providing a way of listening to music privately-in-public, a public privacy located literally within the confines of one's own body-space. The popularity of walkmans among the world's commuting populations confirms the 'need' which this product met. A benign example – maybe – but, once again, one in which the body is presented ambiguously, accentuating embodiment but interceding in what it means to walk around together or share a public space.

In the face of this withdrawal into the private self, critics as diverse as Richard Sennett (1994) and Julia Kristeva (1991) argue that the only way out is by becoming 'strangers to ourselves', fragmenting our inner sense of unity. In Sennett's view this would be achieved through our acknowledging the place of pain:

> Such pain has a trajectory in human experience. It disorients and makes incomplete the self, defeats the desire for coherence; the body accepting pain is ready to become a civic body, sensible to the pain of another person, pains present together on the street, at last endurable – even though, in a diverse world, each person cannot explain what he or she is feeling, who he or she is, to the other. But the body can follow this civic trajectory only if it acknowledges that there is no remedy for its suffering in the contrivings of society, that its unhappiness has come from elsewhere, that its pain derives from God's command to live together as exiles. (1994: 376)

The irony here is that, in rightly recognizing our late-modern desire to escape pain and mortality, Sennett argues for an exacerbation of one of the very processes that is bound up with what he wants to ameliorate. His concern is the increasing privatization of social relations, but because he fails to recognize that this is only one dimension of the broader process of the abstraction of social integration, he ends up advocating another of its associated dimensions, the fragmentation of self. Some forms of feminist theory, we argue, get caught in a similar spiral.

Feminism and the body

Feminist theory has made the constitution of the body a key focus of its analysis. Its insights further explain the phenomenon of disembodiment, but when taken in certain ways they unintentionally feed into the practices of which they are implicitly critical – the abstraction of the body in the late-modern/postmodern world. (Excluded from this criticism are some important new feminist writings which offer the beginning of a reformulation which can both retain the advantages of abstraction of the body and recoup the rich depth of prior forms of embodiment.) We have already considered the way that the emphasis on dieting and honed image, particularly insidious in its targeting of women, separates out the body into fragmented parts. One emerging strand of feminist theorists (see Balsamo, 1996; Elshtain, 1991; Porter, 1991) has begun to emphasize the detrimental way in which technologies intercede in even the most basic of social interactions; intervening, in some cases, as if to make the embodied constraints on the experience of relationships unnecessary and archaic. They have begun to criticize the individualist valorization of 'free choice', the slogans of 'the right to choose' and 'owning one's own body' as thoroughly unsatisfactorily bases for a positive politics of embodiment. However, there are other developments in feminism that we wish to challenge: most notably the very different ideals of achieving androgyny or becoming a cyborg, both of which contribute to extending the disembodying process.

Despite an intention to offer women an 'authentic' experience of their bodies, the ideal of androgyny suggests a desire for an identity which transcends the structure inscribed in the physicality of the body (Caddick, 1986: 62). Androgyny seeks to surpass the contradictions implicit in the nature/culture dichotomy, allowing chosen culture to triumph. Far from knowing the body as a delimiting experience, women are encouraged to use their minds to dissociate the self from the limitation of its physical form. This trend is a revealing example of how the socio-material constituents of a dominant integrative level reconstruct other levels in the terms of that dominant level. Feminism began as an assertion of intimate, authentic and concrete womanhood, yet some traditions of feminism have been deflected by the dominant ideologies, ideologies that they fail to recognize as such. Some radical feminists have sought to reform the problems of gender identity in terms which re-establish a mind/body dichotomy and privilege rational choice over the ontological dictates of bodily inscription. By allowing bodily difference to have little theoretical importance, these feminists have been obliged to frame their critique in the very terms they sought to dismantle.

From another perspective, feminist difference theorists are strongly critical of the androgyny ideal, arguing instead for an embodied subjectivity which avoids what they see as the pitfall of androgyny – a conformity with the implicit assumption that the subject is male 'transcendent in his possession of an ultimate rationality, disembodied in this transcendence' (Caddick, 1986: 64). Difference theorists emphasize the differential influence of the female bodily form. They argue the innate structure of the body distinguishes a grammatical form for the creation of personal and sexual identity. Yet even this perspective, which seeks to centre the body in its theory, is tinged with the reconstructing abstraction of the dominant level. The body on which it is based shows little of the tangibility that characterizes embodied experience. Closeness with the body is to be rediscovered through a deliberate cultural association in order to revolutionize the actual constitution of the self. If androgyny represents the modern ideal of the abstracted body, the difference theorists' version is distinctly postmodern in its sense of the abstracted body instrumentalized in the discovery and presentation of its self.

Difference feminist perspectives on gender and the body are radically separable from androgyny feminism, yet they share the impact that an abstracted sense of body has made in constituting their approaches. We have suggested so far that abstraction of the body has led to a depleted, shallow sense of embodiment. Fragmenting, dichotomizing and partitioning have made it difficult for the body to be experienced as a condensed and reassuring analogue by which to view the social. The body, when lived as a rich and authentic condition of social interrelation and accepted in all its mortal limitations, has provided under different conditions a basis for the security and coherence of communities. This has been historically accompanied by proscriptions against the behaviours of people, particularly women, with cultural and natural morphology being collapsed into each other. The present period has seen a turnaround in this process. Reflexivity about the body in contemporary society has offered, through technologies which transcend embodied form, the opportunity to be liberated from such dictates. Yet its image of the body as a package to be manipulated by the 'looking glass self' of modern consumerism and techno-science (Turner, 1984: 110) has hollowed out our sense of social connection. Bryan Turner aptly characterizes these contemporary contradictions in his description of the body as 'at once the most solid, the most elusive, illusory, concrete, metaphorical, ever-present and ever-distant thing (a site, an instrument, an environment, a singularity and a multiplicity)' (1984: 8). In the final turn of the spiral, one variant of difference feminism – cybernetic feminism – takes computer-generated cyberspace to be homologous with the liberatory possibilities of being 'woman':

> The machines and the women mimic their humanity, but they never simply become it. They may aspire to be the same as man, but in every effort they become more complex than he has ever been. Cybernetic feminism does not, like many of its predecessors, including that proposed in Irigaray's recent work, seek out for women a subjectivity, an identity or even a sexuality of her own: there is no subject position and no identity on the other side of the screens. And female sexuality is always in excess of anything that could be called 'her own'. Woman cannot exist 'like man'; neither can the machine. . . . Her missing piece, what has never been allowed to appear, was her connection to the virtual, . . . computers: they are the simulators, the screens, the clothing of the matrix, already blatantly linked to the virtual machinery of which nature and culture are subprograms. (Plant, 1995: 63)

Conclusion

When nature and culture do *actually* become the subprograms of virtual machinery then we will have reached the stage of post-humanity. In the meantime, the abstraction of embodiment leads in contradictory directions. In the flux of new dominant levels of communion and integration, there is often a desire to repossess past forms. But in this disconnected, de-linked borrowing from the past, there seems inevitably to be a loss. Recouped forms become thinned out as we lose our sense of the forms of historical continuity. The body in our late-modern/postmodern society has become a problem. The paucity of ontological depth it offers is disturbing. The ethical-political task then must be to sift out the benefits of the more concrete, embodied experiences of past ways of life and to present them as forms and principles for living in the present, not as nostalgic slices of the past. These constitutive forms and principles of embodiment must be able to retain the advantages of certain aspects of abstraction – such as the sense of universalizing disembodiment that connects us to the generalized Other; allows us to reflect back on the nature of embodiment; and maintains the dimension of intellect created by the mind/body distinction. However, thinking about it is obviously not sufficient.

In true contemporary style we begin by offering two possible conclusions. The first comes from the final paragraphs of Nicholson Baker's *Vox*; the second is from the closing remarks of the English Marxist Chris Knight in his book *Blood Relations*:

(1) 'Do you think our wires . . . will cross again?'
   'I don't know. I don't know. What do you think?'
   'I don't know. What do you think?'
   'I could give you my number', he said, 'I mean if you still want it. I'll avoid a possibly awkward moment by not asking for yours . . .'
   'All right', she said. 'Let me think about things. Let me absorb the strangeness.'
   'What's strange?'
   'Nothing', she said. 'I guess nothing. I think I should probably sign off now, though. I have to put a load of towels in the laundry.'
   'Certainly. Okay. Thank you for calling this number.'
   'Thank you. Bye Jim.' (Baker, 1992: 164–5)

(2) The revolution's outcome is not simply in 'the future', conceived as something abstracted from the past. As we fight to become free, it is as if we were becoming *human* for the first time in our lives. But in this sense, because it concerns *becoming human*, the birth process we have got to win – our survival as a species depends upon it – has in the deepest sense been won already. None of us would be here had it not been. (Knight, 1991: 533)

The first scenario is sustainable for perhaps an evening or two; the second proposition points up the complex and contradictory nature of our struggle for a long-term future. It is too clever and easy, however, to suggest that the struggle has already been won. Such a struggle, we suggest, will involve an ongoing choice to monitor reflexively, and sometimes to qualify substantially, the 'bounteous' possibilities that the processes of disembodied extension and the techniques of techno-science will throw up in pursuit of extending the nature of what it has meant to be human. It will involve living with others in relations of continuity, mutuality and co-operation. It will involve new forms of community.

Spelling out an 'ethics for living' will be the task of people fighting it out together across overlapping levels of association, near and far, and finding ways of qualifying the ontological dominance of any one level by a contradictory intersection-in-practice of more concrete and more abstract levels of integration. So long as it is not confined to debates conducted through disembodied realms such as writing, or to discussion lifted out of the context of rounds of everyday life (from academic conferences to know-your-own-body encounter groups), then the very process of negotiating a politics of embodiment with others will already be a small step towards recouping the sociality of our bodies. These are cradle-to-grave and cross-generational issues. What is my relationship to somebody else's child? What makes that child 'somebody else's'? What does it mean to emigrate and permanently leave behind long-term associations? When does the 'private' sexual relationship become relevant to community relations? Will my ageing body be indefinitely sustained by the 'wonders of science'? Where will I be buried?

Notes

With thanks to John Hinkson, Alison Ravenscroft, Nonie Sharp and Geoff Sharp for their critical comments. An earlier parallel to this chapter appeared in the journal *Arena* (Carkeek and James, 1992). We must also thank Kathryn Bird for drawing our attention to Nicholson Baker's *Vox*.

1. The question of the week (19 February 1996) on this Canadian site came from a man who was distraught because his partner of 17 years marriage had been engaging in net-sex for the last two months.

2. In the late 1980s articles began appearing in the press on how to choose not only the right person but the right agency. The debut of the first widely marketed computer-to-computer 'inter-facing' agency was in the United States in 1988 (*The Age*, 18 February 1989). It was billed as a 'safe [that is AIDS-free] way to meet people'. (See also *Bulletin*, 26 June 1988.) The first AIDS-free agency in Victoria, Australia, Personal Humanities Service, came to public attention in mid-1987 (*The Age*, 18 July 1987).

3. This possibility qualifies but does not indefinitely hold off the slow crisis of meaning and identity formation brought on with the dominance of relations of disembodied extension.

4. Like this phrase, our title, 'This Abstract Body', is intentionally oxymoronic. Despite the abstraction of social relations, including our relations to our bodies, bodies have a 'this-ness'. To complicate this further, the processes of abstraction, including processes of disembodiment, do not just occur in the realm of ideas and perceptions; they are materially structured.

5. Keep in mind that Baker is a university-trained American male who once worked as a technical specialist in writing computer software manuals. Howard Rheingold also emphasizes the safety of the disembodied.

6. Kathy's Dream Girls are 'Live in full colour video. . . . My Dream Girls are my friends, who are nude dancers, housewives and even some young college students. When you teleconference with one of my Dream Girls, you can explore your biggest fantasies one-on-one with someone eager to share them' (HREF 1, October 1996).

7. Unfortunately there is not the space here to explain and elaborate on these processes. They are listed to give a sense of the complexity of abstraction of social relations and to deter any possible interpretation of a reductive technological determinism.

8. In using terms such as 'abstraction', 'levels', 'extension' and 'reconstitution' we are drawing heavily on the work of Geoff Sharp (particularly Sharp, 1985).

9. While this is not a term we will be elaborating on later in the chapter, it is necessary to a fuller examination of the body question. For example, any discussion of the long history of the body trade or marriage brokerage would need to cover the processes of the institutionalization of intermediating agents.

10. The term is from Anthony Giddens (1981) and refers to the extension, through technological development, of ideas and interactions across time and space such that societal integration remains strong while 'presence availability', social integration through face-to-face encounter, is minimal.

11. While we find this distinction useful, employing it here does not imply any sympathy for Bourdieu's over-emphasis, in our view, of self-interest or group-interest as the motivating basis of action.

12. For a discussion of the way in which in France this separation of private spaces, first limited to the bourgeoisie, spread to the working class after World War II see Prost (1991).

13. For an interesting confirmation of this development by one of its defenders see Bob Mullan: 'Finally, the critics seem to forget that the introduction industry is an industry; the primary terms are supply and demand, and profit . . . it is not a social service, except indirectly, but not by intention. The introduction industry is no more inherently wicked than, say, . . . the car trade' (1984: 2).

References

Anderson, Benedict (1983) *Imagined Communities: Reflections on the Origin and Spread of Nationalism*. London: Verso.

Baker, Nicholson (1992) *Vox*. New York: Random House.

Balsamo, Anne (1996) *Technologies of the Gendered Body: Reading Cyborg Women*. Durham, NC: Duke University Press.

Bourdieu, Pierre (1977) *Outline of a Theory of Practice* (trans. Richard Nice). Cambridge: Cambridge University Press.

Burke, Kenneth (1957) *The Philosophy of Literary Form: Studies in Symbolic Action*. New York: Vintage.

Caddick, Alison (1986) 'Feminism and the Body', *Arena*, 74: 60–88.

Carkeek, Freya and James, Paul (1992) 'This Abstract Body', in *Arena*, 99/100: 66–85.

Cohen, Abner (1974) *Two-Dimensional Man: An Essay on the Anthropology of Power and Symbolism in Complex Society*. London: Routledge and Kegan Paul.

Coward, Rosalind (1984) *Female Desire: Women's Sexuality Today*. London: Paladin.

Douglas, Mary (1970) *Natural Symbols, Explorations in Cosmology*. London: Cresset Press.

Elshtain, Jean Bethke (1991) *Power Trips and Other Journeys*. Madison, WI: University of Wisconsin Press.

Giddens, Anthony (1981) *A Contemporary Critique of Historical Materialism*. London: Macmillan.

Godelier, Maurice (1986) *The Making of Great Men: Male Domination and Power Among the New Guinea Baruya*. Cambridge: Cambridge University Press.

HREF 1: http://www.convict.com/kathy/dream.htm.

Knight, Chris (1991) *Blood Ties: Menstruation and the Origins of Culture*. New Haven, CT: Yale University Press.

Kristeva, Julia (1991) *Strangers to Ourselves*. New York: Harvester Wheatsheaf.

Loose, Julian (1992) 'Keep Talking' (review of *Vox*), *London Review of Books*, 26 March: 18–19.

Lynch, Maryanne (1987) 'The Body: Thin is Beautiful', *Arena*, 79: 128–38.

Mullan, Bob (1984) *The Mating Trade*. London: Routledge and Kegan Paul.

Myers, Fred (1991) *Pintupi Country, Pintupi Self: Sentiment, Place and Politics among Western Desert Aborigines*. Berkeley, CA: University of California Press.

NREF 1: news:51t789$j96@cobweb.aracnet.com.

Plant, Sadie (1995) 'The Future Looms: Weaving Women and Cybernetics', in Mike Featherstone and Roger Burrows (eds), *Cyberspace, Cyberbodies, Cyberpunk*. London: Sage. pp. 45–64.

Porter, Elizabeth (1991) *Women and Moral Identity*. Sydney: Allen and Unwin.

Prost, Antoine (1991) 'Public and Private Spheres in France', in Antoine Prost and Gerard Vincent (eds), *A History of Private Life* (vol. 5). Cambridge, MA: Harvard University Press. pp. 1–143.

Rheingold, Howard (1991) *Virtual Reality*. London: Secker and Warburg.

Sennett, Richard (1994) *Flesh and Stone: The Body and the City in Western Civilization*. London: Faber.

Sharp, Geoff (1985) 'Constitutive Abstraction and Social Practice', *Arena*, 70: 48–82.

Turner, Bryan S. (1984) *The Body and Society: Explorations in Social Theory*. Oxford: Basil Blackwell.

PART II
POLITICS AND COMMUNITY IN VIRTUAL WORLDS

7
VIRTUAL URBAN FUTURES

Michael J. Ostwald

Changing spatial perceptions

When, some time in the late 1980s, the technologies associated with virtual reality first entered the collective consciousness of the popular media, they were frequently presented as aberrant and potentially destructive. Many early newspaper articles and television documentaries focused exclusively on the idea of the 'hacker' or the 'cyberpunk' as embodiment of the social cost of virtual technologies (Chesterman and Lipman, 1988; Sterling, 1992). In such programmes and texts, the dishevelled and socially inept computer nerd was frequently depicted as the most benign expression of the advent of computer-simulated space. However, it was argued that the line between the computer nerd and the criminal hacker was a fine one because the criminal of the 1980s did not break in through the bedroom window but through the computer screen (Hafner and Markoff, 1991). Significantly, while the flat monitor of the computer was regarded as an open window inviting crime, the almost identical screen of the television was somehow seen as more secure because it lacked the two-way interaction that characterized the computer interface. Despite this difference, the computer, like the television before it, was viewed as an active agent of social disintegration. The computer screen was a potential portal into the back-streets and ghettos of the city; a window through which drugs, porno-graphy and violence could exert an influence on the home. Overt virtual technologies, including the Internet, were blamed, like television before them, for the breakdown in the family unit, the rise in street crime and the decay of conventional Cartesian urban spaces.[1] The fear and loathing that suffused popular perceptions of the new technology were not implicitly Luddite but were aligned to the ability of the technology to accelerate the ongoing process of moral, social and urban decline.

By 1993 a significant shift had taken place in the media: the virtual technologies were no longer to be feared but to be tamed and welcomed (Chapman, 1994). The advent of the new technosciences, metaphorically embodied in the concepts of virtual reality and cyberspace, was heralded as a potentially new way of reinstating democracy, reforming the community and redistributing the populace so that urban ghettos could be invigorated with new life (Lénárd et al., 1996; Mitchell, 1995). The rise in popularity of previously underground magazines such as *Mondo 2000* and *Wired* was accompanied by new publications including *21•C* and Internet supplements in the *Financial Review*, the *New York Times* and the *Sydney Morning Herald*. Both television programmes and the popular press provided glossaries of terms to allow the average viewer and reader to be carried away in veneration of the virtual technologies. And, at that moment when major companies started to advertise their World Wide Web addresses on television, the virtual landscape of the net became accepted as an extension of the 'real' world. Virtual technologies were no longer suspected of destroying community and urban space.

While it cannot be denied that the same period, the early 1990s, saw a global outcry against pornography on the Internet, this debate was frequently couched in terms of the problems of greater political freedom or the potential for new software to lock away such sites. Regardless of which side of the argument the media and politicians chose, the debate concerning virtual technologies was argued on social grounds not on technological ones. Significantly, the positive and negative effects of the new virtual realm were seen to impact not only on the community but on the spaces that people inhabit. In the 1980s the computer screen was the unlocked window, the site of paranoid fears of invasion; but by the 1990s software 'locks', 'net-nannies' and 'guard-dog' programs had been developed to secure this so-called window. If, in the 1980s, virtual technologies had been linked to the breakdown in community and, through this connection, to the destruction of urban form, in the Nineties they were seen as the saviour of community life. It did not matter whether the arguments were for or against the virtual technologies, it seemed that no case could be made without referring to both the social consequences of the technologies and their impact on the public spaces of the city. This realization leads to the thought that the rise in virtual technologies had somehow become bound tightly with the decline in amenity of urban communal space.

Also bound up in the complex relationship between virtual technologies and communal spaces is the reason for the rapid shift in media support for the new technology in the early 1990s. Virtual technologies did not, and could not, arise overnight. Virtual technologies and spaces had been slowly and imperceptibly developing for many years in parallel with the decline in popularity of conventional urban spaces in most major Western cities. By the early 1990s, the physical world had already become so virtual that when the new technologies finally impacted on the populace they seemed to be a natural extension of the artificial and temporal spaces that already existed. In a world saturated with television, radio, video, portable stereos and mobile telephones the virtual technologies had already infiltrated society and prepared the ground for their acceptance. By 1990, tele-commuting had become popular, distance learning was back in vogue and it was becoming increasingly difficult to find a real bank in the inner city as they were rapidly being replaced with autotellers, alcoves which served as displaced extensions of the banking world (Mitchell, 1995; Nixon, 1996).

All these technological changes have resulted in a widespread change in perception. The human mind can now perceive a new spatial form, one which derives from the television and computer screen but which has expanded outside the 'thin', 'nonreflecting' surface. Baudrillard's assumption that the 'flat screen' may replace the 'real scene' posits the key to understanding the surrogate urban landscape of the late 1980s and the connection between virtual technologies and Cartesian urban space. The perception of spatiality is becoming increasingly dependent on simulation of an environment which is 'other' to the natural; and, because of this simulation, the new space is inherently unstable. Instability and imper-manence have meant that not only is the new spatiality simulated, it is also temporal. Like a ROM chip, once it is without power the memory fades and waits to be replaced with a new vision.[2] The new space, like the television, simulates something that is *other than the real space* and, also like the television, is impermanent.

The artificial environments created through virtual technologies, like televised space, are not only perfect simulations of 'other' space, they are also dynamic environments wherein cultural and social values become fluid. Yet these twin characteristics of simulation and temporality may be found in the marginal areas of urban society as well as in the environments created by virtual technologies. For this reason, those environments in the real world, where falsification is normal, change is inevitable and there is semblance of community, may be called virtual urban spaces. Virtual urban space, however, is not to be found in the parks, streets and gardens of the city, rather it may be seen most clearly in the shopping malls and the theme parks of the urban fringe (Ostwald, 1996b). However, in order to find urban space which is both temporal and simulated, electronic space must be entered. The virtual electronic matrix of primitive cyberspace already exists and communities have formed in large numbers in cities which cannot be located in conventional Cartesian space. In both the mall and the primitive Matrix, the existing derivation of Gibson's literary cyberspace, the virtuality of urban space may be clearly distinguished.

The rise in virtual technologies is a natural extension of the way in which twentieth-century urban communal spaces already constitute virtual environments. The mall and the primitive Matrix are environments in which sensorial perception has been eroded and the space thus created may only be described as virtual. Such spaces are linked and defined not through technology but through the way that communities form and interact in them. This chapter is concerned with the spaces that promote and define community interaction at the boundary between the Cartesian world and the virtual world. It deals not with high technology but with the interface between physical architecture and virtual architecture: between the most virtual of physical urban spaces and the most prosaic of electronic urban spaces. I will begin with an analysis of the connection between conventional urban spaces and virtual urban spaces, and the communities forming in each. This is followed by a brief review of current theories linking the rise in virtual technology to the decline in urban communal space and an examination of a historical model of urban form, the agora, which embodies that relationship. Finally, I want to consider two contemporaneous examples of virtual urban space, one from the margins of conventional urban space (West Edmonton Mall) and the other from the electronic networks (Lucasfilm's Habitat). Through this analysis we can establish that there is often little or no gap between the so-called 'real world' and the 'virtual world'. With such a realization comes the understanding that conventional means of analysing the city are no longer adequate. There is a strong and growing need to consider that zone where the boundaries between the physical and the virtual are completely blurred.

The changing nature of urban space

The urban centre (in its modern incarnation: the metropolis) has been the focus of intense discussion and theoretical debate since the Renaissance. By the Victorian era massive social and technological changes had caused cities to grow at unprecedented rates until the first urban sprawls developed. However, it is in the last decade that the most striking changes have occurred in the ways in which space and community are perceived. Cities are growing globally and the population explosion has placed pressure on already overcrowded urban spaces. The technological revolution is changing how information is used and global communications networks have reduced the perceived effect of spatial displacement. Moreover, through global money markets all countries are interdependently linked. The modern city is beset with the problems of overpopulation, crime and pollution. Urban public spaces, once the site for recreational activities, have frequently degenerated into wastelands roamed by street gangs and ruled by violence. The nature of urban public space is changing and the ensuing cultural change is not a localized event, although it may not be occurring either simultaneously nor at the same rate in all cities. This change is most apparent in the urban centres of the United States of America, South America, Australia and Asia, while in Europe the overwhelming weight of historical precedence has provided a slightly different form of cultural and spatial change.

    That 'nostalgia is [still] the hegemonic discourse of urbanism' is a major factor influencing the postmodern cityscape (Sorkin in Hennessey et al., 1992: 19). The postmodern solution to urban decay was often the gentrification of depressed regions and communities. For this reason Virilio maintains that the cities of today are monuments to a fictionalized past:

> Neo-geological, the 'Monument Valley' of some pseudolithic era, today's metropolis is a phantom landscape, the fossil of past societies whose technologies were intimately aligned with the visible transformation of matter, a project from which the sciences have increasingly turned away. (1991: 27)

Virilio argues that the cities of today are still too closely aligned with the sciences, transport systems and communications networks of the past, and for this reason they are incapable of reacting to the changes taking place. In a discussion of the new spatial forms that are impacting on architecture and urbanism, Krewani and Thomson question the nature of the city in a tone which closely mirrors Virilio's. They ask whether at 'this point one should stop and ask how real our city experience is and whether our daily city experience has not long since come to resemble its fictitious representation' (Krewani and Thomson, 1992: 124). This tendency for cities to become simulated in non-virtual space is a common component of postmodern urban form and has been widely recognized. Christine Boyer (1994, 1996) has argued that the cities of the 1990s are becoming fictional as they start to represent the collective, mediatized memory of the populace. Michael Sorkin, in *Variations on a Theme Park* (1992), has suggested that the postmodern city is prone to Disneyfication (the concatenation of simulation and artifice) and Deyan Sudjic (1993) has noticed the way in which major international cities are starting to resemble one another through the erasure of difference.

Virilio is also concerned with the dislocations in time perception caused by the same changes in urban space identified by Boyer, Sorkin and Sudjic. 'Unity of place without unity of time', he says, 'makes the city disappear into the heterogeneity of advanced technology's temporal regime' (1986: 19). Through its contact with electronic networks, rapid transit centres and international money markets, the postmodern cityscape is gradually becoming more and more reliant on systems which are both simulated and transient. The idea that technology is erasing the perceived distance between points and the relationship between time and space is not unfamiliar. Cultural critics have often commented on the 'changing pace of life' and 'the shrinking globe'. Both are phenomena related to the advent of technologies which reduce the perceived distance between locations and eliminate the time-lag conventionally associated with all communication (Harvey, 1990). In *The Lost Dimension*, Virilio develops this idea of space–time displacement for the city:

> From here on, urban architecture has to work with the opening of a new 'technological space-time.' . . . Instead of operating in the space of a constructed social fabric, the intersecting and connecting grid of highway and service systems now occurs in the sequences of an imperceptible organization of time in which the man/machine interface replaces the façades of buildings as the surfaces of property allotments. (1991: 13–14)

Advances in technology have impacted on the perceived space-time relationship through the creation of a phenomenological space. The ability to
make phone calls to other countries is now an accepted fact of life and this
has contributed to the development of a global telephone culture which
negates distance. Similarly the television provides an 'eye to the world', and
simulates a global space within the flat screen. While the impact on spatial
perception is reasonably clear, Virilio has linked the perception of space
closely to the formation of community, as outlined in his theory of the
'third window'.

Virilio posits three symbolic types of 'window', using the term to imply a
physical interface between interior and exterior. Historically, the first and
most primitive type of window was used to enter and exit a space; in
modern times this window has become known as a door. The second
window is linked to both community and amenity; it is needed to allow
other people to be viewed and communicated with – it provides visual
stimulation without the requirement for ease of passage. The original needs
for light and air that the second window answered are rapidly fading as
modern technologies replace this function. Virilio's third window is the flat
screen of the television. All these 'windows' provide a communal and spatial
extension of the house. In the case of the third window, the television or
computer screen, this extension is like the space just outside the physical
window: it is a perceived space, one which the senses identify as being
present. The third window is the most stimulating of all three because it
represents a constantly changing space (since it is both temporal and
simulated). As the third window slowly supplants the significance of the first
two, the manner in which people, and especially urban people, experience
the city will change. Virilio's third window may well be seen as more than
television and as all aspects of time- and space-altering technology.

Sobchack and Baudrillard have both studied the spatial characteristics of
the flat screen. Their findings, like Virilio's, suggest that the need for
communal urban space has, at least partially, been provided through the
surrogate media of the television and the computer network. For
Baudrillard, 'the scene and mirror no longer exist; instead there is a
screen and a network'; the third window becomes the 'smooth operational
surface of communication' (1987: 126–7). Sobchack calls the realization that
the flat screen may represent a perceptible space 'the inflation of space'
(1991: 255).

Virilio's third window provides a starting point for an understanding of
the connection between space and community, and how it is possible for
virtual space and virtual community to exist as a natural extension of the
physical world. As already noted, the urban spaces of the physical world
and the virtual world are intricately connected through the notion of
community interaction and social formation. Allucquere Rosanne Stone
supports this by suggesting that communities may exist in non-Cartesian
space. She refers to such societies as 'virtual communities' because they
exist within the virtual space of personal perception, like an extension of

Virilio's third window. Stone's argument calls for the understanding of the phenomenological view of the spatial and the experiential. She identifies four epochs of virtual communities, all of which have spatial connotations. Each epoch is defined by the communication technology around which the communities have been based (Stone, 1991, 1995).

Stone's first epoch identifies studies of scholarly publication. The first virtual communities of this type were made up of 'like minded gentlemen of science' whose researches were painstakingly recorded and circulated for discussion among fellow scientists. The modern incarnation of this community, perpetuated through the medium of the journal and the research paper, still exists in academia. In this sense, the academic journal may be seen as a textual community comprising people separated by displacements in time and space but linked through their interest in a certain topic. Moreover, the academic community of the journal has, like any other community, strict laws and customs. Communications between members of the community may be rigidly ordered to meet accepted forms of language, referencing and format.

The second epoch of virtual communities has grown from the media. In this epoch, the virtual spatiality of radio and television connect people together through perceived experiences and the illusion of participation. Like the academic community spatialized within the journal or paper, the televisual community creates its own particular variations of language and presentation. Also like the journal, the virtual community of the media is capable of creating its own outcasts by forming and directing public opinion. However, the most interesting virtual communities, which most clearly display urban spatial properties, are in the third and fourth epochs.

Stone suggests that the third epoch commenced in May 1978 when Communitree went online. Communitree acted as a bulletin board service, an electronic pin-board on which notices could be left. Theoretically, through such bulletin board services, people from all parts of the world were able to leave messages and conduct conversations from their computer terminals. With the emergence of the first electronic bulletin board the presence of virtual links increased rapidly. Communitree was a rudimentary precursor to the global news-nets where hundreds of thousands converse daily and exchange data in a free-flowing system.

Epoch four in Stone's virtual community is based around Gibson's visions of the Matrix, a form of cyberspace. Novak describes cyberspace as a 'completely spatialized visualization of all information in global information processing systems, along pathways provided by present and future communications networks, enabling full copresence and interaction of multiple users allowing input and output . . . and total integration and intercommunication with a full range of intelligent products and environments in real space' (1991: 225). For the novelist Gibson, cyberspace is a 'consensual hallucination'; a 'graphic representation of data abstracted from the banks of every computer in the human system'. In appearance, cyberspace is like 'lines of light ranged in the nonspace of the mind', it is reminiscent of 'clusters and constellations of data', of 'city lights receding' into the distance along endless highways (1986: 67). Stone's fourth epoch is a projection of the future of virtual space into cyberspace communities. Virtual reality on a small scale already exists in a few research centres around the world and in even fewer private organizations; and the people who have inhabited virtual space simultaneously number only in the low hundreds. Benedikt claims that cyberspace is more than the popular model of virtual reality outlined by Rheingold (1991) or Krueger's 'artificial reality' (1991). Benedikt sees the critical component of any definition of cyberspace as the element of community. A single person does not exist in cyberspace, but in virtual reality. A city may exist in cyberspace, but only as a function of the actions of its inhabitants (see Benedikt, 1991).

The agora: cultural seepage in the physical and virtual environments

Each of Stone's definitions of community has embodied within it the concept of new customs, rules and cultural formations. The textual community of the journal has strict customs which militate against the individual's regional, cultural and political tendencies. In the same way, the televisual community propagates the formation of a global language of consumer logos, slogans and imagery. Global recognition of any product name, regardless of the dominant culture and ideology of the region, is the aim of widespread television advertising. In modern critical theory, the television's role in neutralizing and fragmenting culture is well known. Advertisements and products are increasingly multicultural and multilingual in nature. As a technological device the television is the catalyst for both virtualization and cultural neutralization.

The World Wide Web is the latest extension of the physical world into a medium where advertising competes constantly for high-profile sections of homepages. The language of the Internet is a *mélange* of words which originate in disparate sources: technical jargon, cult television lore and keyboard graphics all combine freely in the patois of the cyberpunk or hacker. Internet terms such as 'spamming', which originated in British comedy in the early 1970s, are now part of a global language despite the fact that in many parts of the world the comedy series that spawned this usage is completely unknown. Netiquette and net slang in the late 1980s were almost entirely derived from British, North American and Japanese cultures. The literary and televisual predilections of the early denizens of electronic bulletin boards thus became the basis for the language of the nets, while those cultures that entered electronic space in the years that followed had to adapt and change. At the 1994 cyberspace conference in Canada, local indigenous communities petitioned the organizers of the conference to leave them out of the event, and indeed out of cyberspace, until their native culture was sufficiently robust to withstand the overpowering influences present in the Internet (Stone et al., 1995). In all Stone's epochs it is clear that as each and every community is constructed, the particular spatial systems they are forming within (be they text, audio, video or virtual world) impact on the way in which cultural and social systems are formed. For example, the cultural and social systems forming in the Internet have certain emotional signs and cues – such as :-), the sideways 'smiley' face signifying humour – primarily because they are limited visually and must often derive emphasis from keyboard notations. For this reason, such cultural cues and signs are frequently unable to be translated into conventional urban space and, in this way, may seem to undermine or at least defy Cartesian social systems. Thus the spatial and communicative medium does influence the intermixing or erasing of social and political systems.

Historically, certain city spaces have been linked to the loss or dilution of social and cultural mores. The city, and any urban space, has as a central function social and cultural orientation. Elizabeth Grosz has even defined the function of the city in terms of its capacity to 'orient sensory and perceptual information, insofar as it helps to produce specific conceptions of spatiality' (1992: 250). Specifically, she sees the spatiality of the city as fundamental to providing the principles that organize 'family, sexual, and social relations'. Importantly, the form and structure of the city 'provide the context in which social rules and expectations are internalized or habituated in order to ensure social conformity' (Grosz, 1992: 250). Seen in this way the spatial form of the Cartesian city, like the virtual environment, influences regional, cultural and social stability. A historical example of this concept is the agora.

In post-Homeric Greece the agora was an urban space separated from the temple precinct because of theological and ontological differences. Spatially, in the cities of ancient Greece and Rome, the agora was defined by an exclusion from the city grid signifying that it occupied a zone outside the order of the city. The architectural and urban historian Lewis Mumford notes that the agora was primarily 'an open space, publicly held and occupiable for public purposes', it was 'open to the passer-by' and contained 'temporary stalls or stands' (1991: 176). Pierre von Meiss records that in the 'regular grid layout of Priene, a colonial town of antiquity, the status of exception' to the rule of the town 'is reserved for the agora, the sanctuary and the theatre' (von Meiss, 1992: 54). This formal exclusion from the city grid, while common in modern cites, had strong symbolic meanings for the inhabitants of an ancient Greek or Roman town. The major cross streets that defined an ancient Roman town frequently passed beside or through the agora so that travellers from other regions would be drawn into the central, non-town space. In this way, such travellers and the cultures they carried with them would tend to reach the agora before being encouraged to remain or depart. The agora was often spatially bounded by street walls and contained (under the eye of the city watch), but within the space it was allowed to change as frequently as required.

Spaces of exclusion like the agora were not only public spaces but also spaces where messages were posted, or chalked on walls, and where news was spread by word of mouth. At that time there was 'probably no urban market-place where the interchange of news and opinions did not . . . play almost as important a part as the interchange of goods' (Mumford, 1991: 176). The agora in this sense functioned as a centre for the passage of information and for free communication; and for this reason it has been linked to the rise in politics and the Greek democratic tradition. In the *Iliad*, the agora is described as a 'place of meeting', although the modern translation has been stripped of much of its original meaning. The agora, in a quotidian sense, fulfilled the ancient Greek requirements for commerce and communication. On one level it was a form of market-place but the original translation, a 'place of meeting', was far more accurate. The agora provided a space through which cultures and languages could mix, a place where produce was bartered and tales were told. It was the site for the intermixing and changing of culture, acting simultaneously as 'market, as place of assembly, and as festival place' (Mumford, 1991: 176). The dimension that controlled this change in culture was anthropocentric, given the necessary dependence on speech. As word of a merchant's travels spread from the agora, the inhabitants of the city were slowly altered by the influx of non-Greek or non-Roman cultures. In Mumford's terminology the agora was a site of 'cultural seepage' where social, political and communal change occurred (1991: 121).

The agora model is still highly relevant to studies of urban social formations. Similarly the complex interplay of communal, spatial, cultural and political forces at work in the agora renders it an appropriate model with which to consider critically those spaces formed through the agency of virtual technologies. The most recent incarnation of the agora is contained in two spatial devices: the shopping mall for commerce and the computer for communication. Mumford has traced the agora and its functions ostensibly to the modern shopping mall:

> Not indeed until the automatism and the impersonality of the supermarket were introduced in the United States in the mid twentieth century were the functions of the market as a centre of personal transactions and social entertainment entirely lost. And even here that social loss has been only partly offset by the development of the larger shopping centre where, in the characteristic style of our over-mechanized age, various media of mass communication at least serve as a vicarious substitute – under the sly control of the guardians of the market. (1991: 176)

Since Mumford shows the historical agora to have been a simulated and temporal space, it can be seen as a precursor to the shopping mall. Similarly the agora model is fitting for analysis of primitive electronic communities since, as Mumford says, if the Greek 'acropolis represents the city in depth . . . the agora represents it in extension, reaching out beyond its visible spatial limits' (1991: 190). Like the Internet, the agora 'expressed no unity' and 'almost any function might be performed there' (1991: 190). The agora is a worthy model for virtual urban space because it encapsulates the concepts of spatial extension, cultural neutralization, community formation and temporality. We can now consider two examples of spaces which are simulated, temporal and, like the agora, sites of 'cultural seepage' – a shopping mall and an electronic environment.

The mall: simulated and temporal urban space

Any introduction to West Edmonton Mall (WEM) reeks of hyperbole, but it is worth the exercise if only to explain the magnitude of it all. WEM is 'larger than a hundred football fields', 353,000 square metres of retail space comprising seven major department stores, 41 large stores, 110 restaurants, 13 night clubs, 20 movie theatres, an interdenominational chapel and approximately 700 other assorted shops.[3] WEM is the epitome of Rabelaisian consumerism, it is the ultimate shopping venue where almost any legal commodity may be found. But, for the developers, the mall's 'shop and buy' nature is secondary to its experiential nature. WEM has grown with a degree of hyperactive Disneyfication which rivals any centre of commerce in the world. Within the vast, architecturally uninspiring, vaulted atrium exists a *mélange* of visions, a concatenation of history and fantasy, each parasitically growing into the other until quotidian boundaries of sense and relationship are diminished. The simulated settings that inhabit WEM are seemingly more important than the shops themselves. The ersatz reality may provoke a carnivalesque nature to the space but the simulation of fantasy is the most noteworthy feature of the mall.

WEM contains a full-size ice skating rink with the potential for spectator seating and a full-size replica of the *Santa Maria* floats in an artificial lagoon. This lagoon is so extensive that a fleet of submarines spiral through floodlit plastic seaweed carrying shoppers on small-scale sanitized adventures to stimulate their leisure time. The lagoon is itself a strange mixture of reality and fantasy – real penguins interact with mechanical sharks and real fish live in plastic caves and eat specially provided food (the plastic seaweed being inedible). A mock Victorian iron bridge carries 'tourists' from cinema to amusement centre by way of a small water-front café where an automaton band plays loud jazz, challenging the surrounding muzak. In another area, the lagoon flows into a beach, the gloomy sun high above WEM is supplemented with artificial sunlight, mechanical waves break on the beach and a few hardy bathers frolic in the specially imported sand. Elsewhere, Siberian tigers (real), Parisian art deco signs (fake), Ching dynasty vases (real) and Doric columns (fake) compete for attention. However, the widespread simulation of history and geography in the shopping mall is not the only example of excessive artifice. Above the mall is a 360-room motel, themed in case the endless kaleidoscopic experiences below are not enough for the most jaded of tastes. Horse-drawn carriages may pick up the visitor and deposit him/her near the medieval English suite with its false timber and stone walls, electric fireplace and flushing toilets. The real medieval is not sanitized enough for WEM. Hollywood-themed rooms are also available, with adjacent suites offering ancient Greek and

Roman decor or the Wild West. Nowhere is the degree of fantasy more evident than in the 'Polynesian rooms where the bed floats in a warrior catamaran under full sail while a volcano erupts behind a waterfall which fills a lava rock jacuzzi pool' (Maitland, 1990: 147). On opening the mall, one of the developers proudly announced that 'What we have done means you don't have to go to New York or Paris or Disneyland or Hawaii. We have it all here for you in one place, in Edmonton, Alberta, Canada' (Henry, 1986: 60). Why go to Paris when WEM can provide a simulacrum of the boulevards right here in Edmonton?

Viewed from above, the main structure of the mall stretches in an east–west direction for almost two kilometres. Inside, a central 'street' runs through a series of spaces and at right angles to this main street are a series of corridors which stretch up to 700 metres in length. These corridors pantomime historical streets: a nineteenth-century Parisian boulevard, Victorian courts and New Orlean's Bourbon Street. Bourbon Street WEM is a whimsical spatial narrative derived from a spurious historical syntax of forms. It is a veritable forest of pediments, balconies, Moorish arches, caryatides and dormer windows. WEM provides a fictional image of the past; a fantasy, no doubt, but one allowing the modern shopper to travel to distant places. The setting has been dislocated through time and space, its relevance is lost, the people are gone and the freestyle interpretation has impoverished the original. Yet, for the viewer of WEM's fictional places – even while recognizing that a copy is being experienced – the copy itself has become transposed onto the signified meaning of the space and has erased the original. The Bourbon Street in WEM is *the Bourbon Street* for most of its visitors; there is no other. In the modern memory, which is palimpsestically erased but imperfectly rewritten, the new urban space becomes a reality even though it is simulated and tainted with hyperreality.

The spatial form portrayed within the mall may be one of fragmented images, distorted vistas and shattered reflections, but this superficial chaos possesses an underlying order and design. The mall is a collage of 'psychographics' designed to suit the specific socio-economic values of the desired shoppers. The 'white noise' that fills mall space, combined with the muzak, dulls the auditory experience and distorts the shopper's sense of time and place. The more heavy-handed visual subliminals, by distracting the senses, alter perception and further exacerbate the already poor definition of space. The outcome of all this altered perception is what William Kowinski names as *mal de mall*: 'a perceptual paradox' which influences the shopper through the layering of 'stimulation and sedation'; a condition which is 'characterized by disorientation, anxiety, and apathy' (Crawford, 1992: 14). And at the same time the mall, through the blurred spatial perceptions, is also a depersonalizing experience. Joan Didion describes the mall as an environment where 'one moves for a while in an aqueous suspension' which militates against informed choice and retention of 'personality' (1979: 183). The mall is a space characterized by a proliferation of conflicting signs and images. These signs interfere with perception and the recorded memory of spatial identity rendering the modern shopping mall intensely virtual.

As malls develop and grow, they have been aiming towards seemingly utopian visions of space and recreation. As Frieden and Sagalyn note in *Downtown Inc*, by 'providing safe, comfortable spaces open long hours, developers made their retail centres inviting to a broad cross section of the population' (1991: 68). Developers made their malls inviting by offering a completely controlled environment. At WEM the entire mall is internalized; someone's work, recreation, indeed life, might all take place inside its walls. Malls have their own generators, water supplies and, in some cases, law-enforcement agencies. They are in effect private cities, places where the inhabitants can escape into simulated comfort and forget about the homeless, the poor and the unemployed. The implications of private space and privately owned cities are far reaching. Social ideologies aside, one of the fundamental characteristics of the mall is the presence of an authoritarian set of controls. Surveillance cameras watch over every space in WEM; it is a price the shopper or tourist must pay to exist in this sanitized new urban space. Moreover, in WEM the visions recorded on the security cameras may be replayed on public display screens, while in shop windows video camera displays simultaneously record and play footage of shoppers as they look into the cameras. In a mall, all activities become both displayed and virtual because everyone is recorded and replayed from multiple angles and in reverse, until even the original shopper is hard to distinguish from the recorded and simulated image.

The spatial reality of the shopping mall is also temporal in nature, being governed by economics and the mathematical mapping of value to topography. Pure topography, in a geographic sense, is not enough to map the ideal location of a shopping mall. It must be combined with demographic and economic data as well as estimates of time and speed of travel. In combination, these factors form coordinates which may be used to map an illusory, virtual terrain. This form of mapping, which over-writes the physical world, is known as econotopography. The concept of economic topographies is not new. The idea of mapping land values to sites has been previously studied in major cities and is also seen most clearly to be analogous to spatial mapping in cities such as New York. This mapping technique is simple to visualize in that the higher the land value, the higher the representation of the bar on the econotopographic map. However, the economic significance of the shopping mall may be mapped onto the landscape even more comprehensively than by land value topographies. The mall, like a river, must have a catchment area which may be marked on a conventional map but which is governed by non-topographic factors. This is the region from which the mall may expect to attract the largest proportion of its customers. The more affluent the region, or the better the public transport, the wider the catchment area.

In WEM, the regularly changing socio-econotopographic mix of the community can be seen. There is a constant instability in the number of stores in WEM at any given moment; the exact mix of shopping is in constant change to meet supply and demand. As the surrounding economic and demographic systems change, they send complex ripples through the econotopographic map until the system settles towards equilibrium and the surety of economic returns reduces. The solution to this problem is to rebuild, revitalize and refurbish. A regional shopping centre in the USA, Canada or Australia may have a life span of between seven and ten years before it needs cosmetic surgery, either major or minor. Unless a new image has been proposed and a new lease of life granted to the ageing shopping centre, equilibrium will change arithmetically into decline and, thence, geometrically into receivership. Thus the econotopographic space of the mall is in cyclical change, and for this reason WEM has a limited life span in its current form, The side-effect of the cyclical nature of the shopping mall is that all of the space it defines is, by virtue of the cycle, completely temporal. Bourbon Street (WEM) has a distinct life span before it will be removed and replaced by some other simulation. The identity of the space will change and, even though the Cartesian relationship between space and location is not varied, the signified presence of new space will erase and then rewrite the new over the old.

Simulation, temporality and the associated transient spatiality are characteristics of the virtuality of urban futures. Space is no longer a constant; the perception of space and time is deconstructed through the synchronous application of simulation and temporality. The space is related to the physical presence of site, but it is even more strongly related to the virtual space of the econotopographic map (and the simulated spatiality of the mall interiors). This is a virtual mapping of space and time derived from the topographic renderings of economic geometries. The shopping mall is the consummate virtual urban space. It is both simulated and temporal. It represents an extant virtual environment present at the boundaries of conventional urban space.

Habitat: simulated and temporal electronic space

Since the late 1980s, a new pattern of communal city has come into existence in electronic space. Perhaps the earliest and most well-documented example of a virtual urban space in an electronic environment is Habitat. While, in once sense, Habitat existed originally as a 35-foot-long mural on the wall of a building in California, this was merely a representation. Online through the electronic networks, 'each area of the mural represents an entirely expandable area in the cyberspace, be it a forest, a plain or a city' (Stone, 1991: 94). Habitat is a virtual urban city which transcends common spatial boundaries. Moreover, Habitat offers a very rare model of a community forming and stabilizing, the interactions of its people, their relationships and commerce. Yet Habitat could never be considered a space in any conventional sense.

In 1986 Lucasfilm and Quantum Computer Services produced Habitat, a graphical computer environment where people could interact and see representations of themselves in virtual space. By 1987 Habitat was the world's first electronic urban environment, a true virtual space both simulated and temporal. In the words of its creators, Morningstar and Farmer:

> The system we developed can support a population of thousands of users in a single shared cyberspace. Habitat presents its users with a real time animated view into an on-line simulated world in which users can communicate, play games, go on adventures, fall in love, get married, get divorced, wage wars, protest against them and experiment with self government. (1991: 273)

Habitat could be accessed through a personal computer with a modem connection allowing for up to 20,000 computers to access the central mainframe simultaneously. Similarly the Habitat world was broken up into 'a large number of discrete locations' called 'regions' and at its height 'Habitat consisted of 20,000 of them' (Morningstar and Farmer, 1991: 276). A person existed in Habitat as a 'toon' – people were depicted as blocky images of colour surrounded by jagged black lines. Each Avatar, as they were called, had a recognizable torso, legs, arms and head. Avatars could walk, turn in a choice of four directions, pick up and use objects, and had a few variations on body position (standing, walking and dead). The bodies were positioned by using a joystick and were viewed in elevation as flat two-dimensional figures. The background landscapes were dominated by primitive child-like renditions of houses with pitched roofs, protruding chimneys, virulent green grass and a vibrant blue sky. Each Avatar could move from one region to another, the scenery changing as the Avatar walked through city and country and forest. As the Avatars moved they could encounter others, and therein lay the interest. When another Avatar was encountered it could be addressed by typing on the keyboard. Above the first Avatar's head would appear a balloon which would stretch to fit the sentences being typed. The second, in real time and on his/her own computer screen somewhere else in the real world, could read what was being typed and reply in turn. This interaction rapidly stripped the basic cartoon images of their perceived simplicity. Habitat became more than a poorly rendered computer game, it was an interactive environment, a place with its own currency, newspaper and traditions.

Morningstar and Farmer produced only the elementary environment and a few simple activities within that environment. Originally, they had attempted to plan the communities themselves but quickly ran into difficulty as 'a virtual world such as Habitat needs to scale with its population' and for 20,000 Avatars they 'needed 20,000 "houses", organized into towns and cities with associated traffic arteries and shopping and recreational areas' (Morningstar and Farmer 1991: 286). In early 1987, with the activities that had been designed failing to attract the envisaged interest and with the towns still only half developed, it was feared that within weeks of going online the community would fail. Yet, for those inhabiting the virtual urban space, the activities were mere sidelines to a far more interesting pastime – setting up a virtual community and political system. Avatars quickly became involved in initiating trade: money, called tokens, could be accrued through interest in the bank and items could be bought, used and sold. Communities developed around the initial cities as Habitat money bought land and developed the sites. Societies grew up and meetings were held with Avatars voting on the naming of the first Habitat city. Habitat became a model urban community with hundreds and eventually thousands of people participating.

Habitat had not been online for long when the first of a series of disquieting events took place. As in the real world, crime sullied the new electronic community. It was discovered that objects currently 'in hand' had a degree of instability, and when one Avatar met another it was possible to take whatever the stationary Avatar was holding and run away with it. Electronic purse snatching soon grew into a major crime-wave. The gods of Habitat, the programmers Morningstar and Farmer, were soon petitioned to stop crime but they were adamant that it was not their business. So the people of Habitat lived in fear for a few weeks as crime escalated further. Because Habitat was originally designed as an adventuring environment, a form of extension of the computer gaming and role-playing market, it was assumed necessary to permit the purchasing of weapons from electronic stores in the Habitat world. These guns and magic wands, originally intended to allow Avatars to fight fantasy monsters, were soon employed for other purposes. An unfortunate young Avatar couple walking hand in hand across the woods found themselves ambushed, killed and looted. Being killed was not as final as it sounds since the next day they were resurrected, but they had lost all their possessions and some of their money. Soon battles broke out and marauding gangs roamed the forests. Back in town, the urban Avatars arranged a meeting of all interested people and called for ideas on what to do about the 'murderers'. It was eventually decided to elect a sheriff and to ask the gods to limit the effectiveness of the guns. Morningstar and Farmer agreed in the face of public pressure; henceforth guns would not function in the city areas and the sheriff would have the power to charge and fine Avatars caught breaking the newly defined laws.

It is interesting to note the parallels between WEM and Habitat. It is also ironic that some of the first locations designed in Habitat were for 'shopping' malls. Both places, by challenging traditional laws regarding public space, have brought to light instances when existing laws might need to be revised. Frieden and Sagalyn have analysed the way in which public laws may not be appropriate for private urban environments such as the mall and private political systems. The realization was only gradual that new laws might be needed to govern the rise in privately owned public space (Frieden and Sagalyn, 1991). But consider Habitat. What if the death of a personal Avatar brought on a real heart-attack in the owner deeply involved in their online existence? Is the Habitat assassin with the fixed cartoon grin now a murderer in the real world? Such violent crimes were more noticeable in the early days of Habitat, but a number of other significant incidents occurred. A church was formed dedicated to non-violence and allowing all Avatars to live in virtual peace. A newspaper was circulated daily listing recent events and unsafe areas, and recording the views of the more urban Avatars. Some other enterprising Avatars formed political parties and ran for government. In time, as Avatars made money and started to enter into the development of communities, the land stabilized, the bandits still thrived in the forests but they would not attack well-armed parties, and then, before the next phase of expansion could occur, Habitat was shut down.

While various incarnations of Habitat continue to operate to this day, Habitat itself fell victim to a combination of circumstances, all of which were largely peripheral to the myriad events which occurred there. Two factors which were certainly instrumental in its demise were the reliance of Habitat on the Commodore 64 computer (which was steadily losing market share) and the widespread growth of the Internet. As is so often the case, commercial not social factors finally determined when it was time to erase the town and move on.

Virtual urban futures

When Habitat started, it was the first electronic communal space ever realized on such a scale; now there are hundreds of similar communities operating on the Internet. Like WEM, Habitat was an internally incon-sistent environment in that it relied on fabrication and proved to be dramatically temporal when it was finally shut down. The mall is also erased when it undergoes the endless and inevitable process of refur-bishment: Bourbon Street will be replaced with the ubiquitous 'Main Street', the submarines will become dinosaurs and before long no-one will be able to remember whether the penguins were real or not. The spatiality of the mall derives its character from both simulation and transience, producing an environment which is as virtual as Habitat. Both Habitat and WEM also relied on a form of omniscient surveillance system to ensure that their urban spaces were safe yet, paradoxically, this also meant that any communities thus formed were a shallow imitation of the social patterns of the outside world. It was outside these isolated conclaves, in the forests of Habitat and in the endless car parks of WEM, that the real world of crime and violence continued to exist largely unperturbed. The virtual space of the mall provides a perfectly sanitized setting, devoid of social problems and controlled by technology to ensure that the sordid realities of the outside world do not intrude. Habitat also attempted to create an ideal world by breaking universal laws: by allowing 'people' to be resurrected and to live without food, water and sickness. Habitat relied on two all-knowing and all-seeing gods, the programmers Morningstar and Farmer, to keep them safe and to control the environment. In both cases the environments became like the panopticon prisons Foucault argued were the ultimate means and form of dehumanization. The panoptic environment, which inscribes spatially the power of the viewer into the body of the prisoner, the shopper or the Avatar, is emphatically not a communal environment.

The agora, like WEM and Habitat, was a place of commerce and communication, a place for mixing cultures and experiences, but the similarities end there. The modern shopping mall is a subversive simulated space, it is a heavily controlled and mediated environment where any semblance of physical or political freedom is illusory. The mall does not encourage 'cultural seepage', rather it actively discourages any cultural and spatial forms which it has not already assimilated. In this sense, it superficially possesses characteristics of urban space but it has little or no capacity to encourage community formation. Like the agora, Habitat sought to provide 'an indiscriminate container' which could be filled with interaction, communication and commerce (Mumford, 1991: 177). Yet the community that formed in electronic space was at best a parody and, instead of fulfilling the agora's role as site of political freedom, Habitat degenerated into the simulation of some idealized place. Like Disneyland's Main Street, with its colourful town hall, church and picket fences, Habitat's community was no more than a shallow façade. Whether or not this situation would have been remedied if the environment had been allowed to continue remains unknown. The possibility of real political and social freedom in Habitat was ignored in favour of commerce and consumption. Although more successful than WEM, the virtual urban space of Habitat was still a poor catalyst for social, political and cultural interaction.

Both Habitat and WEM possess many similarities and strongly support the contentions of this chapter that marginal urban spaces in the real world already constitute virtual environments and that the same characteristics are now being transplanted into the virtual realm. However, these examples offer no strong evidence that genuine communities will form in virtual urban spaces in either the Cartesian or the electronic world. The most recent incarnation of the agora is neither the shopping mall nor the closed electronic environment, but may just be the Internet itself. The agora does not necessarily provide a sense of place, rather it provides a sense of passage, translation and personal freedom. If the Internet can achieve the right balance of interaction, leisure and commerce it may in time develop into a genuine community space. While it continues to mirror the malls, theme parks and office buildings of the Cartesian world it will never become the mythical 'place of meeting' described by Homer in the *Iliad*.

Notes

This chapter has been developed from ideas published in the journal *Transition* (Ostwald, 1993) and in the book *Architecture, Post Modernity and Difference* (Ostwald, 1996a). I also wish to thank Barry Maitland and Sandy Stone and for drawing my attention to WEM and Habitat respectively.

1. In this chapter the term 'Cartesian space' is occasionally used to refer to the 'physical' or 'real' world. Given that the aim of the chapter is to remove the boundaries that separate the 'physical' from the 'virtual', it is doubly ironic that such ambiguous terms must first be created and then used alongside the equally ambiguous terms 'physical', 'virtual' and 'real'.

2. One of the essences of virtual space is that it is phenomenological – it is based on perception. Cartesian experiential space is temporal in that it is limited to a particular time-frame. For example, a house may exist at a given moment in time and may be experienced through direct sensorial perception but if the house is demolished the spatial identity is erased. 'Real' space is therefore also temporal, based on a time-frame relative to our perceptions. Virtual space is no different, but its time frame is not necessarily relative to our own. The perception of a distinct virtual spatial form is derived from secondary sensorial stimulation, which means that not only is the exact identity of the space widely different from one person to another, but the same virtual space may be perceived differently each time it is experienced. Virtual space is highly temporal: 'real' space is also temporal but to a lesser degree.

3. In terms of size, in 1992 the *Guinness Book of Records* listed WEM as the world's largest shopping mall, more than double the size of its nearest rival. WEM also held three other records in 1991: the world's largest indoor amusement park, the world's largest indoor water park and the world's largest parking lot. Despite all of this, the Bloomington 'Mall of America' in Minnesota surpassed WEM in size in 1994. In terms of content, the exact mix of shops in WEM has been listed with many variations in a number of sources. Any discrepancies between these sources relate to the constantly changing mix of shops and attractions present in WEM. The major sources for all of the information on WEM used in this chapter are Maitland (1990), Jackson and Johnson (1991) and Crawford (1992).

References

Benedikt, Michael (1991) 'Cyberspace: Some Proposals', in Michael Benedikt (ed.), *Cyberspace: First Steps.* Cambridge, MA: MIT Press. pp. 119–224.

Baudrillard, Jean (1983) *Simulations* (trans. Paul Foss, Paul Patton and Philip Beitchman). New York: Semiotext(e).

Boyer, M. Christine (1994) *The City of Collective Memory: Its Historical Imagery and Architectural Enhancements.* Cambridge, MA: MIT Press.

Boyer, M. Christine (1996) *Cybercities: Visual Perception in the Age of Electronic Communication.* New York: Princeton Architectural.

Chapman, Gary (1994) 'Taming the Computer', in Mark Dery (ed.), *Flame Wars: The Discourse of Cyberculture. South Atlantic Quarterly*, Special Issue, 92 (4): 297–319.

Chesterman, John and Lipman, Andy (1988) *The Electronic Pirates.* London: Routledge.

Crawford, Margaret (1992) 'The World in a Shopping Mall', in Michael Sorkin (ed.), *Variations on a Theme Park: The New American City and the End of Public Space.* New York: Noonday. pp. 3–30.

Didion, Joan (1979) *The White Notebook.* New York: Simon and Schuster.

Frieden, Bernard. J. and Sagalyn, Lynne. B. (1991) *Downtown Inc.: How America Rebuilds Cities.* Cambridge, MA: MIT Press.

Gibson, William (1986) *Neuromancer.* London: Grafton.

Grosz, Elizabeth (1992) 'Bodies-Cities', in Colomina Beatriz (ed.), *Sexuality and Space.* New York: Princeton Architectural. pp. 241–53.

Hafner, Katie and Markoff, John (1991) *Cyberpunk, Outlaws and Hackers on the Computer Frontier.* New York: Simon and Schuster.

Harvey, David (1990) *The Condition of Postmodernity.* Oxford: Basil Blackwell.

Hennessey, Peter, Mitsogianni, Vivian and Morgan, Paul (1992) 'Interview with Michael Sorkin', *Transition*, 39: 19–27.

Henry, Gordon M. (1986) 'Welcome to the Pleasure Dome', *Time*, October 27: 60.

Jackson, E.L. and Johnson, D.B. (1991) 'Feature Issue, the West Edmonton Mall and Mega-malls', *The Canadian Geographer*, 35: 3.

Krewani, Angela and Thomson, Christian W. (1992) 'Virtual Realities', *Diadalos*, 41: 118–35.

Krueger, Myron R. (1991) *Artificial Reality II*. New York: Addison-Wesley.

Lénárd, Ilona, Oosterhuis, Kas and Rubbens, Menno (1996) *Sculpture City: The Electronic Fusion of Art and Architecture*. Rotterdam: 010.

Maitland, Barry (1990) *The New Architecture of the Retail Mall*. London: Architecture Design and Technology.

Mitchell, William J. (1995) *City of Bits*. Cambridge, MA: MIT Press.

Morningstar, Chris and Farmer, F. Randall (1991) 'The Lessons of Lucasfilm's Habitat', in Michael Benedikt (ed.), *Cyberspace: First Steps*. Cambridge, MA: MIT Press. pp. 273–301.

Mumford, Lewis (1991) *The City in History: Its Origins, Transformations and its Prospects*. London: Penguin.

Nixon, Mark (1996) 'De Recombinant Architectura', *21•C*, 1: 40–5.

Novak, Marcos (1991) 'Liquid Architectures in Cyberspace', in Michael Benedikt (ed.), *Cyberspace: First Steps*. Cambridge, MA: MIT Press. pp. 255–71.

Ostwald, Michael J. (1993) 'Virtual Urban Space: Field Theory (Allegorical Textuality) and the Search for a New Spatial Typology', *Transition*, 43: 4–24.

Ostwald, Michael J. (1996a) 'Virtual Urban Futures: The (Post) Twentieth Century City as Cybernetic Circus', in Wong Chong Thai and Gülsüm Nalbanoglu (eds), *Architecture, Post Modernity and Difference*. Singapore: National University of Singapore. pp. 111–32.

Ostwald, Michael J. (1996b) 'Understanding Cyberspace: Learning from Luna Park', *Architecture Australia*, 85 (2): 84–7.

Rheingold, Howard (1991) *Virtual Reality*. London: Secker and Warburg.

Sobchack, Vivian (1991) *Screening Space: The American Science Fiction Film*. New York: Ungar.

Sorkin, Michael (1992) 'See You in Disneyland', in Michael Sorkin (ed.), *Variations on a Theme Park: The New American City and the End of Public Space*. New York: Noonday. pp. 205–32.

Sterling, Bruce (1992) *The Hacker Crackdown*. New York: Bantam.

Stone, Allucquere Rosanne (1991) 'Will the Real Body Please Stand Up? Boundary Stories about Virtual Cultures', in Michael Benedikt (ed.), *Cyberspace: First Steps*. Cambridge, MA: MIT Press. pp. 81–118.

Stone, Allucquere Rosanne (1995) *The War of Desire and Technology at the Close of the Mechanical Age*. Cambridge, MA: MIT Press.

Stone, Allucquere Rosanne, Ostwald, Michael J. and Duget, Anne-Marie (1995) *Technology and the Second Hand Experience: Cyberspace Forum for the Sydney Biennale*. Sydney: Powerhouse Museum (25 July 1995).

Sudjic, Deyan (1993) *The 100 Mile City*. London: Flamingo.

Virilio, Paul (1986) 'The Overexposed City', in Jonathan Crary, Michel Feher, Hal Foster and Sanford Kwinter (eds), *Zone 1/2*. New York: Zone. pp. 14–38.

Virilio, Paul (1991) *The Lost Dimension* (trans. Daniel Moshenberg). New York: Semiotext(e).

von Meiss, Pierre (1992) *Elements of Architecture: From Form to Place*. New York: Van Nostrand Reinhold.

8

COMMUNITY IN THE ABSTRACT:
A Political and Ethical Dilemma?

Michele Willson

On each side of the political spectrum today we see a fear of social
disintegration and a call for the revival of community.

(Giddens, 1994: 124)

In an age when people have more capacity – through technologically aided
communication – to be interconnected across space and time than at any
other point in history, the postmodern individual in contemporary Western
society is paradoxically feeling increasingly isolated and is searching for
new ways to understand and experience meaningful togetherness.[1]
Nostalgia contributes to this search. Re-presented memories of 1950s-
style communities where moral, social and public order 'flourished' are
contrasted with present social forms, which are portrayed as chaotic,
morally impoverished and narcissistic. However, and at least in theory,
there is also a desire to formulate more enriching ways of experiencing
ourselves 'in relation' which escape the difficulties of earlier, restrictive
forms of community.

Many are looking for a form of 'being together' which can be seen as
valued and, indeed, necessary. In turning to technology, we are presented
with the possibility of virtual communities as a potential solution. Virtual
communities – or communities experienced through technological
mediation over the Internet and possibly enhanced in the future by virtual
reality technologies – are represented by some as a form of postmodern
community. These virtual communities are depicted as the answer to the
theorist's search for a less exclusionary or repressive experience of community. Perhaps this will prove to be the case. But other theorists are
uneasy about whether the unique, 'liberatory' and interconnective potential
of the virtual will provide a vision for future communities. This is not to
claim that celebrations of such a form of community are positing it as the
only form to be practised or experienced, since to some degree 'earlier'
forms will still continue to exist. How the relations between old and new
forms are modelled requires further elaboration and critical attention.

The emergence and functioning of virtual communities has the effect
of 'rounding-out' technological application. Technologically mediated

interactivity balances the rationalistic activities of the 'system' – in Jürgen Habermas's sense – through the insertion and operation of the more communicative activities of the 'lifeworld'. The Internet, in particular, is depicted as being more interactive, accessible and democratizing than previous information technologies. Whether that depiction is valuable is not questioned. But the prospect that such a form of community will achieve anything beyond placing a more acceptable 'front' on technological society – such as providing more meaningful experiences of 'being together' – is indeed questionable.

In view of society's reliance on technology to solve its problems, both scepticism and a further examination of the claims surrounding virtual communities are required. It seems plausible that the hunger for community that is evident in postmodernity is in fact partly driven by the experience and ramifications of being an 'individual' within a technologically organized and aided society.[2] As such, it is interesting that there are similarities between the directions taken by theories of community formulated both within and outside the technological arena. If some see the solution as technological and others, while equally concerned with the issue of more meaningful community, avoid the topic of technology altogether, the same kind of question needs to be asked: namely, whether, in facing the difficulties presented by prior formulations of community, theorists are stripping the complex notion of community down to a superficial, one-dimensional understanding of human interaction. What I want to suggest is that, through the withdrawal of community from an embodied, political and social arena – either to lodge within a philosophical abstraction or to become a disembodied, technologically enabled interaction – an ethical or political concern for the Other is rendered impotent and unrealizable. 'Community' is then produced as an ideal rather than as a reality, or else it is abandoned altogether.

Technologies of individuation

This chapter investigates the political and ethical implications of the rise of cultures of disembodiment. To do that requires separating the applications of information and communication technologies into the areas of administration, surveillance and communications. There is, of course, significant overlap between these areas. For the sake of simplicity I shall be referring to two 'types' of computer technology: the system technologies or databases used by the public and private sectors; and the Internet.[3]

Databases are used by institutions to accumulate, combine and create information on all facets of life (including people's personal lives). These systems operate from diverse, decentred locations, often with different intentions or orientations. Database systems are becoming increasingly interconnected and sophisticated, taking on the form of a global information system capable of infinite analysis, profiling and information combinations.

This has consequences for the subjectivity of social actors through the creation of a technologized Panopticon.[4] The Western individual increasingly experiences her/his life as monitored by technology: being caught on speed camera; captured on video while shopping; monitored for work efficiency by technological surveillance techniques; and taking a loan which is recorded, linked with other financial transactions and purchasing practices, and related to demographic statistics. These are just a few examples of contemporary surveillance. The continuous but often unverifiable surveillance has implications, as Foucault notes in *Discipline and Punish*, for the instigation of normalization practices. The power of normalization refers to the process by which a subject self-imposes or interiorizes particular norms and behaviours to conform to a self-perceived (but socially constructed) understanding of normality. This process is accentuated by the subject's own perception of the depth and pervasive nature of her/his visibility. Databases extend the gaze through disciplinary space, enabling a more pervasive and more widespread surveillance of each and every subject than previously possible. The subject of surveillance is universalized in that s/he is reduced to one file among many, but also individuated through being personally identifiable, trapped within time and space by the continual visibility provided by the database/s. Files can be called up at any time with a simple command typed into a computer terminal (see Chesher in this volume). This has the potential to 'compartmentalize' the individual, separating her/him from others through the isolating qualities of the gaze.

Databases are perceived as a means to assist the surveyor. Given that the surveyor is usually an institution of some description, viewing those outside (or working within) its system, images of Orwell's Big Brother – or many 'little brothers' – are ominously invoked. The technology is oriented towards attaining control through information storage and analysis. Within the data field, information itself becomes an entity. Detached from its referent subject, it is able to be moved, manipulated and transformed.

The Internet also enables information to be moved, transformed and manipulated, bringing into question the issues of authorship and authenticity of material. In contrast to system databases, however, the Internet is depicted as a liberating technology. Its information is accessible to many users and it is interactive in form. The Internet enables the extension of many everyday activities. It is utilized for information collection, discussion of both academic and social topics, dissemination of views and undertaking financial transactions. Like databases, the Internet is unimpeded by state boundaries and is increasingly accessible on a global scale.[5] It is a diverse, decentred communications system with unlimited input – in as much as anybody who is connected to a network can participate in the system – resulting in seemingly uncontrolled and unpredictable development. This is viewed by some institutions as potentially threatening, leading to media exposure of 'illegitimate' or socially destructive activities on the Internet, and attempts by politicians to grapple with this issue through discussions of censorship and guidelines.[6] Yet these institutions also seek a greater involvement in the technology, devising ways through which Internet users can unwittingly provide information about themselves or their practices, and thus contribute to their own surveillance. Howard Rheingold raises the conceivable scenario of those who are information-poor, or have limited access to the technology, being offered 'free time' in exchange for the relinquishing of some personal privacy or control over private information (Rheingold, 1993: 293–4). Technological constructs, such as artificial search engines, are increasing in both ability and number. These may well be able to create profiles and records on individuals' activities and their behaviour within virtual communities. In such a situation, the Internet also operates as a database.

Highlighting in this way the similarities between the Internet – in terms not only of its potential but also of its current capacity – and databases suggests that the application to the technology of terms such as *controlling* or *liberating* is arbitrary. Obviously, the technology itself is neither controlling nor liberating, but the social and cultural uses to which it is put may well be. Insofar as the Internet operates as an interconnected database, it has as much potential for bringing about panoptical kinds of recognition relations as it has for enhancing an experience of freedom and mobility. The Internet is therefore also a powerful form of technology of individuation. It connects and disconnects individuals at the same time. As a paradox of 'connectivity', of participation with others in a virtual space, the technology disconnects the individual from the embodied interactions surrounding her/him. Although it may not individualize through the operation of the gaze to the same extent as presently available through databases, interaction through the Internet still heightens the solitary nature of participation, an activity both singular and universalized.

Equality, fraternity and liberty in a virtual community?

Virtual communities are formed and function within cyberspace – the space that exists within the connections and networks of communication technologies. They are presented by growing numbers of writers as exciting new forms of community which *liberate* the individual from the social constraints of embodied identity and from the restrictions of geographically embodied space; which *equalize* through the removal of embodied hierarchical structures; and which promote a sense of connectedness (or *fraternity*) among interactive participants. They are thereby posited as the epitome of a form of postmodern community within which multiplicity of self is enhanced and difference proliferates uninhibited by external, social structures.

Virtual communities exist within bulletin boards, conference groups, MUDs, MOOs and other interactive networks. Interaction is conducted predominantly through textual means. Descriptions, actions and locations are all communicated textually, produced by a keyboard. This will surely

change over time with the increasing sophistication of virtual reality technology and the continued enhancement of graphic and video technologies
(such as video conferencing). However, while visual information is limited
to text-based description, and auditory or other sensory information is
excluded from the interaction, the 'player' or community member is able to
depict her/himself in whatever shape, form or gender s/he desires. Participants in virtual communities can thus escape their own embodied identities
and accordingly can also escape any social inequities and attitudes relating
to various forms of embodiment. Race, gender or physical disability is
indiscernible over the Internet. Any basis for enacting embodied dis-
crimination is removed, freeing access to participation and granting each
participant equal status within the network.

Disembodiment is seen to carry other liberating potentials. In *Life on the
Screen*, Sherry Turkle (1995) discusses how we can experiment with various
projections – both masculine and feminine – of our selves through cyberspace in what she depicts as a non-threatening (physical) environment.
Mark Poster concurs, suggesting: 'Also one may experience directly the
opposite gender by assuming it and enacting it in conversations' (p. 223, in
this volume). Such a depiction may be experientially liberating and
insightful. It is possible, as Turkle and Poster point out, for someone to
portray her/himself within a virtual community as a member of the opposite sex. This may lead to a gendered interactive experience inasmuch as the
character may find her/himself encountering gender-based reactions and
behaviours from other characters (though, of course, only in a text-based
form). Harassment of, and copious offers to assist, female characters are a
common experience on the Internet. However, the version of gender as
constructed or directed in virtual communities is not equivalent to experiencing embodied gender. Embodiment carries biological and experiential
particularities which have specific consequences for subjectivity. This is
quite apart from (although it can be related to) the social constructions of
gender.

Liberation may also be achieved from the constraints of geographical
space insofar as the physical location of the 'body' of the player is overcome through the extension of interaction in cyberspace, compressing into
a readily transversible medium. Thus virtual communities are also seen as a
way of overcoming the inherent isolation of contemporary life where
people do not know their physical neighbours, are not involved in their
local township decisions and possibly work from home. This 'solution'
overlooks the physically isolated nature of participation, where only the
mind is extended into the mutual interaction. It is worth noting that virtual
community participants often feel the need to reinforce/complement their
disembodied relations by simulating, at the level of ritual, more embodied
or sensorial contacts. For example, participants on the WELL – a virtual
community on the Internet – have regular face-to-face picnics and social
gatherings. The participants develop a more complete understanding of
each other at such gatherings. Howard Rheingold notes that, having met a

particular member of a parenting conference group: 'I discovered that I could never again really be frightened by Albert's fierce online persona – the widely known and sometimes feared "sofia" – after seeing him and his sweet daughter, Sophia, in her clown suit, at a Pickle potluck' (Rheingold, 1993: 21).

The perception of anonymity is presented as a further 'plus' by proponents of virtual community. Liberated from the normative gaze of both institutions and society, identity cannot be verified and attached to the embodied user and behaviour is not constrained by 'real space' norms and values.[7] The degree of anonymity actually achieved is questionable, and will prove increasingly so as information providers and commercial interests devise more effective means of accumulating information about network users. Additionally, the chaos within some communities – as a consequence of anonymity being equated with a lack of accountability – has led them to require participants to provide stable identification. On the WELL, for example, participants are obliged to link all presentations of self with an unchanging referent user-ID, thus enabling identities to be verified (Rheingold, 1993). The need for a kind of order within community interaction has prompted such communities to sacrifice liberatory aspects of anonymity in favour of accountability. The recording and archiving of interactions also creates the 'historical trace' of a character, decreasing the ability for that character to interact unidentified by past behaviours or statements.

Normative guidelines exist within those communities and the gaze – although in a modified form – applies. Marc Smith writes that, as in 'real space' communities, virtual communities must invoke and maintain the commitment of their members; monitor and sanction behaviour; and carry out the production and distribution of essential resources (HREF 1). There are specific rules attached to each community, which participants must agree to follow in order to maintain participatory rights. Many of these rules are fashioned either by the participants themselves or, more frequently, by the person/s who originally constructed the community space. For example, in conference groups the 'host' has control over the topics discussed and the behaviour permitted by conference participants, to the extent that certain topics or users may be banned if necessary.[8]

The question of ethics, or a notion of the common good, within virtual communities themselves (or even within the notion of virtual communities) is related to the existence of the kind of normative guidelines I have been outlining. Communitarian theorists such as Sandel, Taylor and MacIntyre have concentrated on the importance of a certain notion of the common good for 'real space' communities. They examine the incorporation of ethics and norms by the institutions, and within the practices, of such communities. Indeed, MacIntyre argues – along with numerous critics of the postmodern theoretical orientation – that our current life practices are missing common understandings and ethics which provide guidelines, cohesion and meaning for our society. According to MacIntyre, pre-secular times were structured by laws and explanations which placed the world and human interaction within a particular order. This gave rise to a particular understanding or prescription of 'the good life' and of the common good. With the dismantling of these life orders we have simultaneously discarded the notion of commonly held values. Without an intersubjective notion of the good life, he argues, we have turned to a procedural determination of everyday practices and lifestyles (MacIntyre, 1981). This leads to an increasing social reliance on instrumentally rational processes and, correspondingly, on technological assistance.

Something akin to spiritual enlightenment (and therefore a 'world order') is commercially marketed as attainable with the use of information technologies. The recent television advertising campaign by IBM, 'Solutions for a Small Planet™', demonstrates an attempt to link their technologies to the ethos driving current New Age spirituality movements. Two messages are conveyed through these advertisements – one using nuns and another monks, so excited by the computer's capabilities that it interrupts, or even takes the place of, their spiritual contemplations. Firstly, the advertisements suggest the possible realization of a spiritual experience, as religious contemplation comes to stand for or is even replaced by experiencing the technology. Secondly, the very term 'Small Planet' carries with it the possibilities of universal interconnectivity and accessibility. With this technology, the viewer can readily infer, it is easy to be connected with everyone rather than to be lost in a sea of isolation and alienation: a variation on the cliché 'it's a small world' as a response to meeting someone familiar in an unlikely place. It emphasizes the transversality and compression of space into a more manageable concept/experience. A similar kind of suggestion links the communitarian emphasis of interactive technologies. By using these technologies, it is implied, the global can become as manageable and as familiar as your local community (the community that you have, nostalgically, lost).

This message of manageability and familiarity appears to be carried uncritically by all virtual community enthusiasts. They see the good life as achievable through the opportunities of flexible, disembodied identities unconstrained by geographical time and space, and no longer dependent on 'meaningful' others. Which means that it is the *forms* of participation that result in meaningful experiences for participants. Emphasizing multiplicity and choice stresses procedural measures, where the ability to choose identities and location is celebrated, but does not explain the nature of the good life itself.

However, virtual communities must also be understood as multiple and different, making it impossible here to delineate the qualities or understandings of each within one encompassing generalization. Any analysis of virtual community needs to proceed on two different though ultimately related levels: an analysis of the potentialities of the technology that enable virtual communities to exist in their present form; and an analysis of the specific form of each virtual community. The first helps to identify the capabilities and means of all communities within virtual space, allowing certain generalizations; while the second focuses on the specificity of each virtual community, with its own particular norms and regulations.

What is promoted as part of the good life, enabled by the capabilities of the technology, is the accentuation of choice. Within a virtual community individuals are able to choose the level or degree of interaction. They can choose when to participate, they can choose their degree of involvement with others – as long as those with whom they wish to be involved agree.[9] Marriages take place, 'sexual' relationships are formed and hierarchical or administrative relations created. As Sherry Turkle notes: 'Women and men tell me that the rooms and mazes on MUDs are safer than city streets, virtual sex is safer than sex anywhere, MUD friendships are more intense than real ones, and *when things don't work out you can always leave*' (1995: 244; my emphasis). Relationships can be 'broken' at any stage by the simple withdrawal of the character/identity, leaving one to wonder at the level and depth of commitment or investment in these relationships.

Individuals can also choose to have several characters within a community, or to belong to several communities, at any one time. As such they continually 'flit' between one character and another, and between communities. This ability has led observers to analogize the activities of 'character building' and 'flitting' as the concrete depiction of postmodern theory with its emphasis on multiplicity and the navigating of surfaces (Turkle, 1995: 44–5). Nor is it so different from the multiple memberships, social roles and thus identities that individuals hold in modern society, although the rate of transition between these is not as instantaneous as in cyberspace. Such instantaneity accelerates the transformative skills needed to assimilate rapidly into the 'clothes' of each character and may indeed affect a person's experience and means of relating to the world. Parallels can be drawn between this flitting and television 'channel surfing' in the constant search for more rewarding stimuli. Jonathan Crary notes that 'in fundamental ways, we're being drilled to accept as "natural" the idea of switching our attention rapidly from one thing to another' (1995: 66). One wonders whether we are becoming sensory junkies perpetually in search of new experiences; that is, whether this searching for constant yet apparently superficial stimulation is leading to the promotion of instant gratification at the expense of more involved, complex, meaningful investigation and understanding.

In terms of interaction within a virtual community, the emphasis is on fluidity and choice of associations in a social space. Interaction is abstracted from more concrete and embodied particularities and takes place within an environment shaped by the actors themselves. A 'loosening' of connections may appear liberating. But such an understanding devalues many of the positive and ontologically important aspects of those very connections. It appears, for example, contradictory to elevate the enriching aspects of virtual communities while at the same time devaluing or ignoring relations such as those that exist between parent and child, which many theorists would see as fundamental for the basis of any community. As David Holmes has so aptly analogized, the participants of virtual community are like messages in bottles, floating randomly in the oceans waiting to be picked up – a notion connected to the postmodern depiction of the multiplicity of selves in present society (pp. 37–8, in this volume). That there are no bonds or connections 'between' these bottles, apart from communication around a certain interest, is not an anxiety within virtual communities.

Instead, liberatory and postmodern claims about virtual communities are precisely based on the promotion of an anonymity which enables flexible, multiple and anonymous identity construction, and the alteration of spatial and time experiences. What is described in such utopian formulations is the ability to 'play' with identity and to promote communication and information collection. I would suggest that the dissolution or fragmentation of the subject and the instantaneous, transient nature of all communication disconnect or abstract the individual from physical action and a sense of social and personal responsibility to others. A fairly superficial example can be drawn from Sherry Turkle's book *Life on the Screen*. Turkle describes a virtual community participant actively involved in the political machinations of his cybersociety but also completely apathetic about and disengaged from the political situation surrounding him in his 'off-line' life (or embodied location), to the extent that he is not interested in participating in a local senate election (Turkle, 1995: 242).

Blanchot makes a similar point about the disembodied experiences of the broadcast media:

> The whole world is offered to us, but by way of a gaze. . . . Why take part in a street demonstration if at the same moment, secure and at rest, we are at the demonstration [manifestation] itself thanks to a television set. (1993: 240)

Yet the experiential quality of actually attending a demonstration and being surrounded by activity, and the noise and smells of crowd contagion, is a more complex, more involving experience than that achieved via the medium of a television screen. While virtual communities may be interactive, they do not require either physical commitment (other than working with a keyboard) or moral, political or social extension beyond the network. Of those who use the Internet and virtual communities, only a small percentage actively participates. The rest operate from a voyeuristic or 'viewer' position similar to that practised in television viewing.[10]

Since other peripheral distractions are filtered out by the reliance on text-based descriptions, the nature of the interaction becomes intensely focused. Attention is solely placed on the act of communication as perceived through the visual interpretation of text.[11] Such a focus leads to claims that relations on the Internet are more intense than those in real space. In some ways, this view of interaction within a virtual community could be compared to the idea of the singles bar, with the singularity of purpose that this might suggest. Such a singular intention does not equate well with the complex experience of intimacy. And in any case, a very different analogy about interaction with a singular purpose, with a very different result, might just as easily be drawn using Blanchot's example of the street demonstration.

Anthony Giddens writes: 'Intimacy . . . is not, as some have suggested, a substitute for community, or a degenerate form of it; it is the very medium whereby a sense of the communal is generated and continued' (1994: 127). The question is whether intimacy can be achieved in such a public domain as the Internet, with only text-based representation and the imagination. It is necessary to ask if 'community' can be sufficiently defined by the machinations of thin/emptied-out selves interacting via text through cyberspace;[12] or whether, by removing the difficulties and limitations of more traditional communities, we are also stripping away many of the factors that 'make' community meaningful for its participants.

In addressing these issues, it is instructive also to consult the recent work of community theorists working outside the technological debate. To this end, the contemporary thought of Jean-Luc Nancy, when extended to the analysis of virtual communities, enables certain useful analogies and observations.[13] As I want to show, there are similarities between the culture of virtual communities and Nancy's theoretical emphases. Both stress the multiplicity of experience and the dangers of prescribing particular forms of community and identity. Both can also be seen to encounter difficulties in enacting a political ethics concerned with the Other.

The community of Jean-Luc Nancy and the virtual community: a comparison

While the notion of *community* is experiencing a resurgence of interest, many theorists nevertheless overlook the implications of living and experiencing ourselves within a world increasingly reliant on technology. Albert Borgmann explains that society's reliance on, and everyday use of, technology becomes a normalized pattern:

> When the pattern is so firmly established, it also tends to become invisible. There are fewer and fewer contrasts against which it is set off; and meeting us in objective correlates, it attains an objective and impersonal force. (1984: 104; my emphasis)

The technological paradigm has become naturalized and so pervasive that it appears invisible or, at the very least, inevitable. But technological capabilities and uses impact on the subjectivity of the Western individual. Failure to consider the effects here has consequences for the adequacy of some community theories. Yet, despite overlooking technological influences, the formulations advanced by some community theorists reveal similarities in direction to those of virtual community proponents. It will become apparent that both technological and non-technological understandings of community have been abstracted from a 'realizable' embodied form of community, either to an ontological schema (as is the case with Nancy), or to an online network experience in the form of virtual communities.

Nancy rejects the traditional conception of community as a grouping or coalescing around a fixed essence and identity. Community represented this way becomes 'community as communion' (Nancy, 1991: 15). Such a form of community constrains a group of people to a monolithic form of identity, suppressing difference and promoting exclusionary practices. Nancy argues instead for community to be understood as the *incomplete* sharing of the relation between beings. For him, being is not common because it differs with each experience of existence, but being is *in* common: it is the *in* where community 'resides'. Community is to be 'found' at the limit where singular beings meet. The danger is in prescribing or categorizing an essence or form for both community and the beings that it involves.

Some similarities can be drawn between Nancy's theoretical manoeuvres and those celebrating virtual communities.[14] Nancy's discussion emphasizes the fluidity and singularity of being and the importance of the relations between beings. The emphasis on the absence of bonds or ties between these beings allows a non-prescriptive form of relations. Similarly, the virtual communitarians argue for multiplicity, difference and fluidity of experience, although they posit this argument within the notion of multiple, self-constituted selves/identities. They argue for a multiplicity of forms of community existent within the technology, whereby the multiple selves of a subject can belong to one community or to many communities and can freely move between all or any of these. As such, like Nancy, they wish to avoid prescribing particular forms of community and identity. Both orientations understand and encourage a concept of community which promotes relations free from constraint. Yet it appears there are also important differences and these deserve further elaboration.

Nancy would not accept the virtual community argument that a multiplicity of identities within a multiplicity of communities enables a more fruitful experience of community. Instead, identity would be seen to be more in the nature of work, or of a 'fixing' imposed on singular beings. It would therefore be open to the dangers of totalitarianism, oppression and the death/reduction of community (Nancy, 1991). This is similar to the argument in Georgio Agamben's *The Coming Community*. Agamben attempts an understanding of community which does not rely on an idea of identity nor on members belonging to any particularity. Identity involves the accentuation of particular characteristics and the suppression of other characteristics. Instead, Agamben uses the term 'whatever singularity' to emphasize the unique and multiple characteristics of each being. 'Whatever singularity' does not belong to a particular group, nor even to a linguistic designation (Agamben, 1993). Nancy's work carries a similar intention of avoiding the prescription of an essence for his singular beings or their communities.

Nancy asserts that a focus on the subject destroys any conceptualization of community.[15] He draws attention to the significance of the relation *between* beings, rather than to the beings themselves. Singular beings are not fixed totalities: they exist in and through their relations with other singular beings. Indeed, the use of the term 'singular beings' emphasizes these beings' difference, their multiplicity and their relations. A singular being 'ends' at the point where it is exposed to another singular being (or beings) (Nancy, 1991: 27). This is the *limit* where there is a possibility of one singular being and another being existing simultaneously. It is where a consciousness of both separation and togetherness exists at the same time. Nancy's use of these concepts in discussing community and his denunciation of the existence of the 'individual' as an absolute totality without relations intend to highlight the relations between beings. For him, the focus of community is on the relational: the ontological necessity of the relational and, at the same time, the difference in each presentation or experience of the relational. Thus, he claims, we can never lose community despite fears to the contrary.

Such an assertion recognizes the uniqueness of other beings and imposes an implicit ethical responsibility to allow and respect differences. To ignore these differences or attempt to consume them within a totalized whole is to destroy the experience of community. It is precisely this focus on relationships and an ethical consideration for the Other which lacks adequate development in virtual community analyses. If the emphasis of community analysis is on the individual and the effects on/for the individual, then the Other is objectified, becoming a utilitarian instrument for the achievement of the individual's own ends. Understanding the relationship in that way fails to recognize the importance of the Other for self-constitution, and the importance of relations between self and Other for the functioning of community. Any possibility of an ethical responsibility towards the Other encountered by the self (where that self undergoes as a result a formative or boundary experience) is neglected. And the failure to delineate the possibility of an ethics can only accentuate further the compartmentalization and totalization of the individual, despite the potential for fluidity and multiplicity opened by the technology.

In light of the awareness that postmodern theory raises about the suppression of difference and the Other, this is an important point. In virtual communities, we are presented with the description of community where participants appear autonomous, self-indulgent and seeking self-satisfaction. Free-floating beings, whose encounters with others may be formative, are depicted; but these relations are not elaborated sufficiently. Obviously there is a need for other characters to exist to enable interaction within these communities. Indeed, it is the ability for interactivity that is being celebrated and on which meaning is founded for its participants. Yet the celebration is expressed in terms of the possibilities for the subject of these relations. This concentration can be attributed in part to a reluctance to describe or prescribe a particular form of relations and, in that sense, it leaves the way open for multiple, varying experiences of the relational. In turn, it may explain why theorists, even as they concern themselves with an idea of virtual community, are more willing to focus on the potentialities enabled by the technology than on the relations of community.

A further difference between Nancy and the virtual communitarians occurs in the kind of attention paid to notions of subjectivity. Despite a certain ambiguity around his conception of singular beings, Nancy posits his analysis as ontological. Indeed his singular beings could be described as essentialized and ahistorical. Historical and cultural forces are not attributed a formative influence on singular beings. At the same time, an essence is not ascribed to these beings, since each being experiences itself differently. Such an understanding, while devoid of generalizations and oppressive classifications, makes any critique of singularity and community extremely difficult. It also renders any historically situated analysis of community redundant since community is assumed to be impervious to such influences. The virtual communitarians, on the other hand, direct their view to the subjective effects of the discourses and practices enabled through technological application. For writers like Turkle and Poster, there is an emphasis on multiple subjectivities or selves where different experiences, social roles and interactions (languages/discourses) result in the experience of different identities. These selves could be described as more situated and non-essential than the beings depicted by Nancy. However, such a portrayal of multiple selves is reductionist. It removes the complexity and depth from the process of self-constitution by limiting perceived influences on this process to singular events/experiences and the possibility of infinite (unrelated) multiplicity. It also fails to explain adequately the possible implications to the decentred subject of multiple selves of cultural and historical change. Thus, while the approach taken can be clearly distinguished from Nancy's, the criticism of ahistoricism might also be levelled here.

Relations between the various selves of the virtual community member require further elaboration, as does the question of how they are integrated (if at all). Integration need not imply centralization. It is simply an assertion against the insularity of these selves, and thus a recognition of their effect – in whatever degree – on the Other/others. As Marc Smith explains:

> Despite the unique qualities of the social spaces to be found in virtual worlds, people do not enter new terrains empty-handed. We carry with us the sum-total of our experiences and expectations generated in more familiar social spaces. (HREF 1: 138)

New experiences and understandings may be generated in virtual space, leading to the possibility – or expectation – that these new understandings will affect other selves (or, as it might be interpreted, other aspects of the self). It seems a persuasive argument that each self existing 'within' a subject (decentred or otherwise) must impact on the other selves, forcing some self-compromise and modification. Contradictory practices must be self-justified – possibly unconsciously – and relegated to a particular sphere or presentation of the self. For example, the way a person behaves when performing a particular social role may be deemed acceptable only while carrying out that role. Nevertheless, some behaviour required for the role may also be completely contradictory to, and irreconcilable with, the expectations and behaviours of other roles in the person's life. Failure to reconcile these selves in some way would seemingly result in confusion and disorientation. Jane Flax argues that this is indeed the case. She suggests that schizoid and borderline individuals, for example, do not have the subjective fluidity to enable reconciliation and modification of selves to take place, hence their difficulties in functioning within society (Flax, 1993).

Some level of cohesion among selves or, alternatively, a fluid – although sometimes contradictory – unitary subjectivity can be argued. Anthony Cascardi writes that: 'contradictions within modernity are lodged within the divided subject, who may act in different functional roles and as a member of various social groups and who may speak in different voices when in pursuit of different ends or when making different value claims' (1992: 7). This division of the subject is extended through the possibilities produced by mediation in virtual environments. But the virtual communitarians need to elaborate the relationship between, and the influences on, their multiple selves for their position to be convincing.

Attitudes towards the deliberate construction of community uncover other differences between the two theoretical orientations. For Nancy, community cannot be 'made'. It exists at an ontological level within the relation between beings. To attempt to create community is to make it into work, actively constraining the relation between beings by ascribing particular qualities or restrictions, and thus undermining community. For Nancy, the task is to understand the experience of community rather than to describe or create community. Such an orientation is open to the criticism of being politically disengaged and apathetic; of being so careful in avoiding description that the theory disempowers political direction or incentive. It mobilizes a withdrawal from the political arena and thus disregards the possibilities for realizing actual practical benefits or change. Virtual communities, on the other hand, are undeniably 'made', in the sense that the illusion of space is created for the production and operation of community within a humanly crafted technology. Yet this does not mean that interaction will automatically take place, nor that a community will be formed, since people cannot be forced to participate. There must be something which compels or invites their participation. And we would need to reiterate the observation that has already been made: the distancing that occurs through the disembodied processes of participation in a virtual community does not encourage embodied political activity, nor does it draw attention to political activity outside that community.[16]

Both theoretical interpretations of community rely on a tendency towards realization of community in the abstract: a removal of community from the embodied political sphere either to an ontological condition which would not appear to require action, or to a phenomenological experience which engages our minds and not our bodies. Both understandings are ahistorical in orientation; and fail to explain adequately where their notions of community are situated and how those notions can be extended and integrated into a physical realization of community.

Conclusion

Virtual communities are celebrated as providing a space and form for a new experience of community. This experience is depicted as multiple, liberating, equalizing and thus providing a richer experience of togetherness. However, a critical examination of these understandings reveals, paradoxically, a 'thinning' of the complexities of human engagement to the level of one-dimensional transactions and a detaching of the user from the political and social responsibilities of the 'real space' environment. This tendency towards a withdrawal from the active political sphere of real space, or the withdrawal from attempts to realize an embodied form of community, is mirrored in the works of other contemporary community theorists such as Jean-Luc Nancy.

In their desire to avoid placing restrictive or totalizing tendencies on the experience or understanding of community, theorists of both technological and non-technological orientation have removed community from a tangible, embodied or concrete possibility, relegating it either to the sphere of ontological, pre-political, pre-historical existence; or to an experiential existence within the nodes of a computer network system. This general movement towards a separation or abstraction of community from the political possibilities of real space removes any necessity for direct, embodied, political action. The depth of commitment to others within a community also declines, questioning the possibility of responsibility for the Other. As Nancy emphasizes, a concern for the Other is vital for any valid experience of community. But in the case of virtual communities such an ethic is far from apparent.

The growth of virtual culture and technosociality in everyday life carries with it contradictory implications for identity and community. Virtual communities enrich or 'round out' the use of technology by encouraging communication and creative imagination. Children growing up using the medium will see it as an extension of their world, including their relationship base. This in itself will have ramifications for the ways they experience themselves and their interpersonal relations. But we need to be careful in the claims we make about, and the hopes we invest in, virtual communities. By relying on understandings of community which paradoxically work to concentrate our attention on our selves while distancing us from our embodied relations we may be accentuating the very compartmentalization against which we could be striving.

Notes

I would like to thank Paul James, Michael Janover and David Downes for their suggestions and assistance with this chapter.

1. The idea of 'community' is experiencing a resurgence in interest among both theorists and society at large. America has seen the growth of a self-named 'Responsive Community' movement which has emphasized the way in which the community has suffered through the privileging of individual rights and concerns. There has also been an increase in the rhetoric of community employed by politicians like Bill Clinton and Tony Blair (see Willson, 1995).

2. This is not to argue for technological determinism. That is, I am not saying that the technology alone produces specific, unavoidable subjective practices or outlooks. Rather I am arguing that the uses to which the technology is applied by the society/culture; the modes of thought which are accentuated by technological applications; and the practices that are enabled or increased through the technological capabilities available, all have consequences for the experience of subjectivity. Technological capabilities which enable practices otherwise impossible for the society to perform unassisted must, of course, also be granted the potential for subjective effect.

3. The broadcast media would also be situated here and are important because of their cultural and political impact. For more elaboration on broadcast media see (McCoy, 1993) and David Holmes's chapter in this book (Chapter 1).

4. See Foucault (1977) and Poster (1990) for further elaboration on the effects and potential of the Panopticon (as modelled on Jeremy Bentham's construction of a prison). Poster refers to this phenomenon as a Superpanopticon. However, he does not emphasize the role of the gaze, or visibility, in the application and self-imposition of a subject's normalization processes. Databases enable an extension of that visibility into abstracted space, producing a more pervasive and intrusive gaze than that achievable without technological extension.

5. This is not to be trapped within the debate over the universality of access and participation on the Internet while its participants are primarily white male, middle-class English speakers from Western industrialized countries.

6. For example, President Clinton signed the Communications Decency Act, which authorizes the censoring and monitoring of objectionable material on the Internet. China has begun to restrict Internet access, and Victoria, Australia, has already instigated its own online censorship provisions. See van Niekerk (1996: D1).

7. Some difficulty arose in deciding what term to use in describing interaction and experiences outside cyberspace. 'Real life' is problematic as it places a distinction between embodied experience as being real and interaction via technology as not real. Participants in virtual communities would obviously wish to contest the 'unreality' of their interaction, which may well play a very 'real' part in their lives. It also fails to take into account the constructed or perceptual aspects of our interpretations of reality in embodied or real space. 'Embodied space' indicates the realm of face-to-face contact alone, and is therefore also problematic. It is also more unwieldy. The term 'real space' – while still not entirely appropriate – is more suitable.

8. This is a fairly drastic step and usually requires certain consultation with others before action is taken (HREF 1: 29).

9. In the few cases where mutual agreement has not been involved, there has been tremendous discussion around the issue. Virtual rape has provoked significant concern and debate about the impact of text-based acts of violence.

10. Statistics show that 50 per cent of postings on the WELL were contributed by only 1 per cent of users. (HREF 1: 96).

11. Although now graphics and sound are being gradually incorporated.

12. 'Whether virtual systems can sustain the depth and complexity necessary for durable social structures that can withstand time and disruptive circumstances as yet unknown, remains to be seen' (Stone, 1992: 620).

13. I have taken some liberties with the extension and application of Nancy's theory to

allow discussions of virtual communities. According to Poster, Nancy denies the applicability of his theoretical endeavour to technological mediation and indeed elsewhere writes that technological and capitalistic economies work to undermine experiences of community. However, the theory is still useful to elaborate on, and provide a contrast with, aspects of theorizing around virtual communities.

14. Here I am focusing my analysis and assumptions primarily on the work on virtual communities undertaken by Rheingold, Poster and Turkle. Although they have different understandings of subjectivity and also different expectations for these communities, there is sufficient commonality to justify such an approach.

15. Nancy claims that those analyses that focus on the subject, thus ignoring these relations, will fail to understand adequately experiences of community: 'this limit is itself the paradox: namely, the paradox of a thinking magnetically attracted toward community and yet governed by the theme of the sovereignty of a subject. For Bataille, as for us all, a thinking of the subject thwarts a thinking of community' (Nancy, 1991: 23).

16. This is not to assert that political activity oriented towards offline situations does not take place through computer networks. However, in such a situation, the user entering or participating in online dialogue is usually applying the technology as a tool to spread political information rather than accessing a social space.

References

Agamben, Georgio (1993) *The Coming Community* (trans. Michael Hardt). Minneapolis, MN: University of Minnesota Press.

Blanchot, Maurice (1993) *The Infinite Conversation* (trans. Susan Hanson). Minneapolis, MN: University of Minnesota Press.

Borgmann, A. (1984) *Technology and the Character of Contemporary Life: A Philosophical Inquiry*. Chicago: University of Chicago Press.

Cascardi, Anthony (1992) *The Subject of Modernity*. Cambridge: Cambridge University Press.

Crary, Jonathan (1995) 'Interzone', *World Art: The Magazine of Contemporary Visual Arts*, 4: 65–6.

Flax, Jane (1993) 'Multiples: On the Contemporary Politics of Subjectivity', *Human Studies*, 16: 33–49.

Foucault, Michel (1977) *Discipline and Punish: The Birth of the Prison* (trans. Alan Sheridan). London: Allen Lane/Penguin Books.

Giddens, Anthony (1991) *Modernity and Self-Identity: Self and Society in the Late Modern Age*. Stanford, CA: Stanford University Press.

Giddens, Anthony (1994) *Beyond Left and Right: The Future of Radical Politics*. Cambridge: Polity.

HREF 1. Http://www.sscnet.ucla.edu/soc/csoc. Smith, Marc (1992) 'Voices from the WELL: The Logic of Virtual Commons'.

McCoy, T.S. (1993) *Voices of Difference: Studies in Critical Philosophy and Mass Communication*. Creskill, NJ: Hampton Press.

MacIntyre, Alasdair (1981) *After Virtue: A Study in Moral Theory*. London: Duckworth.

Nancy, Jean-Luc (1991) *The Inoperative Community* (ed. Peter Connor; trans. Peter Connor, Lisa Garbus, Michael Holland and Simona Sawhney). Minneapolis, MN: University of Minnesota Press.

Poster, Mark (1990) *The Mode of Information: Poststructuralism and Social Context*. Oxford: Polity.

Poster, Mark (1995) *The Second Media Age*. Cambridge: Polity.

Rheingold, Howard (1993) *The Virtual Community: Homesteading on the Electronic Frontier*. Reading, MA: Addison-Wesley.

Stone, Allucquere Rosanne (1992) 'Virtual Systems', in Jonathan Crary and Sanford Kwinter (eds), *Incorporations: Zone 6*. New York: Zone. pp. 609–21.

Turkle, Sherry (1995) *Life on the Screen: Identity in the Age of the Internet*. New York: Simon and Schuster.
van Niekerk, M. (1996) 'Censor Moves to Shackle Net', *The Age* (Melbourne), 13 February. p. D1.
Willson, Michele (1995) 'Community: A Compelling Solution?', *Arena*, 15, February/March: 25–7.

9

WHAT SPACE IS CYBERSPACE?
The Internet and Virtuality

Mark Nunes

From AT&T advertisements to White House policy statements, the mid-1990s have prepared America for a changed world – or more precisely a new world: one that exists on the shimmering surface of our computer screens. In the first six months of 1994 alone, the number of computers connected to the worldwide network of the Internet jumped by one million to a total of 3,212,000 'host' machines (HREF 2).[1] In response to this rapid growth, the media have refurbished that old American icon of both progress and freedom: the highway. Soon, every American will be back on the open road. New roadside businesses have already begun to emerge as the map of the Internet continues to encompass the globe. But in its current figuration, the Internet does more than network the globe; it creates a metaphorical world in which we conduct our lives. And the more ecstatic the promises of new, possible worlds, the more problematic the concept of 'the world' becomes.

The Internet, both as a technological artefact and as popular image, provides a site for exploring 'the world' and the position of such systems of totality in postmodernity. The geographical metaphors for the Internet quite literally (or perhaps virtually) set themselves up as a place, providing a topological 'ground' beneath the 'Information Superhighway' that allows for travel, distance and speed. 'Cyberspace' no longer strictly refers to the fictional 'matrix' in William Gibson's novel *Neuromancer*; it has now entered into common speech on and off the net as shorthand for the conception of computer networks as a cybernetic space.[2]

The Internet is quickly creating its own world, one which numerous theorists have begun to address. For the most part, approaches to this topic have suggested the extremes of either an apocalyptic moment or the emergence of a cybernetic utopia. In one approach, following Jean Baudrillard, the emergence of the Internet as a kind of cybernetic terrain marks the end of the symbolic distance between the metaphoric and the real. Cyberspace abandons 'the real' for the hyperreal by presenting an increasingly real simulation of a comprehensive and comprehensible world. Baudrillard, Paul Virilio, Jean-François Lyotard and others see 'telematics' as providing a threshold moment for the postmodern: when Enlightenment 'progress' reaches an escape velocity which sends it beyond its own end of comprehending the world. Now, the model of the world becomes the world itself. Still others though, drawing again on Baudrillard and Lyotard, as well as on Gilles Deleuze and Félix Guattari, see cyberspace as a condition of possibility for mutating or derailing the assumptions of Enlightenment thought. These approaches foreground the contemporary challenges to 'the real' in postmodern culture, while at the same time suggesting how theory can be used to dissuade the Internet from its modern closures. Either approach sees the Internet challenging or replacing the one world with possible worlds. As a result, 'cyberspace' as a space presents an instance of both the seductions and subductions of a postmodern 'world'.

Travels in cyberspace

Just as the highways once transformed America, the 'Information Super-highway' offers an image of dramatic change in American lives through a change in virtual landscape. Although the expression originated in the White House as a catchy term for the proposed National Information Infrastructure (NII), 'Information Superhighway' quickly entered popular parlance as a pseudonym for the already-existing worldwide network of the Internet. The overused expression does little to represent the actual network architecture that connects the machines in the infrastructure, yet the metaphor of the highway persists as a media image, functioning as a conceptual model for the world created by this technology. One does not 'go' somewhere when picking up the telephone. But when the computer couples with these same telephone lines, suddenly spatial and kinetic metaphors begin to proliferate. The 'Information Superhighway' depends on a more subtle metaphorical figuration – a virtual topography in which speed, motion and direction become possible. We can see, as Paul Virilio suggests, that the computer could function as 'the last vehicle', one which threatens to resolve all topographical concerns (1989: 108–9). The Internet would then function as a simulated territory we traverse via computer/modem roadster, the computer screen replacing the windscreen. Motion, speed and travel lose their 'real' meanings, while gaining power as techno-logical simulations. Baudrillard, following Barthes, notes how easily automobiles can transform motion into a visual experience in which the driver/viewer interacts with images, rather than with the physical world (Baudrillard, 1988: 13). Unlike this metaphorical transformation of the physical world into images 'on' a windshield, 'cyberspace' blurs the real and the metaphorical as it becomes its own simulation of 'beyond the screen'. The real no longer serves as a referent for this postmodern version of Alberti's Window; now a virtual topography becomes the screen's reality.[3]

In this model, the computer becomes a hyperreal vehicle for travelling through a simulated world. A large number of Internet 'guide' books make use of this geographical metaphor, evoking images of navigation and exploration. Software companies are picking up on the metaphor as well, developing 'geographic interfaces' to augment the virtual desktop; users will now be able to 'jump out [a simulated office] window for an aerial view of information generating sites represented as buildings' (Fisher 1995: F9). Rather than treating this endlessly repeated image of 'travels in cyberspace' strictly as a clever marketing gimmick, I would like to suggest that this conceptual model serves a definite purpose in contemporary culture, one which creates the simulation of a form of power. For Baudrillard, this transference of power from the real to the hyperreal presents the fulfilment of the modern drive to master the world. Geography 'implodes' into one hyperpotential point:

> Where all trips have already taken place; where the vaguest desire for dispersion, evasion and movement are concentrated in a fixed point, in an immobility that has ceased to be one of non-movement and has become that of a potential ubiquity, of an absolute mobility, which voids its own space by crossing it ceaselessly and without effort. (Baudrillard, 1988: 39)

The image of 'cybertravel' has currency precisely because it offers a metaphorical world on/beyond a computer screen, a 'globe' which no longer stands for the world because it has *become* the world.

The Internet, then, would provide an ideal (or rather model) world for economic, political and cultural control: one which is always already conquered and colonized. A virtual potential space replaces real kinetic space or, rather, 'real' potential translates metaphorically into a virtual 'kinetic' energy. According to Arthur Kroker and Michael Weinstein this shift in power presents a form of capitalism sent out of its own orbit. What appears to be an Enlightenment liberation of (mental and economic) energy becomes in practice an abandonment of the flesh to a virtual world of pure circulation. 'Empowerment' is a kind of liberal seduction into virtuality for Kroker and Weinstein (1994: 10–11); the compelling online world 'is a *trompe l'oeil* of possessive individualism covering the individual possessed by the net, sucked into the imploded, impossible world behind the screen' (1994: 9). The virtual class surrenders itself to a 'liquid frenzy' of exchange and circulation, a 'pan-capitalism' freed entirely from 'the real' of labour and flesh (1994: 87–9). In other words, the human now lives for (and through) virtualization. Virilio likewise comments at the very end of *The Vision Machine* that technocratic 'progress' points toward the moment when our bodies perform for the operation of our tools, instead of our tools operating for us (1994: 72–6). McLuhan's relation between humanity and its media-extensions has been reversed: now we extend the media.

This perspective suggests that the conceptual model of a cybernetic 'space' does not augment the world; it abandons the world for one which can be fully realized and fully encompassed – a world of transparency and immediacy. The technology that aims at containing distance eventually creates a virtual world which destroys the conceptual possibility of distance.

In this vertiginous moment of physical stasis and virtual travel, the 'Voyeur–Voyager' experiences an immediacy which dissolves space and time: 'a perpetually repeated hijacking of the subject from any spatial-temporal context' (Virilio, 1991: 101). From this critical perspective, then, the Internet collapses space into one 'hyperpotential point' which implodes all concept of distance, spacing and separation.[4] While this motion may seem liberating, as portrayed in the numerous advertisements for 'surfing the net', in Virilio's view quite the opposite is true: subjectivity becomes a subjecting-to. Nietzsche's 'will to power' transforms into Kroker and Weinstein's 'will to virtuality': 'the will to surrender oneself to technologically-mediated and externalized imaginaries' (1994: 41). As this emerging cyberspace becomes more real, the ability to circumnavigate the globe physically holds less value than the ability to travel that distance electronically.

Thus the Internet does not simply lay down a mesh of connections between real-life nodes/computers, annihilating space; it creates and maintains its own simulated world to replace the physical world of spatial distances. It is no surprise then that businesses are scrambling to 'open shop' on the net: computer networks are no longer simply tools for making a profit; they have become a 'place' to conduct business by establishing 'sites'. International business – internationalism in general – disappears, subsumed by a simulated world of international networks. As the Internet moves closer to its dream of total connectivity, one might imagine with Baudrillard that moment of closure when this metaphorical cyberspace becomes the hyperreal, more important than the real space it once simulated:

> As soon as behavior is focused on certain operational screens or terminals, the rest appears only as some vast, useless body, which has been both abandoned and condemned. The real itself appears as a large, futile body. (1988: 18)

No longer does technology encompass the world; now it replaces it with a 'more real than real' simulation.

Virtual topography

In its 'real' material presence, the Internet consists of a complex redundant network of host machines which communicate over phone lines. As opposed to the elaborate system of bridges, jumps and links that occurs across real space, the geographical figuration of host 'sites' and user 'addresses' creates a simpler virtual terrain for the user – one in which travel amounts to a tracing of connections from site to site. Virtual territory only exists once it has been traced onto a pre-existing code of connectivity. Cyberspace, in other words, functions as a globe to its own world. Fredric Jameson connects the development of the first navigational globe in 1490 to an emerging conceptual model of 'the world' as totality, as well as the realization that 'there can be no true maps', only 'dialectical advance in the various historical moments of mapmaking' (1991: 52). In contrast to the modern conception of the map or globe, and its relation to the unrepresentable totality of the world, the Internet as postmodern map *becomes the totality itself*, superseding the world. Baudrillard refers to this moment as the 'precession of simulacra', when the globe/model defines the world it once approximated (1983: 2). Borges's story of a map so accurate that it completely covers the land provides Baudrillard with an apt allegory for the pre-eminence of simulation over reality itself:

> Henceforth, it is the map that precedes the territory . . . it is the map that engenders the territory and if we were to revive the fable today, it would be the territory whose shreds are slowly rotting across the map. (1983: 2)

One could argue that the Internet as virtual territory is very much a Baudrillardian revival of this fable. Cyberspace presents neither a counter-feit world nor a reproduction of the world; it is a map/model of a reproducible world.[5] This potential for connectivity precedes the virtual world it purports to trace; the 'map' of this territory is itself the territory – both globe and world at the same time.

This metaphorical topography offered up by the Internet presents the simulation of a vast, undiscovered country in which only our imaginations limit our abilities. The immanence of this realm – its very vastness and limitlessness – could be, however, nothing more than the simulation of these significations, simulacra that perform a strategy of deterrence, holding back the *realization* of the spaceless, limited world of the code. Distance disappears into immediacy, and presence becomes a state of simultaneity and transparency. If a host machine 'goes down', it is not absent: it ceases to be part of the virtual world. The code cannot call forth presence from absence; any attempts to 'reach' that site return nothing, not even the equivalent of the telephone's absent ringing (or its tantalizing busy signal). An offline machine no longer exists: *host unknown*. Likewise, the Internet has no frontier because its territory has already been comprehensively mapped. The connections between nodes precede the attempt to explore this terrain – every 'journey' in cyberspace is a repetition and a retracing of steps.

The Internet has no provision for 'undiscovered country', only the simulation of such, just like a planned treasure hunt. Gopher, along with the numerous web-based search engines that have appeared in the past two years, demonstrates that the Internet only simulates an unknown terrain of knowledge. The possibility of reproducing a particular coding of informa-tion precedes – and precludes – any attempt to locate it. One never *discovers* on the Internet; one only *uncovers*. By definition, then, all Internet search tools are comprehensive because information on the Internet exists in a closed system; nothing 'exists' beyond its search parameters. AltaVista™ touts that over 30 million individual pages make up its database, creating the image of an *almost complete* database (and a virtual beyond). But what 'is' online, what has informatic ontological status, so to speak, has always already been mapped. You can only find what has already been found.

More generally, any 'place' not on the Internet simply does not exist. The Internet, in other words, presents a totality without even the possibility of a beyond, an immanent realm in which the operator can only interact with known elements, established sites and comprehensive codes.

This virtual realm is indeed a topography: a writing which both creates and reveals a *topos* or place.[6] While images (*graphics*) work their way into figurations of cyberspace, particularly by way of the World Wide Web, the Internet still functions primarily as a medium of writing. As such, it finds its place within a general history of writing as a material presence for communication (as opposed to the more 'ephemeral' voice). Moreover, by writing a place in which real-time communication can occur, the virtual topography of the Internet allows writing to present itself *as* speech. Derrida calls writing the first communication technology in that it offers a means for 'overcoming' time by aiding memory and by simulating the immediacy of speech (1981: 75). Leibniz's non-phonetic writing, he argues, takes us another step toward the language of the machine, while at the same time moving writing closer to the inferred immediacy of speech (Derrida, 1976: 77–9). Both of these events fall within Derrida's history of the post, the *fort/da* game of absence made presence through writing. From Derrida's standpoint, writing serves as a means of calling forth presence, of making the subject 'here' without being here. This presence appears in idealist (Platonic, romantic) discourses as a kind of dissimulation – writing as false speech. But from the standpoint of writing as technology, the *telos* of writing is to *simulate* the immediacy and transparency, and hence the ideality, of speech. The telegraph, for example, not only allows the spatially absent object to become present for the subject; by shrinking the time between 'gone' and 'here', telegraphy also emphasizes the potential 'hereness' of all writing, its potential as direct discourse. Writing truly becomes tele-graphy (distance writing), in that it 'breaches' the spatial and temporal constraints on a culture (Lyotard, 1991: 49–51). According to Virilio, the speed of telegraphy, along with the accelerating media that follow it, allows for the emergence of a 'teletopology' in place of the world. The simultaneous appearance of the virtual and disappearance of the 'real' produce a 'topographical amnesia' where space as a measure of presence no longer exists (Virilio, 1994: 10). Here is always here and now; real time replaces (substitutes for) real space (1994: 63–4). As communication becomes more immediate, absence/presence and writing/speech distinctions lose meaning; the *fort/da* game of emergence and disappearance begins to implode. No longer a counterfeit or a reproduction, writing achieves its 'transcendence' on the Internet: as third-order simulation of speech. When tele-graphy becomes a virtual topos-graphy, writing has reached the *telos* of the history of the post – and then superseded it. The computer becomes, as Lyotard notes, its own destination/destiny, a closed system of progress 'exercised by remembering its own presuppositions and implications as its limitations' (1991: 53). The postal system for covering distance becomes its own systemic world, a closed loop of circulation.

This vision of telematics is far removed from that of the McLuhan tradition in which the media function as 'extensions of man' into a world of presence. For McLuhan, technology promised the possibility of a global village. McLuhanite faith in television paled in the 1970s, but with the popular emergence of the Internet this technotopic view began to recirculate. A great deal of the online community movement in fact grows from this image that the Internet can capture a communal entity. Howard Rheingold has for some years been at the centre of this vision, but he is far from alone. Though the notion of computer as extension can lead in other directions as well. In Kroker and Weinstein's view, the 'noosphere' of Teilhard de Chardin and the 'global village' of McLuhan are today inhabited not by a liberated humanity, but by 'telematic beings' that exist on 'the Net' only as nodes of input and retrieval in a system of circulating information (1994: 142–3). Instead of providing a 'universalization', these media create a satellitization:

> It is man with his planet Earth, with his territory, with his body, who is now the satellite. Once transcendent, he has become exorbitate. (Baudrillard, 1993: 30)

Satellitization, however, does not yield alienation; rather, this state is one of 'overproximity' to a simulated, transparent world (Baudrillard, 1988: 27).[7] No need to represent the absent other: the simulation is always immanent, waiting to be reproduced.

With increasing immediacy comes the simulation of 'transparent' communication in which the medium appears unmediated. What makes telematics different from other forms of mediated communication is the transparency of the link-up – the distanceless distance, the disappearance of an imagined absence made present. On the Internet for some time now, for example, users have been able to 'talk' via a text-based telephone-like connection. Unlike the telephone, however, the sense of distance becomes transparent the moment connection occurs. The words are 'present' on the screen, yet they have also 'gone' to their destination. No longer a fort/da, the Internet's tele-graphy is here and there at the same time.[8] With the telephone, telematics maintains the same symbol of totality: the globe. Phone lines encircle the globe and allow our voices to travel around the world; and we, remaining comfortably in our homes, can express our wonderment at how close a voice sounds. But because of the topographic metaphors both built into the UNIX backbone of the Internet and laid on top of it by the media, we are invited to interface with our computers in a different way. Those same real phone lines encircling the globe have less of a 'real' presence than the virtual globe of Internet, the hyperpotential world of connectivity.

This 'more real than real' virtual topography presents a cybernetic terrain with a greater degree of control than the 'real world' allows. Once again, comparing Alberti's Window to the computer screen: no longer does the surface represent the world through an illusion of depth, distance and an other side; on the screen all modes of representation collapse into a realm neither real nor imaginary, but simulatory – a fantastic presence made possible by this virtual topography. The more compelling the meta-phorical geography, the closer the Internet comes to complete substitution. Baudrillard writes of this transformation: 'The unreal is no longer that of dream or of fantasy, of a beyond or a within, it is that of a *hallucinatory resemblance of the real with itself* (1983: 142; original emphasis). In place of the symbolic totality of 'the world', the Internet offers up a simulated world of totality, a closed loop of immediacy and transparency. The experience within this simulated globe becomes an experience of the cybernetic real: no longer a reality, but a virtuality.

Virtual worlds

Although we may associate virtual reality with projection goggles and body suits, one need not use any technological prosthesis other than a screen and a keyboard to experience the simulation of reality. While much of the preceding discussion has touched on metaphorical distance, motion and space on the Internet, the technology of networked machines has also led to a more conscious attempt to explore virtual presence: a text-based virtual space called a Multi-User Dimension, Object Oriented (MOO). MOOs are a subspecies of a class of programs known as MUDs – Multi-User Dimen-sions. In its most basic form, a MUD is a multi-user, interactive fantasy game which simulates a terrain through textual descriptions. Players become characters in a world where they can interact with their environ-ment and, most importantly, with other players. Unlike the original MUDs, a MOO allows characters to 'hack at' the code that determines this world. Through the use of a simple programming language, players can create objects in their virtual world: rooms, landscapes, vehicles, food, cameras – even characters.[9] Although plenty of fantasy MUDs still do exist (complete with dragon-slaying elves), MUDs and MOOs have gone far beyond their original gaming focus – including, starting with LambdaMOO in January 1991, attempts at becoming virtual communities (GREF 1). These virtual spaces provide opportunities for individuals to gather for any number of reasons, from professional conferences and business meetings to virtual sex.

PMC-MOO, sponsored by the electronic journal *Postmodern Culture*, provides an appropriate example of this form of 'text-based virtual reality'.[10] Given its declared interests, we might expect postmodern theorists and literary critics to haunt PMC-MOO and, indeed, conferences, meetings and discussion groups are not uncommon. PMC-MOO has also served as a site for poetry 'slams' with the Nujorican Poets' Cafe, as well as annual virtual exhibitions in conjunction with *Blast* and the Sandra Gering Gallery in Manhattan.[11] But alongside these more academic and artistic endeavours, it is just as common to encounter, when 'wandering' from virtual room to virtual room, two players discussing last night's television shows (perhaps MTV's *The Real World*), or this coming weekend's entertainment plans. At the centre of this prototype for a 'global village', the fascinating and the banal overtake one another. Paradoxically, the first-hand experience of the 'ecstasy of communication' is hardly noticeable and ultimately quite ordinary, since this highly mediated form of interaction simulates unmediated communication. 'Where are you in real life?' is a fairly common question in the MOO, but I would argue that the text-generated world works against this sort of interaction, encouraging players to communicate with each other according to metaphors of proximity, not distance. Perhaps more illuminating is the question, 'Where are *we*?' I 'travel' to Virginia by way of a telnet link, where UVA's RISC-based server runs the PMC-MOO program code. Once 'inside' the MOO, I 'meet' others who have also 'arrived' at this destination. Here (wherever that is), the play of *fort/da* no longer makes sense: I am gone and here at the same time. I am present and absent, distant and near. The MOO creates the simulation of space, which players use to present simulations of themselves. The question 'Where are you in real life?' in other words, becomes less important than one's ability to simulate/assimilate oneself in/to this new space.

By calling for the creation of a prosthetic or cybernetic self, one capable of inhabiting this new terrain, the MOO foregrounds the dominant conceptual model that frames the Internet 'as a whole', a metaphorical world treated as a reality. Likewise, the 'naturalness' and comfort of players in this virtual space emphasizes just how 'real' cyberspace has become. Through the Internet distance becomes transparent, making room for a virtual space, an experience quite different from other forms of telecommunication. On the telephone I revel in how close a voice sounds. I gain comfort in knowing that I am overcoming distance. In the MOO, I no longer overcome distance because the screen does not bridge space; it replaces space with a simulation of the world on the surface of my screen. Depthless and infinite, Baudrillard's screen replaces Alberti's Window, a 'superficial abyss' which simulates and denies space at the same time.

MOOs become a kind of 'ideal society', but at the same time it is an often banal ideal, one which re-creates the world as we find it, rather than challenging it. It is a model of closed community. More so, it is a space modelled after the walled-in city: the MOO has its definitional boundaries, but also its behavioural codes which serve as shibboleth and covenant. Community then, no matter how open it may appear, ultimately functions as a kind of affirmation of likes. Deleuze and Guattari refer to this sort of organizational space as a striated space and, as I have suggested elsewhere (see Nunes, forthcoming), the MOO and, more generally, models of community on the Internet which function as closed perimeters do no more than repeat online the assumptions of modernity. While some may dream of 'societies more decent and free than those mapped onto dirt and concrete and capital', most online culture has more to do with an endless repetition and circulation of the same personal, social and political strategies that have served as the dominant expressions of real (modern) space (Dibbell, 1993: 37).

Baudrillard describes this fascination as a mutation in pleasure from *seductio* to *subductio*, from the seduction by the other to a hypnosis of the self, endlessly repeated on the screen (1988: 25). A simulated presence escapes the possibility of counterfeit or of reproducing an original because the original no longer exists (Baudrillard, 1983: 97). The fax machine, for example, sends a reproduction over phone lines, but email produces and sends a simulated document: one that can be copied infinitely, forwarded simultaneously, reproduced in multiple formats. Email obscures the concept of 'the original', but it likewise throws into question both *origin* and destination, since a virtual address is independent of the user's physical location. The move on the Internet from simulation of the post (email) to the simulation of presence (the MOO) is a fated or fatal step toward creating a 'more real than real' reality: the hypertelia of communication technology. One might conclude that telematics only deters the recognition of what has already occurred: the end of space through cyberspace, the end of knowledge through information, and the end of the imaginary through the hyperreal.

This reading of the significance of virtual topographies stands in stark contrast to the many utopic visions of the potentials of the Internet. The attempts to figure the Internet as a space capable of supporting communities indicates both the 'reality' of this vision and the challenges to 'the real' that it presents. Those unfamiliar with virtual communities may not yet appreciate the strength of these interactions between virtual bodies in virtual space. In a 1993 *Village Voice* article, for example, Julian Dibbell describes in some detail an incident of 'cyber-rape' at LambdaMOO, detailing not only the emotional trauma of the female victim, but also the repercussions of such an act for the virtual community.[12] The crime brought players together in a heated discussion over *the state* – literally *the state* – of their virtual community and how to balance justice with liberty. The Whole Earth 'Lectronic Link (the WELL) provides another example of a virtual community and in fact one of the earliest: a set of electronic bulletin boards on which groups of 'citizens' communicate with one another. Howard Rheingold, author of *Virtual Communities* and long-time resident of the WELL, describes this and other virtual communities as electronic *agorae*, offering the possibility of becoming 'informal public places where people can rebuild the aspects of community that were lost when the malt shop became a mall' (1993: 26). Already the Internet has its own civil liberties group, the Electronic Frontier Foundation (EFF), which, as its name implies, connects virtual topography with the American conception of frontiers and liberty. EFF and other groups place great hope in cyberspace (if democratic principles cannot prevail in the 'real' world, perhaps they can in cyberspace). Mitch Kapor, founder of EFF (and Lotus Corp.), argues:

> Life in cyberspace . . . at its best is more egalitarian than elitist, and more decentered than hierarchical. . . . In fact, life in cyberspace seems to be shaping

up exactly like Thomas Jefferson would have wanted: founded on the primacy of individual liberty and a commitment to pluralism, diversity, and community. (1993: 53)

For literally millions of 'netters', cyberspace is a real place with real potentials – and it is precisely this blurring of the real and the unreal that marks a postmodern moment. From this perspective, the compelling image of the 'Internet as world' pushes us beyond the world, beyond its containment, all the while pursuing the same Enlightenment goals that drove the world beyond its own ends and into hyperreality.

One could also argue that these *agorae* are nothing more than simulations of arenas of immense freedom within a limited set of operational parameters. As John Unsworth points out, the predetermined 'core' code of a MOO functions as an inescapable fate, limiting every player's free will (GREF 2). Likewise, the pre-existing operational code of any closed communication system 'restricts itself to putting things that already exist in contact with each other' (Gane, 1993, 57). As noted above, the Internet is ultimately a tracing of a map of connectivity; one cannot 'create' new contacts on the Internet. This inability to 'self-transcend' is what separates communication from community in Baudrillard's work (1993: 12). Cyber-community offers nothing more than a strategy of deterrence; like a Disneyland for Enlightenment conceptions of community, it creates 'an imaginary effect concealing that reality no more exists outside than inside the bounds of the artificial perimeter' (Baudrillard, 1983: 26). The model of community can exist in such an immanent form precisely because it is a model, a simulacrum of community, deferring the moment of realization that community no longer exists. More precisely, community can only exist in a mediated society via the medium itself because no other 'real' exists. No longer fragmented, the self and community become 'fractal', capable of infinite division into self-same parts, each part a simulation of a whole which no longer exists (Baudrillard, 1993: 57). This threat of disappearance by proliferation is far different from the fears of informational 'overlords' or computer-mediated panopticons. In fact, the dream of utopian possibilities and the threat of imminent informational catastrophe provide the same function: deterrence of a crisis in modernity. The promises of an America which will provide its citizens with free access to a world of information and the threat of a world in which this information is controlled, parcelled out or withheld are part of the same strategy. In short, the image of free and infinitely increasing information does nothing more than deter the realization that the Enlightenment pursuit of 'knowledge' has imploded. As Kroker and Weinstein note:

When knowledge is reduced to information, then consciousness is stripped of its lived connection to history, judgement, and experience. What results is the illusion of an expanded knowledge society, and the reality of virtual knowledge. (1994: 24)

Increasing sophistication in technology produces more convincing simulations of information and more convincing strategies of deterrence. 'Information' becomes a term to describe movies on demand, electronic malls and expanding numbers of television channels. The fascination of the depthless screen – 'the superficial abyss' – keeps us firmly rooted. With a wealth of information, we have no time to realize that within the closed circuit of a virtual world we have nothing left 'unknown' and nothing left to learn.

Seductive headings

Given this critique of an emerging postmodern hyperreality, one might ask if there is a way to draw online technology out of its current orbit. For Lyotard, it becomes a question of trying to imagine 'a telegraphic community without *telos*', one which would 'forget' community as its end, so to speak (1991: 54). This 'other' heading (a path for a technologically mediated culture which does not follow an Enlightenment *telos*), if we are to find one, would have to pose a challenge to telematics rather than pursuing it to catastrophe. For Baudrillard, that process involves a game which does not bring about a 'forced realization of the world', but instead allows itself into 'the other' of the system – the accidental, the unaccountable, the accursed share (Gane, 1993, 45). This approach seduces the total vision of a system into becoming 'a locus of that which eludes you, and whereby you elude yourself and your own truth' (Baudrillard, 1988: 66). Rather than attempting to expose (and hence realize) 'the world', Baudrillard dissimulates its totality, leading it off course and out of orbit. Kroker and Weinstein's vision, on the other hand, involves the discovery of an 'Internet equivalent of the Paris Commune' through the hypertexted body (1994: 17). In a similar way though, Kroker's 'data flesh' is no longer concerned with functioning as a node in the net, and instead mutates the Internet into creative relations and models which resist both Enlightenment 'worlds' and (postal) lines of communication (1994: 155). These approaches to the Internet point towards a question rather than an answer, namely: in light of the fascinating transparency of the media, can this 'virtual realm' do other than endlessly repeat its own model?

As I have suggested, the dominant virtual topography places a hyperreal simulation online, a world to replace the world. This model has been adopted wholeheartedly by corporate America, and likewise it has been adopted by the US government as a model of democracy. Democracy and capitalism, twin stars in the orbit of Enlightenment thought, provide a centre of gravity for this production of cyberspace. Likewise, both the underlying panoptic fears and egalitarian aspirations of the online community show a similar prominence throughout of the concerns of modernity. If, however, other spaces are available online, other virtual topographies, we will have to look beyond this system. For Deleuze and

Guattari, the challenge to the (endlessly repeated) striated space of the state, the city and the regulated system comes by way of smooth space and the nomadic process of deterritorialization. While state space allocates and organizes individuals, smooth nomadic space 'distributes' assemblages into multiple lines and crossings (Deleuze and Guattari, 1987: 481). Following this thinking, a new crop of online theorists has seen, particularly with the development of the WWW, the possibility for an emerging smooth cyberspace (see in particular HREF 3). If such a virtual topography is possible, however, it would have to suggest itself not in the 'essence' of the medium, but in relation to it (to do otherwise would be to fall back into an Enlightenment *telos*, one concerned with the destiny/destination of Internet). Might cyberspace, rather than providing a simulated, hyperpotential world of hypertravel, provide for a 'post-global' (and therefore open) terrain?

This challenge contains the potential to derail the very assumptions that have led modernity to its postmodern moment. It could raise the stakes in that MOO question, 'Where are you in real life?' In cyberspace(s), one will expect to find the banal at every turn. One would also hope to find objects of seduction and artifice, objects which turn us away from our intended goals. Rheingold notes that although virtual interfacing facilitates community by obscuring many social barriers (age, race and sex, in particular), this same interface allows for deception and artifice, leaving virtual citizens vulnerable to 'electronic impostors' (1993: 164). The possibility of elusion, illusion and allusion has no place in Enlightenment notions of community. These 'evils', however, may prove to be resistances which prevent closure (assumptions about what it means to be an 'authentic' self in an 'authentic' community), and which keep a system open to experiment, drift and 'peregrination'. Likewise, in a more 'open' topography, unknown contacts and 'monstrous couplings' would replace models of community based on like interests and shared assumptions. This sort of online community, if imaginable, would provide expanses for experimentation, rather than affirmation of givens. Lyotard refers to this resistance as 'possibility', an attempt to rewrite modernity, to displace determination and complexity by writing past the assumptions of its *telos* (1991: 28). He suggests a 'working through' (Freud's *Durcharbeitung*) in place of modernity's directed work, a free play in place of strategic play (1991: 54, 117). Lyotard points to the desirability of escaping the containment of a totalizing system driven towards (and beyond) its own assumptions. In Lyotard's words, 'Being prepared to receive what thought is not prepared to think is what deserves the name of thinking' (1991: 73). The virtual utopian sees the immediate and immanent fulfilment of Enlightenment ideals in a world liberated from itself through virtuality. Perhaps, though, the very immanence of the model can challenge the assumptions that have led to its creation.

Here, we may need to rethink the virtual not in the commercial sense of 'more real than real', but in Bergson's sense: the condition of possibility that occurs the moment before the emergence of the actual. The commercial versions of virtuality promise an online 'world as we find it'. But online spaces need not pursue this promise. Virtual topographies can also present conditions of possibility rather than 'actual' (and determined) spaces. As such, cyberspace would exist between two moments: the stasis of definition (system, globe, world, and so on) and the annihilating kinetics of 'total flow' (disappearance, absolute becoming, infinite enfolding). This approach to Bergson is specifically Deleuzian but, as such, it points to 'the virtual' as an *event*: that moment of becoming, of experimentation, of passing between.[13] Online community would, in this description, not simulate the world but provide a space for passing between the givens of modernity: a condition of possibility for seeing what might emerge.

In this reversed image of a virtual topography, the Internet might offer a virtuality which resists our attempts to totalize it as a world, presenting instead loci for playing with the assumptions that we have taken for granted in modernity: community, information, liberation, self. Virtual communities could pose questions about how individuals construct connections rather than attempting to achieve a determined end (electronic democracy, egalitarian utopia). Rather than working towards (re)producing a model community, cyberspace could just as easily keep us moving beyond our ends, towards new connections: new *'chorographies'* which would demand new discourses (Virilio, 1991: 110). Likewise, the appearance of 'virtual bodies' online can lead us astray from our assumptions about what it means to have a 'real' body. In the virtuality of the Internet, our words are our bodies, an aporetic copula which forces a re-examination of 'the body' as both physiological (noumenal) entity and phenomenological experience. In each instance, the Internet provides the medium for disrupting models rather than confirming them. Following this different course, the Internet might present a seduction rather than a subduction: a challenge to modernity's assumptions about self and body, individual and community. The Internet, rather than presenting a simulation of totality, might provide a space of play. Instead of pursuing ends through this technology, one might turn oneself over to the drift and *dérive* of 'cyberspace'. This vision challenges us to find a depth to the screen, to find – or, rather, lose – ourselves on a different bearing, off our familiar paths.

Notes

An earlier version of this chapter was originally published in *Style*, 29 (1995): 314–27.

1. The original version of this chapter quoted an InterNIC figure of 3,217,000 hosts. That domain survey is no longer available at gopher://is.internic.net. According to the organization Network Wizards, however, the number of hosts has continued to double every year. Network Wizards' 'Internet Domain Survey, July 1996' estimates 12,881,000 hosts worldwide (HREF 2).

2. Although 'cyberspace' may seem metaphorical rather than real, much postmodern theory, and in particular that of Jean Baudrillard, points to how the distance between 'reality' and (topographical) metaphor has ceased to exist (1988: 16).

3. In his book *On Painting* (1436), Leon Battista Alberti describes a technique for painting in perspective in which the artist looks at the subject through a 'grid-screen' and then copies that image sector by sector onto paper marked with a similar grid.

4. Why then all this talk of space if in fact the technology serves to eliminate space? Ironically, Baudrillard suggests, telematics might *require* a distance in order to overcome it. In some of his most direct comments on computer networking technology, he writes that the 'Telecomputer Man' experiences 'a very special kind of distance which can only be described as unbridgeable by the body. The screen is merely virtual – and hence unbridgeable' (1993: 55). Although he cannot cross his screen, he can 'circulate' himself through the media. The implosion of real distance creates the need for a strategy of deterrence: a simulation of space and distance which the body cannot breach, but which a simulated self (complete with computer prostheses) can travel.

5. This non-object corresponds to Baudrillard's third-order simulacrum, valued for its structural potential to be endlessly circulated (and orbited), and hence endlessly reproduced. See Baudrillard (1983: 100–1).

6. For a discussion of the Internet as virtual topography, see Nunes, *Cyberspace Textuality* (forthcoming).

7. Similar concerns appear in Virilio and Lyotard, where overproximity reduces rather than intensifies 'the map of "*I can*"' (Virilio, 1994: 7).

8. One might compare this sort of tele-graphy with the recent emergence of the 'internet telephone'; unlike 'talk', this application simulates telephonic space, returning 'here' and 'there' to their proper places.

9. To some extent, the MOO is void of subjects; the players control programmable 'objects', including their own player-object. 'Self', in other words, becomes object in the MOO, controlled by a set of operational commands.

10. PMC-MOO is no longer affiliated with the journal *Postmodern Culture* and has changed its name to 1K+1 (1001 Plateaux). It is now supported by the Institute for Advanced Technology in the Humanities at the University of Virginia and can be found at telnet:// hero.village.virginia.edu:7777.

11. *Blast* is both a collection of performances and a publication, with a founding editorial council which includes Jenny Holzer, Laurie Anderson, Donna Haraway and Jean-François Lyotard. It defines itself as 'originally a boxed publication containing projects in various media [which] has now extended itself into a multiplicity of traditional and digital forms' (HREF 1).

12. Dibbell's article is by far the most frequently cited example of the investments people make in online community. See also Turkle (1995: 233–54).

13. See Deleuze and Guattari (1987: 92–100, 237–9, 482–8). For a discussion of 'the event' in Deleuze and Guattari, and in particular its relation to the poles of definition and annihilation, see Brian Massumi (1992: 35–41).

References

Alberti, Leon Battista (1996) *On Painting* (trans. John R. Spencer). New Haven, CT: Yale University Press. (Originally published 1436.)

Baudrillard, Jean (1983) *Simulations* (trans. Paul Foss, Paul Patton and Philip Beitchman). New York: Semiotext(e).

Baudrillard, Jean (1988) *The Ecstasy of Communication* (trans. Bernard Schutz and Caroline Schutz). New York: Semiotext(e).

Baudrillard, Jean (1993) *The Transparency of Evil* (trans. James Benedict). New York: Verso.

Derrida, Jacques (1976) *Of Grammatology* (trans. Gayatri Chakravorty Spivak). Baltimore: Johns Hopkins University Press.

Derrida, Jacques (1981) *Dissemination* (trans. Barbara Johnson). Chicago: University of Chicago Press.

Deleuze, Gilles and Guattari, Félix (1987) *A Thousand Plateaus: Capitalism and Schizophrenia* (trans. Robert Hurley, Mark Seem and Helen R. Lane). Minneapolis, MN: University of Minnesota Press.

Dibbel, Julian (1993) 'A Rape in Cyberspace', *The Village Voice*, 21 December: 36–42.

Fisher, Lawrence (1995) 'The Geographic Interface Puts the World on the Desktop', *New York Times*, 5 February: F9.

Gane, Mike (1993) *Baudrillard Live*. New York: Routledge.

GREF 1: gopher://parcftp.xerox.com/Pub/moo/papers/DIAC92. Curtis, Pavel (1992) 'MUDding: Social Phenomena in Text-Based Virtual Realities'.

GREF 2: gopher://jefferson. village.virginia.edu/pubs/pmc/pmc-moo/Virtual.Community. Unsworth, John (1995) 'Living Inside the (Operating) System: Communities in Virtual Reality'.

HREF 1: http://www.users.interport.net/~xaf/blast.html. (1996) *Blast*.

HREF 2: http://www.nw.com/zone/WWW/report.html. Network Wizards (1996) 'Internet Domain Survey, July 1996'.

HREF 3: http://dhalgren.english.washington.edu/~steve/ch12.html. Shaviro, Steve (1995) '12.Bill Gates'. *Doom Patrols*.

Jameson, Fredric (1991) *Postmodernism, Or, the Cultural Logic of Late Capitalism*. Durham, NC: Duke University Press.

Kapor, Mitch (1993) 'Where is the Digital Highway Really Heading?' *Wired*, July–August: 53–9, 94.

Kroker, Arthur and Weinstein, Michael (1994) *Data Trash*. New York: St Martin's Press.

Lyotard, Jean-François (1991) *The Inhuman: Reflections on Time* (trans. Geoffrey Bennington and Rachel Bowlby). Stanford, CA: Stanford University Press.

Massumi, Brian (1992) *A User's Guide to Capitalism and Schizophrenia*. Cambridge, MA: MIT Press.

Nunes, Mark (forthcoming) 'Virtual Topographies: Smooth and Striated Cyberspace', in *Cyberspace Textuality*. Bloomington, IN: Indiana University Press.

Rheingold, Howard (1993) *The Virtual Community: Homesteading on the Electronic Frontier*. Reading, MA: Addison-Wesley.

Turkle, Sherry (1995) *Life on the Screen: Identity in the Age of the Internet*. New York: Simon and Schuster.

Virilio, Paul (1989) 'The Last Vehicle', in Dietmar Kamper and Christoph Wulf (eds), *Looking Back on the End of the World*. New York: Semiotext(e). pp. 106–19.

Virilio, Paul (1991) *The Aesthetics of Disappearance*. New York: Semiotext(e).

Virilio, Paul (1994) *The Vision Machine*. Bloomington, IN: Indiana University Press.

10

ALWAYS ALREADY VIRTUAL:
Feminist Politics in Cyberspace

Patricia Wise

That patriarchal forms of domination and fantasy are re-enacting themselves in cyberspace is perhaps already a given for any feminist exploration of the cultural consequences of virtual reality. At its most visible this takes place across a range of cyber-games, but it can also be noticed in the ways that male-defined occupations of and engagements with virtual spaces carry over assumptions, hegemonies and discourses entirely familiar from modernist culture. However, as Elizabeth Grosz observes: 'All cultural production is phallocentric (that is, covers over women's specificity) but this doesn't mean that we shouldn't use it: it just means that we should use it very carefully, aware of the risks it may entail' (1992: 7). In this chapter, I want to suggest that if feminists are to develop effective politics in virtual spaces, the ways in which women are constituted as always already virtual in modern and postmodern epistemologies and power relations may represent a radical ground to draw on in their political, social and creative engagements with emerging technologies.[1]

The word 'virtual' is, in contemporary culture, most often encountered with specific reference to computer technologies:

> Virtual realities are computer-generated and fed worlds, which simulate key elements of 'real space' or at least its dominant representations – for example, its dimensionality, its relations of resemblance and contiguity – acting as a partial homology for a 'real' space within which it is located. (Grosz, 1992: 7)

In this regard, how the experience and dominant representations of women in the 'real' are transferred into the 'virtualized real' is a major issue for feminists. For many theorists, 'virtual reality' is also a term which incorporates all digitized or pixelized spaces, including, but not confined to, computer-generated spaces; or it refers to the hypermedia effect permeating contemporary culture and contributing to an increasingly fragmented imaginary for the postmodern subject.[2] But before 'virtual' was applied to computers, the media, optics and sub-atomic particles, and before it was applied to whole social formations, it had a common usage of 'not quite there' or 'not quite real' – and a parallel dictionary definition: 'that is so in essence or effect, although not recognized formally, actually, or by strict definition as such; almost absolute' (Brown, 1993) Interestingly, 'virtual' also had another usage suggesting potential: 'capable of producing a certain effect or result; effective, potent, powerful' (Brown, 1993).

In modernity women were always virtually, rather than actually, real, in the sense of the common usage of 'virtual' as 'not quite there' or the dictionary definition of 'almost absolute'. Women, who constituted the lack against which the male presence maintained its own sense of reality, were never themselves a defining presence in the social or the cultural. Their embodied presence was a fact – 'so in essence or effect, although not recognized formally, actually, or by strict definition as such'. But that embodied presence was written over by an absence of autonomy. It did not constitute a presence from which culture or society was spoken and understood. Rather, women were spoken to, for or about. Like other objects, practices and phenomena they were part of nature, culture and society; part of the world outside of the speculating consciousness of men and defined by the same specular economies as the rest of that world. That is, women were something to be understood, though the task may have been difficult due to women's puzzling 'nature'.

In language, woman functions as the 'other' against which masculine identity – the (male) 'I' who speaks, sometimes described as the defining 'phallocentric logos' – defines itself through the operation of difference. Feminists point to the inscription of the logos in the dominant epistemes of Western culture and, following Hélène Cixous, are aware of the dichotomized operations of male/female, culture/nature, public/private, reason/unreason, mind/matter, hard/soft, rational/intuitive oppositions which (paradoxically) form the basis of how the monological intellectual and mythological traditions of the West have read and named the world.

The challenge for feminist philosophers has been how to place the non-present woman in ontology, epistemology, metaphysics; how to theorize, let alone enact, a subjectivity for she who is not a subject in discourse. The discursive construction of women in patriarchy and its effects have been explored across textual and media theory, cultural studies, sociology, political science, history, law, education, medicine, anthropology, mathematics, science. Indeed, the 'otherness', 'lack that is woman', 'object status of women', so permeates the universe of all disciplines that for most feminists the boundaries between disciplines have themselves become extremely blurred. And whatever debates and positions may have arisen, within and between disciplines and feminisms, regarding the ways in which 'she who is not the subject' is constituted and how she might come to make herself a subject, there is no debate as to her definition as 'lack'/'other' in the logos.

The carrying over of these discursive formations into the postmodern is observable in theory and practice. Take, for example, Jean Baudrillard's well-known reference to the Japanese speaking car (a car which of course speaks with a female voice) as an analogy for the role of technologies in the breakdown of the unified subject in the postmodern. Baudrillard places 'the car as deliberating consultant and partner in the general negotiation of a lifestyle' and communication with the car as 'a perpetual test of the subject's presence with his own objects, an uninterrupted interface' (Baudrillard, 1988: 13). The observation is a telling one in relation to a change in the relations between all humans and machines. However, it replays without comment the relations between the male subject and woman – at once object, 'consultant and partner' (nurse-mother-lover), and the necessary other with/through/against which men define themselves. And just as 'uninterrupted interface' with machines is here understood as likely to throw unified subjectivity into disarray or at least into a 'perpetual test of the subject's presence', so too in men's relations with women.

Full 'uninterrupted interface' with women as the 'other' humans remains always to be avoided in the logocentric/phallocentric order because it risks erasure of male subjectivity, yet it remains always seductive because it might heal the Oedipal breach while at the same time creating the illusion of absolute control. If we move this observation into the realm of computer-generated virtual reality experiences, the implications become interesting. Zoë Sofia's analysis of male and female interactions with computer technologies demonstrates

> [a] masculine desire to sexualise – which in the cultural tradition that has defined woman as 'the sex', means to *feminise* – the computer as something exciting to be explored and conquered, contrasting with a feminine penchant for constructing the computer interface as something safe, familiar and utilitarian. (1993: 4; original emphasis)

Sofia explores the 'seductiveness' of cyberspace for male users, and the ways in which they understand the space to be an extension of their own rationality. Returning to Nietzsche, Heidegger, Derrida and others, she notes that '[r]eason can be regarded as a fantasy – a fantasy of mastery and control, a fantasy of domination over less "rule-y" elements' (1993: 26).[3]

Computer-generated interactivity and VR experience can be understood as such a fantasy extended through prosthetic hardware into a virtual 'unreal' where the 'real' is fantastically and spectacularly reproduced but where the prostheses give the subject an edge over the chanciness and unruliness of the 'really real'. In cyberspace and VR, domination and mastery are given more possibility of being attained, enacted or possessed precisely because the real body is imaginatively negated, fantasized to be only marginally involved in the experience. For men caught by the logocentric seductions of VR, the erotic appeal of the embodied experience of a disembodied presence lies in this. The tools 'created' by the logos, by Reason, allow a safe boundary crossing into a space wherein the subject can explore, overcome or at least seek to master the 'irrationality' of the 'really real' without risking death of the body or, worse, death of the mind. In this sense, for the logocentric male subject going into cyberspace or using VR can be understood as something like going to a prostitute, using pornography or privileging the 'bachelor life' of casual sexual encounter over the acquisition of a wife. Entering marriage is frequently constructed in phallocentric discourse as if the male subject were committing an irrational act of voluntary self-sacrifice. In the terms we are using here, he is, because he risks losing his autonomous male subjectivity in 'uninterrupted interface' with a woman. The phallocentric virtual subject believes that because the danger of embodied relational fusion is removed, there is no danger for his unified subjectivity.

The 'fantasy of reason', like the fantasy of uninvolved sex, relies on the central tenet of the logos – that the mind and body are somehow separate entities, which is itself a fantasy. That is, what enables the logocentric male subject to fantasize domination in cyberspace is that he is extending into another fantasy space his fantasy that reason defines him. For feminists considering the political and creative implications of VR and other cyber-technologies this recognition is very useful. In being caught by the fantasy that male domination of real space can be extended to domination of cyberspace, phallocentric subjectivities are problematized. Their presence in cyberspace is a simulation of a fantasy that they fail to recognize in their lived ontology, and encountering this simulation threatens to undo their subjectivities in the real.

Arthur Kroker's discourse in his discussion of Baudrillard in *The Possessed Individual* provides another example of perpetuation of the logos in current theory:

> What if we were to think, with Baudrillard, of technology as seduction? A cold seduction that chills the heart because it charms and entices by its promise of an imminent reversibility, by its horizon of an imminent catastrophe for the sake of which it lures us on but about which it is, of course, forbidden to speak. Not technology as a referent of power which emanates from elsewhere or as reducible to the language of instrumental reason, but the name given to a certain point of fatal disappearance, a violent disintegration towards which everything plunges as its final and ecstatic destiny. (1992: 78)

Such an analysis of the postmodern experience as the fragmentation of the I-dentity of the autonomous male subject in his encounter with sexualized/feminized technologies irresistibly invites analogies with the myths of the Sirens, the Medusa, the witches, the *vagina dentata* – indeed Eve herself. It is an analysis expressed entirely in terms of the destruction of I-dentity in the phallocentric experience of sexual encounter with that other seductive 'other', woman. The discourse reinscribes in the context of postmodern theory the dilemmas and obsessions of the patriarchal logos:

> Here, possessed individualism refers to an opaque amnesic social matter – the society of the soft masses – which is the dark liquid referent through which pass, like invisible neutrinos, all the violent impulses of the mediascape. (Kroker, 1992: 79)

This morbid feminizing of 'social matter' as a referent for technologies explicitly relies on the gendered dichotomies of modernity. Used to forward an argument about 'sacrificial power', the discursive effect of a feminized 'social matter' is to function as the abject against which Reason – here, male subjectivity in danger of becoming 'a fractal zone' – defines itself. If technologies threaten by being the seductive objects which produce the 'cynical sign of imminent reversibility', it would seem that the most dangerous 'catastrophe' site for the postmodern man of this discourse continues to be woman in her ongoing function as seductive object.

Two of the most familiar claims of postmodernism are that we are experiencing 'the death of history' and 'the death of the subject'. These notions stem from the quite sustainable observation that since all cultural signifiers have become floating or unfixed and all sign systems therefore fragmented in the postmodern, and since representations have become simulacra – representations of representations – culture has cut itself loose from any continuity with the modern narrative of history and the post-modern individual is barred from the possibility of a unified subjectivity. 'The point is', observes Fredric Jameson, 'that we are within the culture of postmodernism to the point where its facile repudiation is as impossible as any equally facile celebration of it is complacent and corrupt' (1991: 62).

The difficulty for feminists, to put it bluntly, is that history has been declared dead before women got to be written back into its narrative and the subject has been buried before women got to be subjects. As Rosi Braidotti reminds us:

> Feminists have argued that women have borne both materially and symbolically the costs of the masculine privilege of autonomous self-definition. Women have been physically and symbolically dispossessed of a place from whence to speak. (1994: 119)

Feminists are coming to terms with this problem in various ways, and many feminist theorists and arts/media practitioners are comfortable working with ideas about the postmodern. But the areas of history and subjectivity have been continuing difficulties, even for those who fit the descriptors 'feminist postmodernist' or 'postmodern feminist'. If women are to perceive themselves as disconnected from what Braidotti calls 'women's sense of their own historical struggles' (1994: 120), how do they locate themselves in the postmodern? Is the subject who is woman any longer possible? If so, where can she speak from? And will women be subjects in cyberspace, or in 'virtual communities'?

The technologized woman-object

Since the 1960s feminist theories of the objectification of women in patriarchal culture have highlighted the relationship between capitalist private property relations and representations of women. In these analyses, patriarchal forms of control are infused with economic control over women's bodies, labour, estate, property and income.

During the same period, women were discursively produced as object-extensions of men, their lives represented as confined to spheres defined by that function. However, an extra sign-slide occurred in that women were also produced as object-extensions of male-produced objects. I refer here not only to the use of women draped across cars to render cars more 'desirable' to male consumers – this is merely an expression in consumer marketing of a sexual economy and aesthetic (defined by the male gaze) which has a much longer history in patriarchal culture. More significantly, the 'emancipation of women from household drudgery' in mid-twentieth-century modernity was a manoeuvre which expanded the usefulness of the bourgeois wife as an adjunct to the domestic, social and workplace roles essential for the continuing autonomy of the subjectivity of the bourgeois man. At the same time, the prosthetic extensions of women – their appliances, beauty technologies, fashions, and so on – became indispensable to women, to the extent that their sense of their own identity appeared to be defined by the possession and consumption of the objects and technologies. Finally, the women and the objects/technologies had become inseparable, fused, in their object status. Both were prostheses for men. Women as 'other' humans remained desirable but popularly represented in male-produced media texts as difficult and puzzling seductive objects. 'Man has,' Freud remarked: 'as it were, become a kind of prosthetic God. When he puts on all his auxiliary organs he is truly magnificent; but those organs have not grown on to him and they still give him much trouble at times (1963: 28–9).

In English-speaking cultures the conflation of woman and object is revealed in speech patterns common among men in relation to the technological extensions central to their spheres of social and work activity. Cars, boats, bulldozers and computers are commonly referred to as 'she'. When the technology of a car or computer functions as expected the 'woman-object' is the possession of a proud and satisfied owner, and when the technology behaves unpredictably the 'woman-object' is spoken to and about as if 'she' is 'irrational', animal-like – 'that bitch/cow of a thing'. This is symptomatic of the logocentric 'othering' of woman as lack against which man defines his autonomous subjecthood; the question of ownership and use value (of women and objects) as part of identity formation for men; and the discursive practices of mass media consumerism which render both technologies and women prosthetic extensions of men.

We can track these same formations into popular male cyberspace, where women's 'otherness' and object status is already 'naturalized' and the discourses of dominant practices largely exclude women as users or subjects of cyber action.

The cover of the December 1995 issue of the British magazine *PC Zone*, a vehicle for reviewing and selling computer games, features a blonde model in a red bikini, breasts centred and forward, red lips open, posed astride a racing car bonnet.[4] Behind her, wearing a singlet and what looks like a grotesque codpiece, is an out of focus man looking over his shoulder at the woman. The games highlighted in the cover copy are: Destruction Derby™, John Madden NFL 96™, IndyCar2™, Wipeout™, Mortal Kombat 3™, Crusader™, Screamer™, Dungeon Keeper™. The first full-page advertisement centres a stubble-chinned, blue-eyed, dark-haired white male and the large caption 'Possession is 9/10 of the Law'. In the heavily illustrated 170 pages there are less than 10 representations of women. Readers who are 'fed up with being greeted by flying toasters' can purchase the 'Pamela Anderson Screen Saver' so that the simulacrum of the silicon-breasted model can make 'you (or at least your screen) the centre of attention in the office'. Most of the other representations are metal women/androids. (Why do metal women always have breasts? What precisely are they for?) In this consumer site women are, as in pre-cyber populist sites, objects of the male gaze positioned to attract him to another consumer object or objects to further sexual/sadistic plot development and character definition. The already virtual woman when transferred into virtual space becomes a site for the virtual fantasies of virtual men, who play through the fantasies of embodied men in the wetware space. For a feminist, this is like waking up in Jean Baudrillard's nightmare; as dislocating as a US television advertisement for Playboy Cable TV, in which 'Dr Joy Davies' addresses the viewers with the opening line: 'If your fantasy life is becoming stagnant and predictable. . . .'

There is, however, no surprise for feminists in the fact that when phallocentric culture produces women in virtual space, it produces exactly the same 'models' as it produces in other representations and simulacra. Male subjectivity in Western patriarchy continues to rely for a sense of its own coherence and centrality on positioning women as more like nature – more embodied, more sensate, more irrational, more like animals and earth, and somehow, therefore, more material and concrete; as against men, who are more like gods – more mind, more intellect, more rational and disembodied, and thus more abstract. The irony is that in order to do this, men have abstracted and virtualized women while concretizing and materializing themselves. Women can only be accepted as embodied objects by having a half-life in the patriarchal imaginary. That is, women are 'not quite human' or, as humans, are 'almost absolute'. The measure of what constitutes human is a male measure, and in order to continue to operate comfortably with its own subjectivity, the male defining consciousness in patriarchy requires that women should never *be* like men but always and only 'almost' be like men. If there is no lack or gap or notion of the 'irrational other' keeping women always already virtual, then, as irrational, embodied objects, they cease to have their vital role in the subject formation of men. Women's very embodiment in the phallocentric imaginary is the source of a perpetual virtuality: women are only useful as embodied presences by virtue of being perpetually virtualized.

In the continual quest to refine computer technologies, to attain what Zoë Sofia calls 'Jupiter Space' – that disembodied cyberspace in which the mind of man might be coherently and perfectly reflected back to him as logical, clean, predictable and uncluttered by the distraction of emotions and bodies (1993: 86)[5] – it is nevertheless necessary to continue to have a 'she/other' against which to measure both the embodied and virtual subjectivity of the male. In the imaginary of patriarchal colonizers of cyberspace, the conflated 'woman-object' is both in the machine and the machine itself. When the computer 'creates' a virtual world, thus making its 'creator' or 'controller' more like a god than ever before, the role of the object remains feminized as a means for men to extend and maintain their subjectivities as stable and certain in a real world which continually reminds them that nature and human life are neither stable nor certain, and that men are not immortal.

There is clearly a considerable difference between the ontological terrain for women, particularly bourgeois women in the West, and that for men in how the virtual might be imagined and experienced in the contemporary climate. The virtual woman produced in modernist discursive formations is now encountering virtual reality in cyberspaces which, ironically, are both feminized and being represented, in theoretical discussions at least, as problematic for male subjectivity. However, now present in considerable numbers in workplaces or other spheres which have previously been the sole possessions of men, women can also feel that they are 'at the mercy of machines' rather than 'master of machines'. They can experience their relationship to machines as they can experience relations with men – as if they were 'mistress', in its sexual sense, of machines. In this situation, the machine replaces the man as the mirror which reflects back a woman's powerless object status, passivity and 'otherness'. Women may come to fear machines as they may fear their creators. And emergent virtual spheres are also replete with familiar features that suggest to many women just another extension of patriarchal hegemonics, regardless of some current theoretical analyses regarding the radical possibilities of a new, genderless, classless cybercitizenry.

Rethinking virtual identity

To strategize the possibilities of political actions in virtual worlds, feminists need something more subtle than a notion of techno-liberation breaking down previous alterities/absences. It runs counter to feminist analyses of emergent technological culture to place hope in a shift in social imaginaries and cultural practices through seeing the technologies themselves as enabling the previously oppressed to claim, or be given, a presence in virtual reality. Where might that 'presence' experience itself from? How might it constitute itself in emerging corporeal and virtual politics?

It is equally an over-simplified analysis which leads some feminist commentators (for example, Spender, 1995) to imply that 'technofear' is a discursively constructed inevitability, but that if women can only empower themselves by becoming familiar with new information technologies and naturalizing those technologies in their domestic, educational and work spheres, men can be prevented from continuing to 'own the space' just as they have all public spaces hitherto. Such arguments rely to a considerable extent on an emancipatory ideology that current theory has seriously problematized, and do not take account of women's complicity in their own object status or their 'already virtual' status in pre-cyber-culture.

Besides, the logocentric discursive and epistemological bases of patriarchy have not vanished before women's march into areas of the social that were previously barred to them. Rather, current anti-feminist, anti-immigration, racist discourses would suggest, on the contrary, that the presence of the 'other' in spaces which have conventionally been important sites of Western white male identity formation has precipitated a crisis in male subjectivities which is still playing itself through. It seems that woman cannot be simultaneously a presence and a lack, at once a subject and an object, without logocentric man ceasing to be able to have meaning for himself.

Clearly strategies of familiarization, education and access should be pursued in relation to women and technologies, and will result in considerable benefits. But women's always already virtual status is not automatically disturbed or displaced by the act of adapting technologies to the service of their lives. In 'A Manifesto for Cyborgs', Donna Haraway (1991) alerted us to the probability that the 'feminizing' of work practices in information technology capitalism carries with it new opportunities for exploitation and oppression. She outlined an increasing trend in Western capitalism towards a technologized 'homework economy':

> Work is being redefined as both literally female and feminized, whether performed by men or women. To be feminized means to be made extremely vulnerable; able to be disassembled, reassembled, exploited as a reserve labour force, seen less as workers than as servers; subjected to time arrangements on and off the paid job that make a mockery of a limited work day. . . . [T]he concept indicates that factory, home, and market are integrated on a new scale and that the places of women are crucial – and need to be analysed for differences among women and for meanings for relations between men and women in various situations. (1991: 166)[6]

Part of this analysis might include noting a trend of the 1990s for highly skilled women who have become dissatisfied with deteriorating bourgeois workplace conditions to turn to computer technologies as the basis for a new kind of 'techno-cottage industry', or home-based work using information technologies. This can provide a solution and a challenge for women who want to spend more time with their families and/or less time in the stressful phallocentric environments of corporations. For other women, such work could result in familiar oppressive capitalist patterns. There is no guarantee that technological piecework, simply because it is undertaken by bourgeois women, will be any the less prone to exploitation through overwork and underpayment.[7] It is also more than possible that, as for other casual women outworkers, home-based technological labour might come to 'justify' continued or renewed isolation in the home and responsibility for the bulk of domestic labour and child-rearing. As with the 'labour-saving devices' of the mid-century, women's 'emancipation' and 'freedom of choice' through technologies might just as easily become entrapment. Many women may find that they and their computers remain prosthetic extensions of male partners and/or male-directed capitalism.

Cyberspace can, and should, continue solidarity among alienated 'others' who gain access to cyber-technologies, but I would suggest that Spender's 'nattering' is a term which does not suggest an intervention likely to unsettle the phallocentric cultures of corporations, government, law, economics, work and family. There may be value in thinking about the more powerful thing of gossiping – of maintaining underground cultures of connection through powerful 'talk' with 'gossips' (or friends) – which can constitute, as it always has, a crucial counter-cultural network of support and solidarity. And while it is certainly useful, particularly in the context of pedagogies, to pursue the notion that some women may have particularly 'female' needs in relation to technologies and that women should exercise initiative in fashioning 'female' ways of interacting with technologies, such strategies also risk a kind of essentialism which discursively reinscribes women's difference as 'otherness from Man' and simultaneously blocks possibilities for notions of difference and partiality which might constitute the basis for ethical and/or ideological positions that value diversity among women and men.

A more practical basis for feminist interventions in cyberspace could lie in noticing that women's already virtual experience actually constitutes an advantage in cyber-citizenry. Women have developed various complex means of continuing to believe they have presence and continuing to share decontextualized knowledges every since they were colonized and objectified. In addition to the many personal, domestic, community and workplace counter-cultural ways in which women subvert the daily virtualizing of their lived experiences, feminisms themselves constitute an ideological and epistemological insistence on presence against representation as virtual. Women have a great deal of valuable expertise about 'presence in virtuality'.[8]

Among these is the capacity to read, speak and write from two or more positions at once which has enabled women thus far to function *within* the logos, indeed to disturb it from time to time. For women to participate in logocentric discourses with agency, they have had to read both from a male viewpoint and as a female object of that viewpoint, interpreting what happens on the matrix between those positions. And in order to construct themselves as speaking subjects undoing the logos, women have had to speak and write in discourses which themselves exclude women from the logos. Multiple literacies and polyvocality are a feature of women's lives and, among reflexive feminists conscious of their uses, they have achieved particularly sophisticated expressions. Cyberspace is especially suited to exploring and developing a diversity of literacies and expressions. Kroker observes of Lyotard's analysis of the postmodern that 'here, everything is a matter of double discourses, of the asymmetry of the *dissoi logos* of the early Sophists' (1992: 150). In that case, feminists enter cyberspace already in advance of the univocal discursive practices of phallocentric culture, particularly in terms of how they might use multiple discourses to unsettle or sabotage patriarchal hegemonics.

For feminists who recognize that currently we have the novel opportunity to affect outcomes in the early stages of a major transformation in the social, the project remains one of fashioning subjectivities and spaces from which to intervene in ways that do unsettle, disturb or even destroy the patriarchal hegemonic. This requires a carefully nuanced reading of contemporary positions. To have an understanding of the relation between cyber-politics and male-theorized postmodernity is an important starting point. At the same time, women need to pay attention to the strategies already developed and being developed by women to express their subjectivities, to be change agents, despite being constructed as always already virtual in modernity *and* postmodernity.

Donna Haraway's work, particularly, 'A Manifesto for Cyborgs', posits feminist affinity groups based in 'cyborg' identity as a form of writing into women's mythos an idea of 'a hybrid machine and organism, a creature of social reality as well as a creature of fiction' (1991: 149). Hers is an argument for '*pleasure* in the confusion of boundaries and for *responsibility* in their construction' (1991: 150; original emphasis):

> The cyborg is resolutely committed to partiality, irony, intimacy, and perversity. It is oppositional, utopian, and completely without innocence. No longer structured by the polarity of the public and the private, the cyborg defines a technological polis based partly on a revolution of social relations in *oikos*, the household. Nature and culture are reworked; the one can no longer be the resource for appropriation or incorporation by the other. The relationships for forming wholes from parts, including those of polarity and hierarchical domination, are at issue in the cyborg world. (1991: 151)

There is a great deal of value in Haraway's unravelling of patriarchal technological epistemes, her recognition that female identities are already partial and strategic, and her suggestion that there are 'great riches for feminists in explicitly embracing the possibilities inherent in the breakdown of clean distinctions between organisms and machines' (1991: 174). However, I am not convinced that a 'cyborg feminism' constitutes a sufficient basis for political positions adequate to cyberspace embodiment, especially since virtual reality is currently proliferating, and acculturating subjectivities to it, regardless of gender. It would seem useful to collide Haraway's ideas with the wider terrain of recent feminist work interested in embodied, sexed, differentiated and partial subjectivities in cultural spaces.

Elizabeth Grosz, for example, in *Volatile Bodies* (1994) and *Space, Time and Perversion* (1995) undertakes a thorough revisiting of a wide range of male and female theory concerning how the logos operates and how that affects the embodied experiences of men and women. Like Haraway, Grosz rejects essentialism. She offers a range of suggestions as to how people might move beyond the constraints of the logos through a subject 'no longer seen as an entity – whether psychical or corporeal – but fundamentally an effect of the pure difference that constitutes all modes of materiality' (1994: 208). Embracing ideas about inscription of the social on the body and about 'intensities and flows', Grosz posits ways of thinking about non-dualized, non-unified notions of subjectivity based in 'pure difference', including the model of the Möbius strip,[9] which:

> enables the mind/body relation to avoid the impasses of reductionism, of a narrow causal relation or the retention of the binary divide. It enables subjectivity to be understood not as the combination of a psychical depth and a corporeal superficiality but as a surface whose inscriptions and rotations in three-dimensional space produce all the effects of depth. It enables subjectivity to be understood as fully material and for materiality to be extended and to include and explain the operations of language, desire and significance. (1994: 209–10)

Grosz's approach offers a theoretical space from which feminists can undo the impact of logocentric discourses on their capacities to think their own subjectivities. Her reworking of familiar epistemes to develop a basis for the postmodern subject also produces a shift in ontological possibilities, enabling women to resist essentialist positions as they dispense with alienation from their own subjectivities. That alienation was produced by an object status necessary for maintenance of the I-dentities of dualistic, dichotomized male subjects who imagine themselves to be unified subjects. If we accept Grosz's play of differences, not only can feminists leave that role behind, but they also can attain enough distance from it to notice how effectively most women have actually maintained a sense of their own subjectivities within and against alienation. This is a recognition which might also inform how women constitute subjectivities in cyberspace.

Some descriptions of the postmodern subject recoil in horror from sexual boundary transgressions: 'transexuality too: a fatal sign-slide between the genders, really an amnesia on the question of the sexual referent, as the meaning of the sexual is obliterated in the cold light of the "obscenity of communication"' (Kroker, 1992: 79).[10] Indeed, the dispersed and disassociated cultural signifiers of postmodernity in general are, in such descriptions, understood to pose a 'catastrophic' threat to unified subjectivity. But women have long been denied the experience – or fantasy – of unified subjectivity. A (male) view in which the 'sign-slide' equals death contrasts dramatically not only with Grosz's ideas but with those of many other feminist theorists of the body, whose emphasis tends to be on how the play of signs and bodily possibilities opens out when women reject object status and transgress gender boundaries imposed on them in the phallocentric sexual economy.[11] Much current feminist theory about bodies is characterized by a celebration of fluidity, the abject, the 'dark liquid' potentialities of female sexualities when they break through or explode the mythos and logos of patriarchy. It also frequently challenges the conventions of academic discourse in its expression. And current feminist writing, visual art, music, theatre, film, video and cyber-art about bodies is cross-disciplinary, transgressive of genre conventions, multi-media, multi-sited and widely informed by notions of carnival, confusions, perversions, dressing up, undressing down, partialities, disarray, unruliness in the lived experiences of women. Feminist theorists and arts practitioners have found what Gilles Deleuze and Félix Guatarri, theorists of flows, rhizomes and nomadology, would call 'lines of flight' out of the 'molar assemblages' of patriarchal hegemonics into the disassembled 'molecular' of a yet to be determined becoming.[12] As with bodies, so with virtual bodies. As with spaces, so with virtual spaces.

Virtual presence

Feminist politics in cyberspace must continue to explore and extend on these understandings and practices. But it is important to be alert to any propensity on the part of feminisms themselves to 'molarize', or be caught in the modernist trap of a perception that because men have so far controlled the production and distribution of cyber-technologies, *ipso facto* they will therefore control the spaces those technologies generate. Such recursiveness must be stepped over if women are to step into the cyberspaces as subjects and citizens. Likewise, to fear that women may not be able to understand, manipulate and work with emerging technologies and technological spaces is a meaningless extension of modernity into the postmodern. Fear is, anyway, the speciality of those male theorists who re-enact the same old oppressive mantras, who fail to undo, when they enter postmodernity and cyberspace, their own continuing fantasy of possession of themselves, the spaces they occupy and their virtual representations of women – the men who come to fear 'the black hole of fragmented subjectivity' when they feel themselves falling for the seductive object as if it was an embodied woman. That is, they are unsettled by their own technological 'creations'.

Feminists are not necessarily unsettled to find themselves in a space in which their subjectivity is virtualized, nor unfamiliar with the idea of imaginary fragmentation or dispersion. Because of their experience in the modern, in the real, women are perfectly placed for cyber-citizenry. They do not fear 'uninterrupted interface' – indeed, have been known to court it. And it would be highly ironic if feminists were to be dislocated by what Baudrillard calls the '*trompe l'oeil*' effect of postmodern technologies, in which an 'undermining of the privileged position of the gaze' means that the subject becomes the object in a 'realm of appearances, where there is nothing to see, where things see you' (1990: 61); which is developed by Kroker into: 'that point where subjectivity inscribes itself in the commodity first, then in the sign, and finally in the sacrificial violence immanent to seduction (1992: 79–80). These could serve as descriptions of the experience of women in patriarchy – as 'mirrors' for male subjects: first becoming complicit in their own inscription as commodities, then signs and finally victims. 'How dreadful', it is tempting to remark, 'for these men so suddenly to experience the horror of being the subject-as-object.' Feminists already have a wide range of personal and political strategies for dealing with that experience.

Women also have nothing to fear from the 'seductions' of technologies precisely because women *were* the seductive and terrifying 'sign of imminent reversibility' against which phallocentric culture guaranteed an illusion of unified, god-like subjectivities long before computer technologies enabled them to enact and fantasize their own reproduction in Jupiter Space. It follows, then, that just as women can develop understandings of bodies, spaces and subjectivities which reject and dismantle the logos as it has affected their imaginaries and their lived experiences, they can also develop understandings of virtual bodies and spaces which make use of their subjectivities, their play with sign-slides, their long experience of ontologies of virtual being.

As always already virtual, women were never the possessors of social and cultural spaces. But there are many ways in which they have always been traversers of spaces, nomads in patriarchy. This has been particularly the case for bourgeois feminist intellectuals.[13] What Grosz calls 'feminist reoccupations of space' (1995: 120) might become a matter of drawing on both emerging theoretical understandings about bodies, subjectivities and spaces, and analysis of the history of women's survival in phallogocentric culture. Empirically, that survival is evidenced in the very existence of bourgeois feminism as well as in the role of gossip, kinship and affinity in sustaining women's underground culture in all classes and ethnic groups.

I am suggesting a praxis for feminists in cyberspace that goes beyond naturalizing women with the technologies, or technologies with women, and has little faith in utopian visions of the disintegration of entrenched oppressive structures in a gender/race/class-neutral global cyber-community. For an effective feminist politics in virtuality, it is necessary to take the radical step of enfolding and accepting women's history as objects – as always already virtual subjects. The history and theory of women's alienation, and the strategies developed in order to survive it, can be carried over into new cultural spaces. Feminist ideas about cyberspace and virtual reality, and feminist practices with and within them, can be fashioned in what Moira Gatens calls 'a web of intertextuality/intersexuality' (Maras and Rizzo, 1995: 65). In practical terms, this means that feminists need to let go of a desire for a unified subjectivity, which was always a phallocentric fantasy, a trick of the logos. They need to explore, critique and further ideas about permanent partialities, temporary collectivities and diasporic processes; about speeds, fractals, vectors; about lines of flight, rhizomes, intensities and flows.

Interventions in cyberspace might include fashioning various political, academic or creative affinity groups. Difference will find different means and expressions. Strategies will emerge which enable various ethics, ideological projects, political actions, theoretical analyses, creative productions, intertextual experiments, cross-media excursions, feminist virtual reality parlours and feminist teledildonics, for that matter. To all think the same about or do the same with cyberspace and virtual reality would be a rerun of the well-meaning projects of liberation feminism before feminists came to terms with the constant problematics of difference.

'Desire', Deleuze and Guattari suggest, 'never needs interpreting, it is it which experiments' (1987: 95). Feminists have thus far launched themselves into cyberspace with enthusiasm, confidence, diversity and irony. Because technological objects and the spaces they enable are tools – like chisels, paintbrushes, vacuum cleaners, typewriters, sewing machines – feminists who have analysed and resolved the problematics of modernist woman–object fusions have no difficulty picking up the cyber-gadgets and getting on with using them. While this nevertheless requires careful strategizing, there are some ways in which virtual worlds are prime sites for feminist politics even before strategies are clearly theorized or articulated.

Feminist projects in and about cyberspace can be understood as nomadic movements, because existing 'territories', concepts of 'ownership' and structures of 'power' can be understood as incoveniences, not barriers. The patriarchal defences, it would seem, are already weakened by the shock value of women's presence just beyond the horizon of Jupiter Space. If feminists notice that the apparent domination by men of the emerging spaces of the virtual world is marked by a considerable degree of dis-location and uncertainty in phallocentric subjectivities, they can also notice that alterity can become a strength for political interventions in virtual reality. And having addressed their previous complicity in alienation from their own subjectivities by undoing women's seduction by the signs of seduction, feminists are well placed to express and extend diverse, unfixed, unconfined subjectivities in virtual spaces.

Interventions in cyberspace can be intensely political, but subject definition is what feminist praxis should avoid. As Rosi Braidotti puts it: 'one of the issues at stake here is how to reconcile partiality and dis-continuity with the construction of new forms of interrelatedness and collective political projects' (1994: 5). Feminist political actions in the twentieth century have profoundly disturbed male subjectivities because women have 'leaked' into spaces previously barred to them – in the social, in corporate, intellectual and creative cultures – and they have refused to be fixed into any particular place within those spaces. When feminists speak and act with agency, it is not from all the same positions and they therefore remain doubly 'difficult'. Just when patriarchal representations had feminists marginalized and de-sexed in boiler-suited stereotypes which allowed them to be ignored, lots of them turned up with shaved legs and lipstick, often right in the middle of male cultures. Just when there seemed to be a neat divide sustainable between feminists and 'real women' (that is, 'virtual women'), feminisms produced an avalanche of sign-slides.

In naively reproducing in virtual space the object that has for many become a source of I-dentity crisis in the real, some men are unwittingly aiding and abetting feminist cyber-politics. Ironically, simulacral women being virtualized by phallocentric culture in cyberspace already represent for the patriarchal imaginary the disturbing seepage of the 'animal' female into the pure mind space of the male hegemonic. Feminists need only keep popping up in unexpected places in unexpected guises to put a virtual cat among the virtual pigeons.

Notes

1. I should stress that the ideas developed here are focused on feminists and feminist positions in relation to cyber-culture. That is, I assume a largely informed and/or relatively privileged group of women, who might, at present, be concerned about ways to move their activism into cyberspace. This being the case, I do not in this instance seek to provide a comprehensive critique concerning cyber-technologies and women in general, nor do I address in any detail important broader issues of class, global economic disparities, developed capitalist cultures' domination of cyberspace, and so on. My project is necessarily limited in its purview and does not pretend to offer practical solutions to large-scale access and equity questions.

2. For example, Arthur Kroker's *The Possessed Individual*, in which 'virtual reality' is used to evoke postmodern culture *per se*. Kroker views 'virtuality now as the dominant sign of contemporary technological society' and argues that 'virtual reality – the world of digital dreams come alive – is what the possessed individual is possessed by' (1992: 2).

3. Sofia draws on Melanie Klein's object relations theory, various other psychoanalytic and textual theories, philosophy and the philosophy of science in her wide-ranging analysis. See also Cathryn Vasseleu's chapter in this volume, especially her discussion of the desire to 'escape' the 'limits' of the body, of how 'teledildonics avoids the issue of negotiating sexuality as a corporeally mediated exchange. Instead of messy and tenuous interpretations, sexuality becomes an intelligible exchange of information, the erotogenic effects of which depend on where your autonomy "interfaces" with the tactile s(t)imulator' (p. 54).

4. We might dwell briefly on the word 'model' as used in modernity for a woman who poses for mass market material. Its primary meaning as a noun is 'Representation of structure', its second meaning is 'Type of design' and its third 'An object of imitation'. Under the third, we find 'b. A person (without qualification, usu. a woman) employed to display clothes by wearing them. E20 c. *euphem*. A prostitute M20' (Brown, 1993). Here we have that slide again, between the male-conceived 'design', the 'object', the 'woman as object' in consumerism and the woman as a commodity in a more explicit sexual economy. We might also note the ways in which cars, computers and software come in 'models', mass produced and rapidly replaced, 'generation after generation'. Virtual woman in cyberspace, I would suggest, is discursively produced as the next model, the next generation from virtual woman in 'real space' modernity and postmodernity, whose representation still changes models each year.

5. Sofia takes the term 'Jupiter Space' from *2001: A Space Odyssey*

> where it was used to refer simultaneously to the womby red brain-womb of the computer HAL . . . and to the outer space near the planet Jupiter, from whence the astronaut is reborn as an omnipotent extraterrestrial foetus. . . . Subsequent elaborations of the constellation reinforce parallels between the technological spaces of the masculinist/rational brain, the computer and its interior, outer space, etc. Often a male face is shown with the top part of the head opening onto and/or overlain with images of outer space (space as brain-womb), or of electronic circuitry (the brain equals computer idea), and/or of a luminous grid of lines passing into infinity. In some variants, these kinds of images are shown reflected onto the faces, spectacles or helmet masks of male viewers of video displays, computer screens or outer space. Other texts draw equations between, say, computer microcircuitry and city maps, or invoke extraterrestrialism and mathematical order in scenes of the grid of light-lines formed by urban streets and freeways at night, or the Cartesian precision of skyscraper façades. . . . The grid motif reiterates a visual pun on the concept of the 'matrix' as womb and as mathematical geometrical grid, signifying the fertile technoscientific intellect. (1993: 84)

Noting that often in television and news promotions 'the grid gives way to images of a smooth and luminous sphere with featureless land masses', Sofia reads through Heidegger to suggest that

> the featureless and glowing planet pictures an Earth whose contents have all been sucked up into the objectless *Bestand*, the standing-reserve, no longer showing resistance to the zooming extraterrestrial superpowers that encircle and enframe them: reality has been swallowed up, digested and re-sourced (through the corporate matrix and the C^3I) into luminous hyperreality. (1993: 86)

6. Haraway takes the notion of the 'homework economy' from the work of Richard Gordon (1991).

7. *Excellence in Content: The Focus for Australian Investment in Multimedia Content*, a government-commissioned report, refers for example to a finding that the major investment into multimedia content is 'Sweat Equity . . . the amount of unpaid time development teams put into their product' (HREF 1). Government-commissioned research I have recently undertaken with Gillian Swanson shows that women working in freelance capacities in multimedia are contributing 'sweat equity' in commissioned projects, while women in salaried positions are undertaking unpaid development work with new technologies, embedded in their salaried work context but beyond their normal duties and/or hours.

8. Kroker comments that Paul Virilio 'sums up in the brilliant theoretical concept – dromology – the double sign of presencing and absence, which is surely the epochal consciousness of the postmodern condition' (1992: 30). But this is a sign under which women have always lived in patriarchies. Virilio develops a particularly useful and astute reading of postmodernity, precisely because he does notice this feature of it. See especially *Speed and Politics* (1986).

9. The model of the Möbius strip has, of course, been used elsewhere, notably by Lacan, but I am particularly interested in Grosz's use of it to rethink body/subject possibilities in a feminist context.

10. Kroker is here engaged with Baudrillard.

11. See, for example, various chapters in Rosalyn Diprose and Robyn Ferrell, *Cartographies: Poststructuralism and the Mapping of Bodies and Spaces* (1991); Barbara Caine, E.A. Grosz and Marie de Lepervanche, *Crossing Boundaries: Feminism and the Critique of Knowledges* (1988), especially Moira Gatens' contribution, 'Towards a Feminist Philosophy of the Body'; Jane Gallop, *Thinking Through the Body* (1988); also the works of Luce Irigaray, especially *This Sex Which Is Not One* (1985).

12. See Gilles Deleuze and Félix Guatarri, *A Thousand Plateaus: Capitalism and Schizophrenia* (1987); and Gilles Deleuze and Claire Parnet, *Dialogues* (1987). Deleuze and Guatarri's ideas are explored, critiqued and developed in a feminist context in Grosz's *Volatile Bodies* (1994) and *Space, Time and Perversion* (1995), in Braidotti's *Nomadic Subjects* (1994), Moira Gatens' *Imaginary Bodies* (1996) and Elspeth Probyn's *Outside Belongings* (1996).

13. See, for example, the introduction to Braidotti's *Nomadic Subjects* (1994).

References

Baudrillard, Jean (1988) *The Ecstacy of Communication*. New York: Semiotext(e).

Baudrillard, Jean (1990) *Seduction* (trans. Brian Singer). New York: St Martin's Press.

Braidotti, Rosi (1994) *Nomadic Subjects: Embodiment and Sexual Difference in Contemporary Feminist Theory*. New York: Columbia University Press.

Brown, Lesley (ed.) (1993) *The New Shorter Oxford Dictionary on Historical Principles*. Oxford: Clarendon Press.

Caine, Barbara, Grosz, E.A. and de Lepervanche, Marie (eds) (1988) *Crossing Boundaries: Feminism and the Critique of Knowledges*. Sydney: Allen and Unwin.

Deleuze, Gilles and Guatarri, Félix (1987) *A Thousand Plateaus: Capitalism and Schizophrenia* (trans. Brian Massumi). Minneapolis, MN: University of Minneapolis Press.

Deleuze, Gilles and Parnet, Claire (1987) *Dialogues* (trans. Hugh Tomlinson and Barbara Habberjam). New York: Columbia University Press.

Diprose, Roslyn and Ferrell, Robyn (eds) (1991) *Cartographies: Poststructuralism and the Mapping of Bodies and Spaces.* Sydney: Allen and Unwin.

Freud, Sigmund (1963) *Civilisation and Its Discontents* (trans. James Strachey). London: Hogarth Press.

Gallop, Jane (1988) *Thinking Through the Body.* New York: Columbia University Press.

Gatens, Moira (1996) *Imaginary Bodies.* London: Routledge.

Gordon, Richard (1983) 'The Computerization of Daily Life, the Sexual Division of Labour, and the Homework Economy'. Paper presented at Silicon Valley Workshop Conference, University of Santa Cruz.

Grosz, Elizabeth (1992) 'Lived Spatiality: Insect Space/Virtual Sex', *Agenda* 26/7: 5–8.

Grosz, Elizabeth (1994) *Volatile Bodies.* Sydney: Allen and Unwin.

Grosz, Elizabeth (1995) *Space, Time and Perversion.* Sydney: Allen and Unwin.

Haraway, Donna J. (1991) *Simians, Cyborgs and Women: The Reinvention of Nature.* New York: Routledge.

HREF 1: http://www.dist.gov.au/pubs/reports/excon/exconmmi.html. Coopers and Lybrand, Multimedia Industry Group (1995) *Excellence in Content: The Focus for Australian Investment in Multimedia Content.* (Report commissioned by the Australian Government.)

Irigaray, Luce (1985) *This Sex Which Is Not One* (trans. Catherine Porter with Carolyn Burke). Ithaca, NY: Cornell University Press.

Jameson, Fredric (1991) *Postmodernism, Or, the Cultural Logic of Late Capitalism.* London: Verso.

Kroker, Arthur (1992) *The Possessed Individual.* Montreal: New World Perspectives Culture Text Series.

Maras, Steven and Rizzo, Teresa (1995) 'On Becoming: An Interview with Moira Gatens', *Southern Review*, 28 (1): 53–67.

Probyn, Elspeth (1996) *Outside Belongings.* New York and London: Routledge.

Rheingold, Howard (1991) *Virtual Reality.* London: Secker and Warburg.

Sofia, Zöe (1993) *Whose Second Self: Gender and (Ir)rationality in Computer Culture.* Geelong: Deakin University Press.

Spender, Dale (1995) *Nattering on the Net.* North Melbourne: Spinifex Press.

Virilio, Paul (1986) *Speed and Politics* (trans. Mark Polizotti). New York: Semiotext(e).

11

THE TECHNOLOGIZATION OF THE SACRED:

Virtual Reality and the New Age

Christopher Ziguras

A central feature of New Age thought is the notion that underlying the 'exterior' reality perceptible to the senses is an inner reality perceptible only through heightened awareness. Thus the concreteness of external physical reality is considered merely a façade which provides the seeker of Truth with clues to the underlying reality it hides. Take, for example, a self-help audiotape entitled 'Your Car and its Parts: What is the Symbolism for Your Life?' When one explores the deeper meaning of mechanical failure, the greasy materiality of the automobile is seen as an expression of a more real underlying reality in which all things make sense: 'What is the message when your car blows a gasket, your battery goes dead, or you get a flat tyre? How is this reflecting the choices you are making? This isn't a discussion about car parts. It demonstrates the symbolic nature of how your reality is projected . . .' (Samuel Weiser Inc., 1995: 52). The world of objects which surrounds us is seen within the New Age movement as a projection of a sacred reality, which exists within, or below, the concrete.

This chapter explores the ways in which New Age constructions of the sacred are creating a form of religiosity which spiritualizes the contemporary fascination with high technology and science, and in particular with the 'virtual' realities of contemporary information technology. I argue that this sacred and increasingly high-tech virtual inner reality, by not acknowledging the social forces at work in shaping their experience of the sacred, is the means by which New Agers attempt to make sense of the world. Rather than actually discovering a radically new paradigm on which to model belief and action, the New Age has become celebratory of the same processes which it set out to provide an alternative to.

Because New Age practices of representing the world are actively used as tools for self-transformation, these ideas are powerfully constitutive of New Agers' sense of self-identity and the way in which they comprehend physical reality and social relations. The reflexive process in which the person is actively (and perpetually) engaged in attempting to re-create his/her self-identity is (unlike conventional psychotherapy) understood as a process of peeling away layers of the socially constructed and hence inauthentic external self, in order to discover the pre-social and 'authentic' inner person. New Age spirituality has often been referred to as 'self-religiosity', in which the sacred is equated with the authentic self, and the search for God leads one to deep introspection (Heelas, 1992).

As a project which regards desocialization as a utopian value, New Age self-identity is naive to the extent that it is unwilling to provide a coherent critique or alternative to the conditions which lead its members to seek radical changes in their lives. The New Age, while seeing itself as a force for social change which undermines the mechanistic, rationalistic and consumerist expressions of culture, has itself become a vehicle for the heightening of those very tendencies it claims to oppose, although in new forms. Throughout the New Age movement there is an unwillingness to comprehend the nature of social structures; instead, this spiritual movement maintains an idealistic belief in the power of thought to change social forms. Although some extreme illustrations of New Age culture are drawn on in this chapter, which some New Agers would consider to be unrepresentative of the movement as a whole, these instances are consistent with the underlying beliefs of the New Age.

After describing the central features of New Age thought, this chapter will then detail the ways in which the New Age espouses new forms of scientization of social life through the modelling of the sacred inner reality on the 'new science' and urging the realignment of social life in line with this inner reality. Subsequent sections focus on the New Age celebration of the technologization and commodification of relaxation through high-tech meditation techniques, and the ways in which New Age techniques are being incorporated into management training in order to foster behavioural and attitudinal traits in workers consistent with the contemporary demands of corporate life. The New Age movement, I will argue, is not a force which poses a humanistic counterpoint to the dominant systemic imperatives of our time, but is instead a major force for the modernization of outmoded forms of an earlier modernity and their replacement with the less rigid but more pervasive 'fluid' structures of postmodernity. The New Age does not counter but rejuvenates these forces by providing a spiritual framework which attempts to normalize the new expressions of corporeality that are related to the new technologies discussed throughout this book which penetrate ever deeper under our skins.

The New Age

The term 'New Age' is a particularly slippery one given that it is routinely used in very different ways to refer to a number of discrete but in some senses related phenomena – a dawning historical epoch, a syncretic religious orientation, a post-hippie subculture, a holistic world-view, a spiritual-political social movement, and so on. On closer inspection the diverse and often bizarre array of cultural practices which are commonly labelled New Age seldom appear to have much in common. However, when one looks at the discursive construction of practices as different as crystal healing, tarot reading, Celtic rituals and Hollywood Buddhism, it becomes apparent that the meaning of all these practices is constituted with reference to the same, more or less coherent, system of beliefs. One thorough account by a New Age writer summarizing the central features of New Age thought is that formulated by William Bloom, which is worth quoting at length:

- All life – all existence – is the manifestation of Spirit, of the Unknowable, of that supreme consciousness known by many different names in many different cultures.
- The purpose and dynamic of all existence is to bring Love, Wisdom, Enlightenment . . . into full manifestation.
- All religions are the expression of this same inner reality.
- All life, as we perceive it with the five human senses or with scientific instruments, is only the outer veil of an invisible, inner and causal reality.
- Similarly, human beings are two-fold creatures – with:
  (i) an outer temporal personality and
  (ii) a multi-dimensional inner being (soul or higher self).
- The outer personality is limited and tends towards materialism.
- The inner being is infinite and tends towards love.
- Our spiritual teachers are those souls who are liberated from the need to incarnate and who express unconditional love, wisdom and enlightenment. Some of these great beings are well known and have inspired the world religions. Some are unknown and work invisibly.
- All life, in all its different forms and states, is interconnected energy – and this includes our deeds, feelings and thoughts. We, therefore, work with Spirit and these energies in co-creating our reality.
- Although held in the dynamic of cosmic love, we are jointly responsible for the state of our selves, of our environment and of all life.
- During this period of time, the evolution of the planet and of humanity has reached a point when we are undergoing a fundamental spiritual change in our individual and mass consciousness. That is why we talk of a New Age. . . . (quoted in Heelas, 1993: 104)

All New Age practices are attempts to escape from the outer personality and from outer reality in order to experience a sacred inner reality. In this chapter I am interested in how the 'Unknowable' is known; that is, the way in which inner reality and Spirit are in fundamental ways reflections of the here and now. The notion of energy, which will be a recurring theme here, derives, on the one hand, from appropriations of similar concepts from traditional cultures and their religious systems and, on the other, from the pervasive influence of high-technology in shaping postmodern urban environments.

Many New Age 'tools' are inspired by, or are anachronistic appropriations of, pre-modern cultural practices. Given that the self-transformative
project is so enmeshed in a characteristically postmodern fluidity of self-
identity, it is peculiar that the New Age constantly harks back to pre-
modern cultures, attempting to legitimate new fads through drawing on
ancient wisdom. Although New Agers insist otherwise, and the content of
the practices may sometimes change little, the social relations which
surround these practices are fundamentally different. In more traditional
cultures than our own, the practices and beliefs which are drawn on by the
New Age, such as Celtic solstice rituals or Tantric massage, are connected
by a dense web of meanings with the cosmology, the forms of identity and
the lifestyles of their original cultural form – and in this sense it is fair to
describe them as having been holistic. Once disembedded from these
connections which give the practices deep meanings for their original
practitioners they risk being reduced to shallow therapeutic devices. This
frequently happens, and has led to strong and legitimate criticisms of the
disrespectful way in which traditional cultures have been selectively
exploited by the West in recent years. New Age spiritual practices are often
construed as more or less equivalent paths to the same sacred space; they
are interchangeable tools to attain higher consciousness. The only criterion
for evaluation of any particular practice is whether it works for you, and
the thousands of autobiographical texts which fill the shelves of New Age
bookstores urge the seeker to constantly experiment in finding the self-
transformation technique appropriate to that stage of his/her own spiritual
journey.

If traditional beliefs and practices were merely hollowed-out and stripped
of meaning, though, there would be no New Age – it is hard to imagine
these pseudo-traditional discourses arousing the passions they do if that
were the whole story. As well as being disembedded from older social
contexts, the practices are re-embedded in contemporary frameworks of
meaning as tools in the active project of working upon one's self-identity,
and with reference to a quite distinct spiritual system. Traditional
spiritualities and healing practices are reconstituted in relation to other
radically different practices, all of which are unified by their common
medium (energy), to form the eclectic cross-cultural grab-bag which is the
New Age. Thus the introduction to *The Healing Arts* treats health-care
modalities as different as Yoga, traditional Chinese medicine, chiropractic
and naturopathy as interchangeable techniques for the tuning of the life
current:

> Attunement may be described as the increased experience in a person's body and
> consciousness of the healing or life current. Although the healer facilitates
> attunement in another using whatever external technique is appropriate, the
> increased experience of life and health comes from within. (Hetzel, 1989: 12)

The New Age attempts to ground the uncomfortably free-floating seeker
of meaning and ontological security in a new form of holism – one in

which the increasingly disparate spheres of personal experience are reunited in relation to an inner reality which is a field of energy. If contemporary capitalism sets about making all things interrelatable through the medium of money, the New Age 'counters' this materialist integration of spheres with its own techno-spiritual universal medium in which the body, mind, spirit and emotions are all thought of as interrelated systems of energy. Rather than countering the scientization of social life, the New Age provides a stopgap way of glossing over this major area of cultural conflict. Virtually all New Age practices and the accompanying gadgetry work on the body's energy in some way. Channelling, psychic healing, crystals and pyramids – all do similar (but slightly different) things with similar (but necessarily distinct, for marketing purposes) forms of energy. They either claim to focus, balance, harmonize and fine-tune energies, or else they claim to improve the circulation of energy by removing obstructions and blockages. Energy should flow uninhibited through the body, and through their relationships with nature and with others – there should be no disruption between the energy of the individual and the energy of the cosmos.

Science and 'the other side'

For over a century, the precursors of the New Age have been drawing on the popular science of the day to construct a model of 'the other side' in terms of various conceptions of energy. In most Western societies in the late nineteenth century, groups of eccentric but otherwise respectable middle-class and aristocratic men and women sought to legitimate their spiritual humanism by extending the bounds of science to include questions previously relegated to theological inquiry or the philosophy of consciousness. Various conceptions of energy were employed to provide natural explanations for the supernatural phenomena of the time, and in particular to provide a mechanism for psychic communication (Albanese, 1990; Alder, 1968).

The counter-culture of the late 1960s and early 1970s devoured and reproduced nineteenth-century spiritualist and occult discourses with unprecedented vigour, often combining them with elements drawn from Asian religions. The counter-culture also drew on the romantic celebration and exploration of nature – the inner nature of altered psychological states and the unconscious, and the outer nature of raw wilderness – which were seen as untainted by modernity's objectifying and desacralizing tendencies. This reinstated a dichotomy evident in psychoanalysis (and especially the sexual liberationist psychoanalytic theories of Willhelm Reich, which had been popular in California) in which a wild and chaotic nature was a powerful weapon to draw upon to undermine a rigid and repressively ordered society. Lewis Mumford, writing in the late 1960s, captured this spirit in observing that:

Since ritual order has now largely passed into mechanical order, the present revolt of the younger generation against the machine has made a practice of promoting disorder and randomness. . . . (1967: 62–3)

The disorder and randomness to be found in the (stoned) mind or in nature came to be seen by the spiritual edge of the counter-culture as antithetical to the dominant values of contemporary Western societies – materialism, egocentrism and militarism. Daniel Bell was to comment a few years later that there was a fundamental cultural contradiction emerging in Western societies, 'a disjunction between the kind of organization and the norms demanded in the economic realm, and the norms of self-realization that are now central in the culture' (1976: 15).

While many on the spiritual end of the counter-cultural spectrum saw science as anathema to the new consciousness, others who sought parallels between scientific and spiritual thought found in quantum physics a branch of science which seemed not only to capture the ultimate disorder and arbitrariness of the universe, but also to emphasize the interrelatedness of apparently discrete phenomena. This was advocated as a more accurate picture of reality than the wishful thinking of a Newtonian physics which painted a picture of a simple mechanical system made up of discrete parts, and which seemed to be, along with Cartesian mind–body dualism, the fundamental assumption made by most branches of science in producing the current mismatch between the material and religious branches of modern human inquiry. Fritjof Capra, drawing on the work of Thomas Kuhn, argued that not just physics, but all of science and the popular understandings which were informed by it, were in the grip of a struggle between two competing paradigms. Science had reached the point, with the advent of quantum physics, at which a reintegration of science and mysticism was possible at last (Capra, 1977). These together made a 'new vision of reality' which was now posing a challenge to the dominant paradigm, 'Cartesian–Newtonian thought'. The new paradigm Capra elaborated drew on Taoist philosophies as expressed in the *I Ching* and which appeared to be complementary with the new physics. Capra posited that '[t]he Chinese philosophers saw reality, whose ultimate essence they called Tao, as a process of continual flow and change' (1983: 17).

According to a New Age reading of the 'new science', inner reality is a continual dance of matter/energy. And although this body of theory deals with the behaviour and nature of sub-atomic particles (which would seem to me to have little to do with the human condition and politics), the New Age seeks to model outer reality on inner reality, thus allowing quantum theory to be claimed as lending scientific credibility to a certain social and political outlook.

The following sections of this chapter deal with the type of social and political beliefs which are based in applying the form of an inner reality to the world of people and things. Throughout this I will explore the contemporary construction of inner reality, and the ways in which this construction leads to a particular understanding of the nature of external reality, the nature of the body, of self-identity and of the more generalized socio-political outlooks which these ontological positions entail.

Technologizing the sacred

The USS *Enterprise*, twenty-third-century spacecraft and setting for *Star Trek: The Next Generation*, features a space called the holodeck which is an empty room where a three-dimensional virtual reality is created by the ship's computer. This virtual space is used for recreation, training and research purposes; and in it simulated objects and people not only look life-like but have physical properties such as weight and texture, so that the show's characters have trouble making out the difference between the simulated and the real when in the holodeck. One episode involves a number of the crew realizing that for a period of a few days, when they thought they were going about their day-to-day tasks but encountering mildly strange occurrences they have actually been trapped inside the holodeck. Their illusion of being on the outside is created by a simulated personality which mysteriously develops a consciousness and is living (as far as the Federation's definition of life is concerned) trapped inside the ship's computer.

There are curious parallels between the reality of the virtual space of the holodeck and the reality of the physical world as conceived by many New Agers. However, according to a New Age ontology, rather than being programmed by the ship's computer, the observable world is shaped from energy into physical form by thought. David Spangler and William Irwin Thompson, in describing Vernor Vinge's *True Names*, an early cyberpunk novel, argue that the virtual worlds of cyberspace described by Vinge (and later William Gibson) provide a model of the relationship between the astral plane and the material world. Cyberspace consists only of data, which are arranged so as to give the appearance of materiality or reality by triggering associations in the user's unconscious. According to Spangler and Thompson, 'this is a computerised version of the astral realms in which patterns and geometries of energy become interpreted by a human con-sciousness as beings, landscapes, and so forth.' (Spangler and Thompson, 1991: 101). The astral plane, the underlying reality, is comprised of energy, as cyberspace is of data, and we interpret this reality by imposing upon it recognizable forms. That is, the physical world, like the reality of the holodeck, is merely a surface which masks the unstable reality underneath:

> Our world is really a buzz of energy that our imaginations interpret as the physical objects and people that we normally see. It is not that those people and objects aren't really there, but they may not be there in the manner in which we perceive them. (Spangler and Thompson, 1991: 101)

Starhawk (formerly Miriam Simos) is one of the biggest names in goddess worship, the feminist wing of the New Age movement. For her,

> the physical world is formed by . . . energy as stalactites are formed by dropping water. If we cause a change in the energy patterns, they in turn will cause a change in the physical world – just as, if we change the course of an underground river, new series of stalactites will be formed in new veins of rock. (Starhawk, 1979: 183)

The appearance of fixity of objects should not be taken too seriously, since underneath at a deeper level of reality all is fluid and changeable by will. At this deeper level,

> all things are swirls of energy, vortexes of moving forces, currents in an ever-changing sea. Underlying the appearance of separateness, of fixed objects within a linear stream of time, reality is a field of energies that congeal, temporarily, into forms. In time, all 'fixed' things dissolve, only to coalesce again into new forms, new vehicles. (Starhawk, 1979: 181)

For this reason goddess-worshipping women prefer to employ powerful rituals which work directly on the underlying flow of energy instead of pursuing more conventional forms of social empowerment, much to the dismay of more materialist feminists such as Rene Denfeld, who has recently launched a tirade against spiritual feminism (Denfeld, 1995).

The practice of using will or imagination to change reality is referred to here as creative visualization. Shakti Gawain, in her seminal work on the subject, explains how creative visualization works:

> Our physical universe is not really composed of any 'matter' at all; its basic component is a kind of force or essence which we call *energy*. . . . Thought is a quick, light, mobile form of energy. It manifests instantaneously, unlike the denser forms such as matter. . . . The idea is like a blueprint; it creates an image of the form, which then magnetizes and guides the physical energy to flow into that form and eventually manifests it on the physical plane. (1982: 5–6; original emphasis)

This is as close as the New Age comes to a scientific explanation of prayer, and Starhawk shares such faith in wishful thinking:

> When our energy is concentrated and channelled . . . it can move the broader energy currents. The images and objects used in spells are the channels, the vessels through which our power is poured and by which it is shaped. When energy is directed into the images we visualize, it gradually manifests physical form and takes shape in the material world. (1979: 183–4)

This particular way of using science for a thorough reconstruction of the sacred has led the New Age to a radically idealist and voluntaristic attitude towards physical reality. It has also allowed for a rethinking of the reality of the mind and its relationship to modern information technology. However, Starhawk has sufficient political understanding to acknowledge that the New Age idea that we create our own reality 'can only conceivably make sense to white upper-middle-class Americans, and then only some of the time' (1990: 37). And while the politicized wing of the New Age acknowledges that 'reality also has the power to shape us', a politics based purely on a 'psychology of liberation', as Starhawk describes her own endeavours, can conceive of collective ritual but not meaningful collective political action (1990: 37).

Selling fast enlightenment

At the same time, the failure to think through the implications of tech-nologization of the sacred has undermined the earlier counter-cultural defence of the 'human' in the face of the 'mechanical' reshaping of lived experience, and resulted instead in the New Age playing a central role in the technologization of self-identity in late capitalism. It is a truism in New Age circles that most of us use only 10 per cent of our mental capacity. According to any number of mind expansion advocates, neuroscience has found that 90 per cent of the brain's neurons go unused in cognitive activities, although what this figure might mean is never fully elaborated. Einstein supposedly estimated that he only ever used 35 per cent of his brain. In commenting on this phenomenon, Andrew Ross has argued that desires for increased mental efficiency are part of a broader 'yuppie work ethic' of relatively well-paid intellectual workers who have more spare money than time. A blurring of the boundaries between work and leisure for this group results in notions of productivity and efficiency spreading into the private sphere – where one 'works' on a tan or spends smaller amounts of 'quality' time with loved ones, and where the difference between socializing and networking becomes confused. It is in this cultural context that an obsession with mental performance readily takes hold (Ross, 1991).

Numerous psychotechnologies claim to be able to improve mental performance to a full 100 per cent of potential. This is achieved by syn-chronizing energy levels in the left and right hemispheres of the cerebellum, and lowering the frequency of brainwaves. At the low-tech end of the spectrum, Transcendental Meditation claims to be able to improve the efficiency of brain activity through the chanting of secret mantras, but only after the client signs a contract promising not to disclose the secret mantra and agrees to pay hundreds of dollars to learn the closely guarded technique.

Others, keen to apply new technologies to assist in self-transformation and in order to facilitate a closer relationship between the inner and outer realities, have developed electronic equipment which they maintain is able to work directly on the innate energies. Digital tools for higher con-sciousness, or 'consciousness tech', are rather crude applications of the logic that a better arrangement of energy in the mind and body, facilitating personal growth and accelerated learning, is able to be achieved through a direct interface between mind and machine, in some cases bypassing the consciousness of the participant completely. Given the appropriate inter-faces, computing power and software, inner reality can be reprogrammed (Hooper and Teresi, 1990).

One of the most prominent of the mind technicians is Master Charles (formerly Brother Charles). His genius was to realize that what he and other devotees had actually been doing during the years they had spent in an ashram while performing Vedic rituals, meditating and chanting was using mantras to rescript their databases. He concluded that the psychic effects of caves, long noted by high-country yogis, are actually due to the correspondence and harmonizing of the cave's echo interval with certain brainwave frequencies. Master Charles left the ashram and set about producing a shortcut to nirvana in the form of a series of audiotapes which exploit the consciousness-altering properties of certain frequencies in a more convenient manner. Master Charles claims to have accelerated traditional spiritual growth by 75 per cent, boasting 'we've got the cave experience of fifty years down to twelve – that's a big breakthrough!' (quoted in Hooper and Teresi, 1990: 168). In doing so he developed 'contemporary high-tech meditation' and founded an organization he called Multidimensional Synchronicity Through Holodynamics to spread the word, the tapes and the seminars. 'After all,' he says, 'we are Americans. We have created McDonald's. If we can create fast foods, can we not create fast enlightenment?' (quoted in Hooper and Teresi, 1990: 71).

In employing external energy sources the New Age advocates of consciousness tech must argue that, rather than overwhelming the body's energies, external energy sources are compatible with life-force energy (Ross, 1991). Medicine is routinely criticized in New Age circles, for example, for working against the life-force energy with pharmaceuticals and invasive procedures, in contrast to 'natural' therapies which are said to foster innate energies which facilitate self-healing. There are many New Agers who are unwilling to equate electrical energy in digital form with the body's own life-force. But this is not a problem for Master Charles, who refers to the mind as a 'conceptual database' and calls his brand of meditation a 'precision brain-enhancement technology' (1994: 39–41).

The more sophisticated brain machines comprise a small computerized black box attached to a set of earphones and pair of goggles with a number of multi-coloured lights inside them. These crude virtual reality headsets function by accompanying audio signals similar to those used by the mono-sensory audio systems (such as Master Charles's), with lights flashing in carefully chosen combinations of frequency and colour for the desired mental state. A 1993 advertisement for Melbourne's Innerquest Mind Fitness Centre challenges psychic sloths to '[i]mprove your inner vision, tone up your mental muscle!' by merely relaxing while wearing one of these light and sound sets. 'Mental clarity. . . . Some are born with it [picture of Einstein]. For the rest of us there exists a unique way to improve our mental fitness . . . Synetic Systems' light/sound technology.' According to the advertising literature, the flashing lights and digital tones induce altered brain states without any effort on the part of the purchaser, who remains completely passive. 'No mantra, no guru, no kidding!' Another such virtual reality spin-off, the SuperMind™ system, comes with software, or 'mindware' as the advertisers have dubbed it, which creates 'moodscapes' on environmental themes such as Spring Day ('Bathe in a warm breeze, as the scent of flowers fills the air. A soothing stream and the sounds of birds celebrate the ecstasy of aliveness'). The sensuality of the scene being painted is repeatedly referred to, yet the product is attempting to commodify a replicated feeling of aliveness which only comes from the bodily experience of feeling warm air, smelling flowers, and so on. In order to impress consumers with the prospect of such a tacky simulation, the product's promoters rely on allusions to the New Age's favourite government agency, NASA, and its pathbreaking advances:

> I put on my space age shades, plugged in the Thunderstorm soundtrack, and programmed the *SuperMind*™ computer for a 'heavy-duty' Theta session. As I punched the start button I was reminded of NASA's virtual reality machines. Those billion dollar video games that transport your consciousness into an artificial computer world you manipulate with voice commands and gestures. (SuperMind advertisement, 1993)

High technology and the evolution of consciousness

Quite apart from desires for personal productivity and efficiency, the expansion of mental capabilities is positioned as a central factor in the next phase of human evolution. New Age writers claim that humanity is passing from a phase of physical evolution, which emphasizes external forms of power over others and over nature, to a phase of evolution of consciousness and soul, whose corresponding form of power is a non-dominative self-empowerment (Zukav, 1989: 19–32). A notable mainstream expression of the connection between the virtual reality interface and the evolution of consciousness is Stephen King's *The Lawnmower Man*, one of Hollywood's first encounters with virtual reality. While experimenting with a full-body virtual reality interface, the researcher undergoes a strange transformation and develops superhuman physical strength, astounding intelligence and the ability to communicate telepathically; and finally he achieves a God-like state of being able to exercise control over physical reality, making objects fly around and overturning cars, through an exercise of will. The mental control over external reality by mastery of inner reality, which Starhawk and the advocates of creative visualization argue is possible, is mastered through the Lawnmower Man's accelerated rate of psychic evolution. With his mental efficiency enhanced by smart drugs and liberated from the constraints of embodiment, the mind of the Lawnmower Man is able to interact with the mountain of information in cyberspace, and in the end his soul escapes his body to exist as a pure consciousness in an electronic neural network made up of digital information. In this case the awesome power which is attained through technological enhancement of psychic abilities falls into the hands of one who lacks spiritual and emotional maturity. *The Lawnmower Man* plays out a New Age fantasy in which information technology allows for heightened experience of inner reality through more efficient tools for working with energy. The connection of minds in cyberspace through much more direct virtual reality interfaces is equated with the unification of souls on the astral plane. This is the absurd end-point of an alignment of energy with spirituality with digital information, in which computer networks provide an opportunity for transcendence and escape from the confines of embodiment, and in which the flow of electronic information is more like inner reality than flesh is. With a New Age understanding of energy as the stuff of the inner reality, high-tech spiritual connection on an electronic higher plane becomes merely a problem of translation.

Another way in which the 'holistic' New Age seeks to get around the limitations that embodiment places on the striving of the will is to reconceptualize the body as an infinitely malleable fluid object, able to be thoroughly reshaped in line with any self-transformative project. A New Age understanding of embodiment has in recent decades found its way into the mainstream through the popularizing of alternative health care modalities. Objecting to mechanical models employed by the biosciences, most alternative therapies prefer a model of embodiment which emphasizes the fluid. Wellbeing is maintained by the healthy flow of internal energies by which the body heals itself (Fulder, 1996). A flyer for Mary-Lou Myers' Psychodynamic Massage and Somatic Integration Therapy, distributed in Melbourne in 1994, is a typical expression of the fluid ontology of the inner body. It quotes Stanley Keleman (author of the curiously titled *Living Your Dying*), who observes that: 'The body is not an object, it is not even a concrete event, it is not even materialistic. It's a molecular process. It's a moving event.' Because these energies which comprise the inner reality of the body are able to be manipulated by the power of will, and since, as far as the body is concerned, New Age discourse is replete with references to physical reality as the outward expression of the 'programming' of inner reality, it follows that by rescripting one's inner self one can alter one's own physical reality. Deepak Chopra, author of numerous top-selling self-help books including *Quantum Healing*, argues that in order to be able 'to change the printouts of our bodies, we must learn to rewrite the software of our minds' (Chopra, 1993). While the emphasis of alternative therapies on the interrelationship between mental, emotional and physical health is very valuable, there is often a tendency towards a naive individualism which can result in victim blaming through a lack of attention to the social (as opposed to personal) nature of health and illness (Coward, 1989).

The inner self conceived of by the New Age is at once eternal and universal, but also ever-changing and unstable. The more unstable outer identity becomes, and the more readily one transforms one's own sense of self with regard to the latest commodified identity form, the more one is said to be getting in touch with the fluidity of the underlying reality. This essentialism is a means of coping with the ontological crises which are associated with such unstable forms of self-identity. In the present, as the comparatively stable social structures of modernity such as the nuclear family, class identities, and so on, give way to seemingly less restrictive postmodern institutions, numerous cultural movements (and here we can lump together the New Right and the New Age as well as neo-nationalism) search for existential anchors to ground the destabilized self amid this sense of flux.

The mainstreaming of the New Age

My argument so far has been that the New Age movement has acted to facilitate rather than counter the contemporary techno-scientific redefinition of what it is to be human. By relying on individualistic and idealist understandings of power and social change, and on a corresponding failure to articulate a critique of the structural features which produce the characteristically postmodern sense of alienation driving the inward search for the sacred, the New Age too often ends up encouraging the disillusioned to embrace the ontological fluidity which produces such deep personal crises in the first place. By stripping away the outer socialized layers of the self, the New Age encourages the abandonment of those older and deeper forms of social meanings constituted within communities and across generations, in favour of the commodified pop-psychological packages peddled by the slick and soft-focused Aquarian salespeople.

Perhaps the most visible sign of the New Age's encouragement of personal transformation in order to accommodate oneself to depersonalizing systems is in the shifting of New Age attitudes to materialism and corporate culture (Ostrow, 1995). In studying the prevalence of New Age ideologies and self-transformative techniques in management training in the late 1980s and 1990s, Paul Heelas and Richard Roberts have been interested in how, given that the New Age has so much in common with the counter-culture which emphasized dropping out of the rat race to avoid modernity's contamination of the soul, the same spiritual beliefs are now seemingly so much at home in the world of big business (Heelas, 1992; Roberts, 1994).

While alternative New Agers who have retained a counter-cultural opposition to mainstream lifestyles consider the 'external' trappings of consumerism as unhealthy distractions from inner happiness, mainstream New Agers often treat success in the market as expressive of an inner godliness, in much the same way as those early capitalists who were the subject of Weber's classic study (Heelas, 1992). Success in work and material wealth are not revered in themselves but as signs of general wellbeing, of being in touch with one's inner self and therefore able to control one's material reality at will. Heelas argues that the contradiction Bell describes between the cultural demands for self-realization and systemic need for rational organization is able to be overcome in the mainstream New Age by spiritualizing the rewards of working life: finding meaning by interpreting conventional materialism through the filter of an inward-looking religiosity.

At the same time as this transformation has taken place in the New Age's attitude to wealth and work, far-reaching changes have occurred in the nature of the work with which New Agers have recently been involved. Increasingly, working life in contemporary Western societies demands a degree of ontological flexibility. Personality is increasingly becoming a raw material for commercial exploitation by employers who view their employees' motivations, attitudes and interpersonal skills as 'resources' (McDonald, 1993/4). New Age self-transformative practices are tools with which people can remake themselves much more readily while attaching some greater meaning to the loss of a stable sense of self and loss of a predictable social environment, thereby enabling some people to thrive in the ontological turbulence surrounding postmodern flexibility. Richards describes the role of New Age ideologies in encouraging workers to be autonomous, self-steering and entrepreneurial in the face of the dismantling of corporate structures which are claimed to have encouraged dependency (Roberts, 1994). As management adopts models of organizational control which emphasize the devolution of power and enhanced reflexivity on the part of individuals and groups within the organization, there is a need to change the 'culture' of the workplace, either by retrenching and rehiring on a casual basis or through personality and behavioural modification of existing workers. In this latter project of instilling desired motivations in a workforce, the New Age has been very successful in selling its services to corporations, governments and the self-employed, to the extent that it is now not uncommon for management training to employ New Age notions of 'empowerment' and 'enabling' to facilitate 'self-transformation' (Roberts, 1994). The New Age's celebration of constant change as meaningful in itself and closer to the natural state of affairs is put to corporate use in allaying the very real personal fears involved in losing job security. Whether it be in the workplace, at the interface between the high-tech and the human, or more generally in celebrating the fluid forms of personality created by the commodification of self-identity, the New Age is not in any major way working against the dominant structural forces but is instead trying to clear the psychological and social barriers which stand in their way.

Note

Thanks to Paul James for valuable insights and comments on early drafts of this chapter.

References

Albanese, Catherine (1990) *Nature Religion in America*. London: University of Chicago Press.
Alder, Vera Stanley (1968) *The Finding of the Third Eye*. London: Rider.
Bell, Daniel (1976) *The Cultural Contradictions of Capitalism*. London: Heinemann.
Capra, Fritjof (1977) *The Tao of Physics: An Exploration of the Parallels between Modern Physics and Eastern Mysticism*. New York: Bantam Books.
Capra, Fritjof (1983) *The Turning Point: Science, Society and the Rising Culture*. London: Fontana.
Chopra, Deepak (1993) Flyer for a seminar entitled 'It's Real Magic: The A–Z of Wealth Consciousness', Melbourne.
Coward, Rosalind (1989) *The Whole Truth: The Myth of Alternative Health*. London and Boston: Faber and Faber.

Denfeld, Rene (1995) *The New Victorians: A Young Woman's Challenge to the Old Feminist Order*. St Leonards, NSW: Allen and Unwin.

Fulder, Stephen (1996) *The Handbook of Complementary Medicine*. New York: Oxford University Press.

Gawain, Shakti (1982) *Creative Visualization*. New York: Bantam.

Heelas, Paul (1992) 'The Sacralization of the Self and New Age Capitalism', in Nicholas Abercrombie and Alan Warde (eds), *Social Change in Contemporary Britain*. Cambridge: Polity. pp. 139–66.

Heelas, Paul (1993) 'The New Age in Cultural Context: The Premodern, the Modern and the Postmodern', *Religion*, 23: 103–16.

Hetzel, Richard (1989) 'A Healing Perspective', in Richard Hetzel (ed.), *The Healing Arts*. Ferntree Gully, VIC: Houghton Mifflin.

Hooper, Judith and Teresi, Dick (1990) *Would the Buddha Wear a Walkman? A Catalogue of Revolutionary Tools for Higher Consciousness*. New York: Simon and Schuster.

McDonald, Kevin (1993/4) 'On Work', *Arena Journal*, 2: 33–42.

Master Charles (1994) 'Nirvana Access – 1990's Style', *Golden Age* (Sydney), 21: 39–41.

Mumford, Lewis (1967) *The Myth of the Machine*, Vol. I, *Technics and Human Development*. San Diego: Harcourt Brace Jovanovich.

Ostrow, Ruth (1995) 'The Taming of the Beast', *The Australian* (Weekend Review supplement), 9–10 September: 3.

Roberts, Richard H. (1994) 'Power and Empowerment: New Age Managers and the Dialectics of Modernity/Postmodernity', *Religion Today*, 9 (9): 3–13.

Ross, Andrew (1991) *Strange Weather: Culture, Science, and Technology in the Age of Limits*. London: Verso.

Samuel Weiser Inc. (1995) *Distribution Catalog*. York Beach, ME: Samuel Weiser.

Spangler, David and Thompson, William Irwin (1991) *Reimagination of the World: A Critique of the New Age, Science, and Popular Culture*. Santa Fe: Bear.

Starhawk (1979) *The Spiral Dance: A Rebirth of the Ancient Religion of the Great Goddess*. San Francisco: Harper and Row.

Starhawk (1990) *Truth or Dare: Encounters with Power, Authority and Mystery*. San Francisco: Harper.

Storm, Rachel (1991) *In Search of Heaven on Earth*. London: Bloomsbury.

SuperMind advertisement (1993) *Magical Blend*, 39: 24.

Zukav, Gary (1989) *The Seat of the Soul*. New York: Simon and Schuster.

12

CYBERDEMOCRACY:
The Internet and the Public Sphere

Mark Poster

I am an advertisement for a version of myself.

(David Byrne)

The stakes of the question

The discussion of the political impact of the Internet has focused on a
number of issues: access, technological determinism, encryption, commodification, intellectual property, the public sphere, decentralization, anarchy,
gender and ethnicity. While these issues may be addressed from a number
of standpoints, only some of them are able to assess the full extent of what
is at stake in the new communications technology at the cultural level of
identity formation. If questions are framed in relation to prevailing political
structures, forces and ideologies, for example, blinders are being imposed
which exclude the question of the subject or identity construction from the
domain of discussion. Instances of such apparently urgent but actually
limiting questions are those of encryption and commodification. In the case
of encryption, the United States government seeks to secure its borders
from 'terrorists' who might use the Internet and thereby threaten it. But the
dangers to the population are and have always been far greater from this
state apparatus itself than from so-called 'terrorists'. More citizens have
been improperly abused, had their civil rights violated, and much worse, by
the government than by terrorists. In fact terrorism is in good part an effect
of government propaganda; it serves to deflect attention from governmental
abuse toward a mostly imagined, highly dangerous outside enemy. If the
prospects of democracy on the Internet are viewed in terms of encryption,
then the security of the existing national government becomes the limit of
the matter: what is secure for the nation-state is taken to mean true security
for everyone, a highly dubious proposition.[1] The question of the potential
for new forms of social space which might empower individuals in new
ways is foreclosed in favour of preserving existing relations of force as they
are viewed by the most powerful institution in the history of the world, the
government of the United States.

The issue of commodification also affords a narrow focus, often restricting the discussion of the politics of the Internet to the question of which corporation or which type of corporation will be able to obtain what amount of income from which configuration of the Internet. Will the telephone companies, the cable companies or some amalgam of both be able to secure adequate markets and profits by providing the general public with railroad time-tables, five hundred channels of television, the movie of one's choice on demand, and so forth? From this vantage point the questions raised are as follows: Will the Internet be used to deliver entertainment products, like some gigantic, virtual theme park? Or will it be used to sell commodities, functioning as an electronic retail store or mall? These questions consume corporate managers around the country and their Marxist critics alike; though here again, as with the encryption issue, the Internet is being understood as an extension of or substitution for existing institutions. There is no doubt that the Internet folds into existing social functions and extends them in new ways, translating the act of shopping, for example, into an electronic form. But the ways in which it institutes new social functions, ones that do not fit easily within those of characteristically modern organizations, are far more cogent in suggesting possible long-term political effects of the Internet. The problem is that these new functions can only become intelligible if a framework is adopted that does not limit the discussion from the outset to modern patterns of interpretation. For example, if one understands politics as the restriction or expansion of the existing executive, legislative and judicial branches of government, one will not be able even to broach the question of new types of participation in government. To ask then about the relation of the Internet to democracy is to challenge or to risk challenging our existing theoretical approaches and concepts as they concern these questions.

If one places in brackets political theories that address modern governmental institutions in order to open the path to an assessment of the 'postmodern' possibilities suggested by the Internet, two difficulties immediately emerge: (1) there is no adequate 'postmodern' theory of politics and (2) the issue of democracy, the dominant political norm and ideal, is itself a 'modern' category associated with the project of the Enlightenment. Let me address these issues in turn.

Recently theorists such as Philippe Lacoue-Labarthe (1990) and Jean-Luc Nancy (1991) have pointed to the limitations of a 'left/right' spectrum of ideologies for addressing contemporary political issues. Deriving from seating arrangements of legislators during the French Revolution of 1789, the modern ideological spectrum inscribes a grand narrative of liberation which contains several problematic aspects. First, it installs a linear, evolutionary and progressive history which occludes the differential temporalities of non-Western groups and women, and imposes a totalizing, strong interpretation of the past which erases from view gaps, discontinuities, improbabilities, contingencies, in short a panoply of phenomena that might better be approached from a non-linear perspective. Second, the

Enlightenment narrative establishes a process of liberation at the heart of history which requires at its base a pre-social, foundational, individual identity. The individual is posited as outside of and prior to history, only later becoming ensnared in externally imposed chains. Politics for this modern perspective is then the arduous extraction of an autonomous agent from the contingent obstacles imposed by the past. In its rush to ontologize freedom, the modern view of the subject hides the process of its historical construction. A postmodern orientation would have to allow for the constitution of identity within the social and within language, displacing the question of freedom from a presupposition of and a conclusion to theory, to become instead a pre-theoretical or non-foundational discursive preference. Postmodern theorists have discovered that modern theory's insistence on the freedom of the subject, its compulsive, repetitive inscription into discourse of the sign of the resisting agent, functions to restrict the shape of identity to its modern form, an ideological and legitimizing gesture of its own position rather than a step towards emancipation. If a postmodern perspective is to avoid the limits of modern theory, it is proscribed from ontologizing any form of the subject. The postmodern position is limited to an insistence on the constructedness of identity. In the effort to avoid the pitfalls of modern political theory then, postmodern theory sharply restricts the scope of its ability to define a new political direction. This theoretical asceticism is a contemporary condition of discourse imposing an unusual discipline and requiring a considerable suspension of disbelief on the part of the audience. To sceptics it can only be said that the alternatives, those of 'modern' positions, are even less desirable.

But there are further difficulties in establishing a position from which to recognize and analyse the cultural aspect of the Internet. For postmodern theory still invokes the modern term 'democracy', even when this is modified by the adjective 'radical', as in the work of Ernesto Laclau (1990). One may characterize postmodern or post-Marxist democracy in Laclau's terms as one that opens new positions of speech, empowering previously excluded groups and enabling new aspects of social life to become part of the political process. While the Internet is often accused of elitism (a mere 30 million users), there does exist a growing and vibrant grass-roots participation in it organized in part by local public libraries (Polly and Cisler, 1994: 22–3). But are not these initiatives, the modern sceptic may persist, simply extensions of existing political institutions rather than being 'post', rather than being a break of some kind? In response I can assert only that the 'postmodern' position need not be taken as a metaphysical assertion of a new age; that theorists are trapped within existing frameworks as much as they may be critical of them and wish not to be; that, in the absence of a coherent alternative political programme, the best one can do is to examine phenomena such as the Internet in relation to new forms of the old democracy, while holding open the possibility that what might emerge might be something other than democracy in any shape that we may conceive it given our embeddedness in the present. Democracy, the rule by all, is surely preferable to its historical alternatives. And the term may yet contain critical potentials since existing forms of democracy surely do not fulfil the promise of freedom and equality. The colonization of the term by existing institutions encourages one to look elsewhere for the means to name the new patterns of force relations emerging in certain parts of the Internet.

Decentralized technology

My plea for indulgence with the limitations of the postmodern position on politics quickly gains credibility when the old question of technological determinism is posed in relation to the Internet. For when the question of technology is posed we may see immediately how the Internet disrupts the basic assumptions of the older positions. The Internet is above all a decentralized communication system. Like the telephone network, anyone hooked up to the Internet may initiate a call, send a message that he or she has composed, and may do so in the manner of the broadcast system, that is to say, may send a message to many receivers, and do this either in 'real time' or as stored data or both. The Internet is also decentralized at a basic level of organization since, as a network of networks, new networks may be added so long as they conform to certain communications protocols. As a historian I find it fascinating that this unique structure should emerge from a confluence of cultural communities which appear to have so little in common: the Cold War Defense Department, which sought to insure survival against nuclear attack by promoting decentralization, the counter-cultural ethos of computer programming engineers, which had a deep distaste for any form of censorship or active restraint of communications, and the world of university research, which I am at a loss to characterize. Added to this is a technological substratum of digital electronics which unifies all symbolic forms in a single system of codes, rendering trans-mission instantaneous and duplication effortless. If the technological structure of the Internet institutes costless reproduction, instantaneous dissemination and radical decentralization, what might be its effects upon the society, the culture and the political institutions?

There can be only one answer to this question, which is that it is the wrong question. Technologically determined effects derive from a broad set of assumptions in which what is technological is a configuration of materials which affect other materials; and the relation between the tech-nology and human beings is external, that is, where human beings are understood to manipulate the materials for ends that they impose upon the technology from a preconstituted position of subjectivity. But what the Internet technology imposes is a dematerialization of communication and, in many of its aspects, a transformation of the subject position of the individual who engages within it. The Internet resists the basic conditions for asking the question of the effects of technology. It installs a new regime of relations between humans and matter, and between matter and non-matter, reconfiguring the relation of technology to culture and thereby undermining the standpoint from within which, in the past, a discourse developed – one which appeared to be natural – about the effects of technology. The only way to define the technological effects of the Internet is to build the Internet, to set in place a series of relations which constitute an electronic geography. While this may be true as well for other communications technologies, none but the Internet so drastically reconfigures the basic conditions of speech and reception.

Put differently, the Internet is more like a social space than a thing so that its effects are more like those of Germany than those of hammers. The effects of Germany on the people within it is to make them Germans (at least for the most part); the effects of hammers is not to make people hammers, though Heideggerians and some others might disagree, but to force metal spikes into wood.[2] As long as we understand the Internet as a hammer we will fail to discern the way it is like Germany. The problem is that modern perspectives tend to reduce the Internet to a hammer. In this grand narrative of modernity, the Internet is an efficient tool of communication, advancing the goals of its users who are understood as preconstituted instrumental identities.

The Internet, I suppose like Germany, is complex enough so that it may with some profit be viewed in part as a hammer. If I search the database functions of the Internet or if I send email purely as a substitute for paper mail, then its effects may reasonably be seen to be those on the order of the hammer. The database on the Internet may be more easily or cheaply accessed than its alternatives and the same may be said of email in relation to the post office or the fax machine. But the aspects of the Internet that I would like to underscore are those which instantiate new forms of interaction and which pose the question of new kinds of relations of power between participants. The question that needs to be asked about the relation of the Internet to democracy is this: are there new kinds of relations occurring within it which suggest new forms of power configurations between communicating individuals? In other words, is there a new politics on the Internet? One way to approach this question is to make a detour from the issue of technology and raise again the question of a public sphere, gauging the extent to which Internet democracy may become intelligible in relation to it. To frame the issue of the political nature of the Internet in relation to the concept of the public sphere is particularly appropriate because of the spatial metaphor associated with the term. Instead of an immediate reference to the structure of an institution, which is often a formalist argument over procedures, or to the claims of a given social group, which assumes a certain figure of agency that I would like to keep in suspense, the notion of a public sphere suggests an arena of exchange, like the ancient Greek agora or the colonial New England town hall. If there is a public sphere on the Internet, who populates it and how? In particular one must ask what kinds of beings exchange information in this public sphere? Since there occurs no face-to-face interaction, only electronic flickers on a screen, what kind of community can there be in this space?[3] What kind of peculiar, virtual embodiment of politics is inscribed so evanescently in cyberspace? Modernist curmudgeons may object vehemently against attributing to information flows on the Internet the dignified term 'community'. Are they correct, and if so, what sort of phenomenon is this cyberdemocracy?

The Internet as a public sphere?

The issue of the public sphere is at the heart of any reconceptualization of democracy. Contemporary social relations seem to be devoid of a basic level of interactive practice which, in the past, was the matrix of democratizing politics: loci such as the agora, the New England town hall, the village church, the coffee house, the tavern, the public square, a convenient barn, a union hall, a park, a factory lunchroom, and even a street corner. Many of these places remain but no longer serve as organizing centres for political discussion and action. It appears that the media, especially television but also other forms of electronic communication, isolate citizens from one another and substitute themselves for older spaces of politics. An example from the Clinton health-care reform campaign will suffice: the Clinton forces at one point (mid-July 1994) felt that Congress was less favourable to their proposal than were the general population. To convince the Congress of the wisdom of health-care reform, the administration purchased television advertising which depicted ordinary citizens speaking in favour of the legislation. The ads were shown *only in Washington, DC*, because they were directed not at the general population of viewers but at congressmen and congresswomen alone. The executive branch deployed the media directly on the legislative branch. Such are politics in the era of the mode of information. In a context like this, one may ask where is the public sphere, where is the place citizens interact to form opinions in relation to which public policy must be attuned? John Hartley makes the bold and convincing argument that the media *are* the public sphere: 'Television, popular newspapers, magazines and photography, the popular media of the modern period, are the public domain, the place where and the means by which the public is created and has its being' (1992: 1).[4] The same claim is offered by Paul Virilio: 'Avenues and public venues from now on are eclipsed by the screen, by electronic displays, in a preview of the "vision machines" just around the corner' (1994: 64). 'Public' tends more and more to slide into 'publicity' as 'character' is replaced by 'image'. These changes must be examined without nostalgia and the retrospective glance of modernist politics and theory.

Sensing a collapse of the public sphere and therefore a crisis of democratic politics, Jürgen Habermas published *The Structural Transformation of the Public Sphere* in 1962. In this highly influential work he traced the development of a democratic public sphere in the seventeenth and eighteenth centuries and charted its course to its decline in the twentieth century (Habermas, 1989). Then, and arguably since, Habermas's political intent was to further 'the project of Enlightenment' by the reconstruction of a public sphere in which reason might prevail, not the instrumental reason of much modern practice but the critical reason that represents the best of the democratic tradition. Habermas defined the public sphere as a domain of uncoerced conversation oriented towards a pragmatic accord. His position came under attack by poststructuralists like Lyotard (1984), who questioned the emancipatory potentials of its model of consensus through rational debate. At issue was the poststructuralist critique of Habermas's Enlightenment ideal of the autonomous rational subject as a universal foundation for democracy. Before deploying the category of the public sphere to evaluate democracy on the Internet, I shall turn to recent developments in the debate over Habermas's position.

In the 1980s Lyotard's critique was expanded by feminists like Nancy Fraser (1989, 1990), who demonstrated the gender blindness in Habermas's position.[5] Even before the poststructuralists and feminists, Oskar Negt and Alexander Kluge began the critique of Habermas by articulating the notion of an *oppositional* public sphere, specifically that of the proletariat. What is important about their argument, as demonstrated so clearly by Miriam Hansen, is that Negt and Kluge shifted the terrain of the notion of the public sphere from a historico-transcendental idealization of the Enlightenment to a plurality and heterotopia of discourses. This crucial change in the notion of the public sphere assumes its full significance when it is seen in relation to liberal democracy. The great ideological fiction of liberalism is to reduce the public sphere to existing democratic institutions. Habermas's critique of liberalism counterposes a radical alternative to it but one that still universalizes and monopolizes the political. Negt and Kluge, in contrast, decentralize and multiply the public sphere, opening a path of critique and possibly a new politics (Negt and Kluge, 1993).[6]

The final step in the development of the concept of the public sphere came with Rita Felski's synthesis of Negt/Kluge with both feminist gender analysis and the poststructuralist critique of the autonomous subject. For Felski the concept of the public sphere must build on the 'experience' of political protest (in the sense of Negt and Kluge), must acknowledge and amplify the multiplicity of the subject (in the sense of poststructuralism), and must account for gender differences (in the sense of feminism). She writes:

> Unlike the bourgeois public sphere, then, the feminist public sphere does not claim a representative universality but rather offers a critique of cultural values from the standpoint of women as a marginalized group within society. In this sense it constitutes a *partial* or counter-public sphere. . . . Yet insofar as it is a *public* sphere, its arguments are also directed outward, toward a dissemination of feminist ideas and values throughout society as a whole. (1989: 167)

Felski seriously revises the Habermasian notion of the public sphere, separating it from its patriarchal, bourgeois and logocentric attachments perhaps, but nonetheless still invoking the notion of a public sphere and more or less reducing politics to it. This becomes clear in the conclusion of her argument:

Some form of appeal to collective identity and solidarity is a necessary precondition for the emergence and effectiveness of an oppositional movement; feminist theorists who reject any notion of a unifying identity as a repressive fiction in favor of a stress on absolute difference fail to show how such diversity and fragmentation can be reconciled with goal-oriented political struggles based upon common interests. An appeal to a shared experience of oppression provides the starting point from which women as a group can open upon the problematic of gender, at the same time as this notion of gendered community contains a strongly utopian dimension. . . . (1989: 168–9)

In the end Felski sees the public sphere as central to feminist politics. But then we must ask how this public sphere is to be distinguished from any political discussion. From the heights of Habermas's impossible (counterfactual) ideal of rational communication, the public sphere here multiplies, opens and extends to political discussion by all oppressed individuals.

The problem we face is that of defining the term 'public'. Liberal theory generally resorted to the ancient Greek distinction between the family or household and the polis, the former being 'private' and the latter 'public'. When the term crossed boundaries from political to economic theory, with Ricardo and Marx, a complication set in: the term 'political economy' combined the Greek sense of public and the Greek sense of private, since economy referred for them to the governance of the (private) household. The older usage preserved a space for the public in the agora, to be sure, but referred to discussions about the general good, not market transactions. In the newer usage the economic realm is termed 'political economy' but is considered 'private'. To make matters worse, common parlance nowadays has the term 'private' designating speeches and actions that are isolated, unobserved by anyone and not recorded or monitored by any machine.[7] Privacy now becomes restricted to the space of the home, in a sense returning to the ancient Greek usage, even though family structure has altered dramatically in the interim. In Fraser's argument, for example, the 'public' sphere is the opposite of the 'private' sphere in the sense that it is a locus of 'talk', 'a space in which citizens deliberate about their common affairs' and is essential to democracy (Fraser, 1990: 57). There are serious problems then in using the term 'public' in relation to a politics of emancipation.

This difficulty is amplified considerably once newer electronically mediated communications are taken into account, in particular the Internet. Now the question of 'talk', of meeting face-to-face, of 'public' discourse, is confused and complicated by the electronic form of exchange of symbols. If 'public' discourse exists as pixels on screens generated at remote locations by individuals one has never met and probably will never meet, as it is in the case of the Internet with its 'virtual communities', 'electronic cafés', bulletin boards, email, computer conferencing and even video conferencing, then how is it to be distinguished from 'private' letters, printface, and so forth. The age of the public sphere as face-to-face talk is clearly over: the question of democracy must henceforth take into account new forms of electronically mediated discourse. What are the conditions of democratic speech in the mode of information? What kind of 'subject' speaks or writes or communicates in these conditions? What is its relation to machines? What complexes of subjects, bodies and machines are required for democratic exchange and emancipatory action? For Habermas, the public sphere is a homogeneous space of embodied subjects in symmetrical relations, pursuing consensus through the critique of arguments and the presentation of validity claims. This model, I contend, is systematically denied in the arenas of electronic politics. We are advised then to abandon Habermas's concept of the public sphere in assessing the Internet as a political domain.

Against my contention, Judith Perrolle turns to a Habermasian perspective to look at conversations on bulletin boards and finds that the conditions of the ideal speech situation do not apply. She contends that these conversations are 'distorted' by a level of machine control: here validity 'claims of meaningfulness, truth, sincerity and appropriateness . . . appear to be physical or logical characteristics of the machine rather than an outcome of human negotiation' (Perrolle, 1991: 351). The basic conditions for speech are configured in the program of the virtual community and remain outside the arena of discussion. She continues: 'Most computer interfaces are either not designed to allow the user to question data validity, or else designed so that data may be changed by anyone with a moderate level of technical skill' (1991: 354). While this argument cannot be refuted from within the framework of Habermas's theory of communicative action, the question remains whether these criteria are able to capture the specific qualities of the electronic forms of interaction.

Now that the thick culture of information machines provides the interface for much if not most discourse on political issues, the fiction of the democratic community of full human presence serves only to obscure critical reflection and divert the development of a political theory of this decidedly postmodern condition. For too long critical theory has insisted on a public sphere, bemoaning the fact of media 'interference', the static of first radio's, then television's role in politics. But the fact is that political discourse has long been mediated by electronic machines: the issue now is that the machines enable new forms of decentralized dialogue and create new combinations of human–machine assemblages, new individual and collective 'voices', 'spectres', 'interactivities', which are the new building blocks of political formations and groupings. As Paul Virilio writes, 'What remains of the notion of things "public" when public *images* (in real time) are more important than public *space?*' (1993: 9; original emphasis). If the technological basis of the media has habitually been viewed as a threat to democracy, how can theory account for the turn toward a construction of technology (the Internet) which appears to promote a decentralization of discourse, if not democracy itself, and appears to threaten the state (unmonitorable conversations), mock at private property (the infinite reproducibility of information) and flaunt moral propriety (the dissemination of images of unclothed people often in awkward positions)?

A postmodern technology?

Many areas of the Internet extend pre-existing identities and institutions. Usenet newsgroups elicit obnoxious pranks from teenage boys; databases enable researchers and corporations to retrieve information at lower costs; electronic mail affords speedy, reliable communication of messages; the digitization of images allows a wider distribution of erotic materials, and so it goes. The Internet, then, is modern in the sense of continuing the tradition of tools as efficient means and in the way that prevailing modern cultures transfer their characteristics to the new domain. These issues remain to be studied in detail and from a variety of standpoints, but for the time being the above conclusion may be sustained. Other areas of the Internet are less easy to contain within modern points of view. The examination of these cyberspaces raises the issue of a new understanding of technology and finally leads to a reassessment of the political aspects of the Internet. I refer to the bulletin board services that have come to be known as 'virtual communities', to the MOO phenomenon and to the synthesis of virtual reality technology with the Internet.

In these cases what is at stake is the direct solicitation to construct identities in the course of communication practices. Individuals invent themselves and do so repeatedly and differentially in the course of conversing or messaging electronically. Now there is surely nothing new in discursive practices that are so characterized: reading a novel,[8] speaking on CB radio, indeed watching a television advertisement, I contend, all encourage the individual to shape an identity, in varying degrees and in different ways, in the course of engaging in communication. The case of the limited areas of the Internet listed above, however, goes considerably beyond, or at least is quite distinct from, the latter examples. The individual's performance of the communication requires linguistic acts of self-positioning that are less explicit in the cases of reading a novel or watching a television advertisement. On the Internet, individuals read and interpret communications to themselves and to others and also respond by shaping sentences and transmitting them. Novels and TV ads are interpreted by individuals who are interpellated by them but these readers and viewers are not addressed directly, only as a generalized audience, and, of course, they respond in fully articulated linguistic acts. (I avoid framing the distinction I am making here in the binary active/passive because that couplet is so associated with the modern autonomous agent that it would appear that I am depicting the Internet as the realization of the modern dream: universal, 'active' speech. I refuse this resort because it rests upon the notion of identity as a fixed essence, pre-social and pre-linguistic, whereas I want to argue that Internet discourse constitutes the subject as the subject fashions him- or herself. I want to locate subject constitution at a level which is outside the oppositions of freedom/determinism, activity/passivity.) On the Internet individuals construct their identities, doing so in relation to ongoing dialogues not as acts of pure consciousness. But such activity does not count as freedom in the liberal-Marxist sense because it does not refer back to a foundational subject. Yet it does connote a 'democratization' of subject constitution because the acts of discourse are not limited to one-way address and not constrained by the gender and ethnic traces inscribed in face-to-face communications. The magic of the Internet is that it is a technology that puts cultural acts, symbolizations in all forms, in the hands of all participants; it radically decentralizes the positions of speech, publishing, filmmaking, radio and television broadcasting, in short the apparatuses of cultural production.

Gender and virtual communities

Let us examine the case of gender in Internet communication as a way to clarify what is at stake and to remove some likely confusions about what I am arguing. In real-time chat rooms, MOOs and MUDs, participants must invent identities which consist, as a minimum, of a name and a gender. Gender, unlike age or ethnicity, is thus a general attribute of Internet identities. This gender, however, bears no necessary relation to one's gender in daily life. The gendered body is replaced by the gendered text. Studies have pointed out that the absence of bodily gender cues in bulletin board discussion groups does not eliminate sexism or even the hierarchies of gender that pervade society generally.[9] The disadvantages suffered by women in society carry over into 'the virtual communities' on the Internet: women are underrepresented in these electronic places and they are subject to various forms of harassment and sexual abuse. The fact that sexual identities are self-designated does not in itself eliminate the annoyances and the hurts of patriarchy. Yet Internet social relations are often taken seriously by participants, so much so that gender problems in daily life take on new dimensions in cyberspace. There is an articulation of gender on the Internet that goes beyond the reproduction of real-life hierarchies to instantiate new conditions of inscription.

The case of 'Joan' is instructive in this regard. A man named Alex presented himself on a bulletin board as a disabled woman, 'Joan', in order to experience the 'intimacy' he admired in women's conversations. Alex wanted to talk to women as a woman because of the limitations he perceived in real-life masculine identities. Van Gelder reports that when his 'ruse' was unveiled, many of the women 'Joan' interacted with were deeply hurt. But Van Gelder also reports that their greatest disappointment was that 'Joan' did not exist (1991: 373). The construction of gender in this example indicates a level of complexity not accounted for by the supposition that cultural and social forms are or are not transferable to the Internet. Alex turned to the Internet virtual community to make up for a perceived lack of feminine traits in his masculine sexual identity. The women who suffered his ploy regretted the 'death' of the virtual friend 'Joan'. These are unique uses of virtual communities not easily found in 'reality'. In cyberspace, one may create and live a gendered identity which differs from one's daily life persona; one may build friendships through this identity and experience joy and sadness as these relations develop, change and end. Still in the 'worst' cases, one must admit that the mere fact of communicating under the conditions of the new technology does not cancel the marks of power relations constituted under the conditions of face-to-face, print and electronic broadcasting modes of intercourse.

Nonetheless the structural conditions of communicating in Internet communities do introduce resistances to and breaks with these gender determinations. The fact of having to decide on one's gender itself raises the issue of individual identity in a novel and compelling manner. If one is to be masculine, one must choose to be so. Further, one must enact one's gender choice in language and in language alone, without any marks and gestures of the body, without clothing or intonations of voice. Presenting one's gender is accomplished solely through textual means, although this does include various iconic markings invented in electronic communities such as, for example, emoticons or smilies (:-)). Also one may experience directly the opposite gender by assuming it and enacting it in conversations.[10] Finally the particular configuration of conversation through computers and modems produces a new relation to one's body as it communicates, a cyborg in cyberspace who is different from all the embodied genders of earlier modes of information. These cyborg genders test and transgress the boundaries of the modern gender system without any necessary inclination in that direction on the part of the participant.[11]

If Internet communication does not completely filter out pre-existing technologies of power as it enacts new ones, it reproduces them variably depending on the specific feature of the Internet in question. Some aspects of the Internet, such as electronic mail between individuals who know each other, may introduce no strong disruption of the gender system. In this case, the cyborg individual does not overtake or displace the embodied individual, though even here studies have shown some differences in self-presentation (more spontaneity and less guardedness).[12] From email at one end of the spectrum of modern versus postmodern identity construction, one moves to bulletin board conversations where identities may be fixed and genders unaltered but where strangers are encountered. The next, still more postmodern example would be where identities are invented but the discourse consists in the simple dialogues, as with the case of 'virtual communities' like the WELL. Further removed still from ordinary speech is Internet Relay Chat,[13] in which dialogue occurs in real time with very little hierarchy or structure. Perhaps the fullest novelty enabled by the Internet is in the Multi-User Dimensions, Object Oriented or MOOs, which divide into adventure games and social types. More study needs to be done on the differences between these technologies of subject constitution.

On the MOOs of the social variety, advanced possibilities of postmodern identities are enacted. Here identities are invented and changeable; elaborate self-descriptions are composed; domiciles are depicted in textual form and individuals interact purely for the sake of doing so. MOO inhabitants, however, do not enjoy a democratic utopia. There exist hierarchies specific to this form of cyberspace: the site administrators who initiate and maintain the MOO are able to change rules and procedures in ways which most regular players cannot. After these 'Gods' come the players themselves, who, by dint of experience in the electronic space and with the programming language, accumulate certain skills, even privileges for ease of access to an array of commands. These regular members are distinguished from 'guests' who, as a result of their temporary status, have fewer privileges and fewer skills in negotiating the MOO.[14] Another but far more trivial criterion of political differentiation is typing skill since this determines in part who speaks most often, especially as conversations move along with considerable speed. Even in cyberspace, asymmetries emerge which could be termed 'political inequalities'. Yet the salient characteristic of Internet community is the diminution of prevailing hierarchies of race,[15] class, age, status and especially gender. What appears in the embodied world as irreducible hierarchy plays a lesser role in the cyberspace of MOOs. And as a result the relation of cyberspace to material human geography is decidedly one of rupture and challenge. Internet communities function as places of difference from and resistance to modern society. In a sense, they serve the function of a Habermasian public sphere, however reconfigured, without intentionally or even actually being one. They are places not of the presence of validity-claims or the actuality of critical reason, but of the inscription of new assemblages of self-constitution. When audio and video enhance the current textual mode of conversation the claims of these virtual realities may even become more exigent.[16] The complaint that these electronic villages are no more than the escapism of white, male undergraduates may then become less convincing.

Cyborg politics

The example of the deconstruction of gender in Internet MOO communities illustrates the depth of the stakes in theorizing politics in the mode of information. Because the Internet inscribes the new social figure of the cyborg and institutes a communicative practice of self-constitution, the political as we have known it is reconfigured. The wrapping of language on the Internet, its digitized, machine-mediated signifiers in a space without bodies,[17] introduces an unprecedented novelty for political theory. How will electronic beings be governed? How will their experience of self-constitution rebound in the existing political arena? How will the power relations on the Internet combine with or influence power relations that emerge from face-to-face relations, print relations and broadcast relations? Assuming the US government and the corporations do not shape the Internet entirely in their own image and that places of cyberdemocracy remain and spread to larger and larger segments of the population, what will emerge as a postmodern politics?

If these conditions are met, one possibility is that authority as we have known it will change drastically. The nature of political authority has shifted from embodiment in lineages in the Middle Ages to instrumentally rational mandates from voters in the modern era. In each case a certain aura becomes fetishistically attached to authority holders. In Internet communities such an aura is more difficult to sustain. The Internet seems to discourage the endowment of individuals with inflated status. The example of scholarly research illustrates the point. The formation of canons and authorities is seriously undermined by the electronic nature of texts. Texts become 'hypertexts' which are reconstructed in the act of reading, rendering the reader an author and disrupting the stability of experts or 'authorities'.[18] Similar arguments have been made by Walter Benjamin regarding film and Roland Barthes regarding novels.[19] But the material structure of Internet relations instantiates the reversibility of authorial power at a much more fundamental level than that in film and the novel.

If scholarly authority is challenged and reformed by the location and dissemination of texts on the Internet, it is possible that political authorities will be subject to a similar fate. If the term 'democracy' refers to the sovereignty of embodied individuals and the system of determining office-holders by them, a new term will be required to indicate a relation of leaders and followers that is mediated by cyberspace and constituted in relation to the mobile identities found therein.

Notes

1. For an intelligent review of the battle over encryption see Steven Levy (1994: pp. 44–51, 60, 70).

2. When I wrote this I had forgotten that Heidegger uses the example of the hammer in his discussion of technology in *Being and Time* (1962: 69ff.). I was reminded of this while reading Don Ihde's illuminating work, *Technology and the Lifeworld: From Garden to Earth* (1990: 31–4). Heidegger does not exactly speak of human beings becoming hammers as I suggest but something pretty close: *Dasein* is 'absorbed' in equipment (Heidegger 1962: 102).

3. See N. Katherine Hayles, 'Virtual Bodies and Flickering Signifiers' (1993).

4. Hartley's text is a study of the role of the media in the formation of a public sphere. He examines in particular the role of graphic images in newspapers.

5. See especially Chapter 6, 'What's Critical about Critical Theory? The Case of Habermas', in *Unruly Practices* (Fraser, 1989). For a critique of Habermas's historical analysis see Joan Landes (1988).

6. The foreword to this work, by Miriam Hansen, is essential and important in its own right (Negt and Kluge, 1993: ix–xli).

7. See the discussion of privacy in relation to electronic surveillance in David Lyon, *The Electronic Eye: The Rise of Surveillance Society* (1994: 14–17).

8. Marie-Laure Ryan (1994) presents a subtle, complex comparison of reading a novel and virtual reality. She does not deal directly with MOOs and Internet virtual communities.

9. Lynn Cherny in 'Gender Differences in Text-Based Virtual Reality' (forthcoming) concludes that men and women have gender-specific communications on MOOs. For an analysis of bulletin board conversations which reaches the same pessimistic conclusions, see Susan C. Herring, 'Gender and Democracy in Computer-Mediated Communication' (1993). Herring wants to argue that the Internet does not foster democracy since sexism continues there, but she fails to measure the degree of sexism on bulletin boards against that in face-to-face situations, nor does she even indicate how this would be done.

10. One example of education through gender switching is given by K.K. Campbell in an email message entitled, 'Attack of the Cyber-Weenies'. Campbell explains how he was harassed when he assumed a feminine persona on a bulletin board. I wish to thank Debora Halbert for making me aware of this message.

11. For an excellent study of the cultural implications of virtual communities see Elizabeth Reid, 'Cultural Formations in Text-Based Virtual Realities' (GREF 2).

12. In 'Conversational Structure and Personality Correlates of Electronic Communication', Jill Serpentelli studies the differences in communication pattern on different types of Internet structures (GREF 4). Kiesler, Siegel and McGuire (1991) report that spontaneity and egalitarianism are trends of these conversations.

13. For a fascinating study of IRC see Elizabeth Reid, 'Electropolis: Communication and Community on Internet Relay Chat' (GREF 3).

14. I wish to thank Charles Stivale for pointing this distinction out to me and for providing other helpful comments and suggestions.

15. See Lisa Nakamura (1995), who argues that race persists on MOOs but is constructed differently from 'real life'.

16. For a discussion of these new developments, see Pavel Curtis and David A. Nichols, 'MUDS Grow Up: Social Viritual Reality in the Real World' (GREF 1).

17. On this issue see the important essay by Hans Ulrich Gumbrecht, 'A Farewell to Interpretation' (1994).

18. 'The Scholar's Rhizome: Networked Communication Issues' by Kathleen Burnett explores this issue with convincing logic (EREF 1).

19. Walter Benjamin: 'the distinction between author and public is about to lose its basic character. . . . At any moment the reader is ready to turn into a writer. . .' (1969: 232). See also Roland Barthes (1974) for the concept of readerly texts.

References

Barthes, Roland (1974) *S/Z* (trans. Richard Miller). New York: Hill and Wang.

Benjamin, Walter (1969) 'The Work of Art in the Age of Mechanical Reproduction', in *Illuminations* (trans. Harry Zohn). New York: Schocken Books. pp. 217–51.

Cherny, Lynn (forthcoming) 'Gender Differences in Text-Based Virtual Reality', *Proceedings of the Berkeley Conference on Women and Language*, April 1994.

EREF 1: Kburnett@gandalf.rutgers.edu. Burnett, Kathleen, 'The Scholar's Rhizome: Networked Communication Issues'.

Felski, Rita (1989) *Beyond Feminist Aesthetics: Feminist Literature and Social Change*. Cambridge, MA: Harvard University Press.

Fraser, Nancy (1989) *Unruly Practices*. Minneapolis: University of Minnesota Press.

Fraser, Nancy (1990) 'Rethinking the Public Sphere', *Social Text*, 25/6: 56–80.

GREF 1: ftp.parc.xerox.com in /pub/Moo/Papers. Curtis, Pavel and Nichols, David A., 'MUDs Grow Up: Social Virtual Reality in the Real World'.

GREF 2: Ftp.parc.xerox.com in /pub/Moo/Papers. Reid, Elizabeth, 'Cultural Formations in Text-Based Virtual Realities'. (Also available as 'Virtual Worlds: Culture and Imagination' in Steven G. Jones (ed.), *CyberSociety: Computer-Mediated Communication and Community*. Thousand Oaks, CA: Sage. pp. 164–83.

GREF 3: Ftp.parc.xerox.com in /pub/Moo/Papers. Reid, Elizabeth, 'Electropolis: Communication and Community on Internet Relay Chat'. (Also published in Intertek, 3 (3), Winter 1992: 7–15.)

GREF 4: Ftp.parc.xerox.com in /pub/Moo/Papers. Serpentelli, Jill, 'Conversational Structure and Personality Correlates of Electronic Communication'.

Gumbrecht, Hans Ulrich (1994) 'A Farewell to Interpretation', in Hans Ulrich Gumbrecht and K. Ludwig Pfeiffer (eds), *Materialities of Communication* (trans. William Whobrey). Stanford, CA: Stanford University Press. pp. 389–402.

Habermas, Jürgen (1989) *The Structural Transformation of the Public Sphere* (trans. Thomas Burger). Cambridge, MA: MIT Press.

Hartley, John (1992) *The Politics of Pictures: The Creation of the Public in the Age of Popular Media*. New York: Routledge.

Hayles, N. Katherine (1993) 'Virtual Bodies and Flickering Signifiers', *October*, 66, Fall: 69–91.

Heidegger, Martin (1962) *Being and Time* (trans. John Macquarrie and Edward Robinson). New York: Harper and Row.

Herring, Susan C. (1993) 'Gender and Democracy in Computer-Mediated Communication', *Electronic Journal of Communications*, 3 (2). (May be found at: info.curtin.edu.au in the directory Journals/curtin/arteduc/ejcrcc/Volume_03/Number_02/herring.txt.)

Ihde, Don (1990) *Technology and the Lifeworld: From Garden to Earth*. Bloomington, IN: Indiana University Press.

Kiesler, Sara, Siegel, Jane and McGuire, Timothy (1991) 'Social Psychological Aspects of Computer-Mediated Communication', in Charles Dunlop and Rob Kling (eds), *Computerization and Controversy*. New York: Academic Press. pp. 330–49.

Lacoue-Labarthe, Philippe (1990) *Heidegger, Art and Politics* (trans. Chris Turner). New York: Basil Blackwell.

Laclau, Ernesto (1990) *New Reflections on the Revolution of Our Time*. New York: Verso.

Landes, Joan (1988) *Women and the Public Sphere in the Age of the French Revolution*. Ithaca, NY: Cornell University Press.

Levy, Steven (1994) 'The Battle of the Clipper Chip', *New York Times Magazine*, 12 June. pp. 44–51, 60, 70.

Lyon, David (1994) *The Electronic Eye: The Rise of Surveillance Society*. Minneapolis, MN: University of Minnesota Press.

Lyotard, Jean-François (1984) *The Postmodern Condition: A Report on Knowledge* (trans. Geoff Bennington and Brian Massumi). Minneapolis, MN: University of Minnesota Press.

Nancy, Jean-Luc (1991) *The Inoperative Community* (ed. Peter Connor; trans. Peter Connor, Lisa Garbus, Michael Holland and Simona Sawhney). Minneapolis, MN: University of Minnesota Press.

Nakamura, Lisa (1995) 'Race in/for Cyberspace: Identity Tourism and Racial Passing on the Internet', *Works and Days*, 13 (1–2), Spring–Fall: 181–93.

Negt, Oskar and Kluge, Alexander (1993) *Public Sphere and Experience: Toward an Analysis of the Bourgeois and Proletarian Public Sphere* (trans. Peter Labanyi, Jamie Daniel and Assenko Oksiloff). Minneapolis, MN: University of Minnesota Press.

Perrolle, Judith (1991) 'Conversations and Trust in Computer Interfaces', in Charles Dunlop and Rob Kling (eds), *Computerization and Controversy*. New York: Academic Press. pp. 350–63.

Polly, Jean Armour and Cisler, Steve (1994) 'Community Networks on the Internet', *Library Journal*, 15 June: 22, 24.

Ryan, Marie-Laure (1994) 'Immersion vs. Interactivity: Virtual Reality and Literary Theory', *Postmodern Culture*, 5 (1), September.

Van Gelder, Lindsy (1991) 'The Strange Case of the Electronic Lover', in Charles Dunlop and Rob Kling (eds), *Computerization and Controversy*. New York: Academic Press. pp. 364–75.

Virilio, Paul (1993) 'The Third Interval: A Critical Transition', in Verena Conley (ed.), *Rethinking Technologies*. Minneapolis, MN: University of Minnesota Press. pp. 3–12.
Virilio, Paul (1994) *The Vision Machine* (trans. Julie Rose). Bloomington, IN: Indiana University Press.

GLOSSARY

Abstract communities

While all manifestations of COMMUNITY, from tribal kinship associations to the virtual communities of the internet, are formed through the ABSTRACTION and EXTENSION of social relations, the concept is used in its general sense to refer to those associations of people whose relationship to each other is characterized by a more abstract mode of integration than that found in face-to-face communities. The dominant form of abstract community of the twentieth century is the nation-state, but this is increasingly being reconstituted through processes of globalization, including the mobility enabled through space- and time-altering technologies (see James, 1996). In their computer-mediated forms, abstract assemblies, sometimes called virtual communities, enable an increase in interactivity between individuals while at the same time increasing the anonymity of each member of that community.

Abstraction

Abstraction is usually used to denote the drawing away from the 'concrete' and particularized referents of ideas. In the more comprehensive sense used here, a socio-material dimension is added to the ideational. It is not just words that can become more abstracted, but also social relations (see Sharp, 1985). For example, a commodity is more abstract than a gift, especially when the gift is given under conditions of reciprocity. Firstly, COMMODIFICATION involves an abstraction of value which allows unrelated objects to be assessed in terms of a medium of equivalence – namely money; and secondly, a commodity can be exchanged between persons whose embodied relationship to each other is irrelevant for the purposes of the exchange. Similarly, electronic communication is abstracted to the extent that the embodied particularities of persons are attenuated by the form of the interchange.

Agency-extended integration

According to the 'levels' argument (q.v. James and Carkeek, Chapter 6, this volume; see also Holmes, Chapter 1, this volume), when agency-extended integration becomes dominant, the form of social integration is abstracted beyond being based predominantly on the directly embodied and/or particularized mutuality of persons in social contact. It is at this level that persons act in the capacity of being the representatives, the agents or mediators, of institutions – including church and state, guild and corporation – and their various constituencies. It is only at this level that it makes sense to use abstract terms such as 'constituency' or 'citizenry'.

Agora

A term dating from post-Homeric Greece, the agora was a public space unregulated by the state or church, in which unfettered political expression existed. It was an open space, usually a market-place where goods and information were exchanged. Information was relayed either by word of mouth or by messages posted on walls. Throughout European modernity, the cosmopolitan coffee house predominates as the most significant continuation of a public agora. But also, as Mark Poster points out, 'the New England town hall, the village church, the coffee house, the tavern, the public square, a convenient barn, a union hall, a park, a factory lunchroom, and even a street corner' may perform agora-like functions (see p. 217, this volume). However, while these places might still exist, they no longer serve as organizing centres for political discussion and action. Instead, the agora either dissipates, or is replaced by simulation, as in the shopping mall, or CYBERSPACE.

Artificial reality

Artificial Reality can be distinguished from VIRTUAL REALITY in that it retains a reference to the REALITY that it is simulating. The plasticity of artificial environments is typically recognized as secondary to 'reality' because of its lack of comprehensiveness. Virtual reality (VR), on the other hand, tends to be far more convincing insofar as it works directly on the senses and achieves a comprehensiveness which erases, in experience, the possibility that it could be distinguished from a state of affairs that is more 'real'. Artificial Realities tend to be 'passive' rather than active simulations. As active simulation, VR generates a depthlessness of perception, shifting from matter-based (passive) to light-based mediations. An extreme example of this is the way stereopsis works in VR headgear. Stereopsis is simply the process of splitting the images received in each eye to give the impression of depth. What is significant with VR is that the goggles or helmet used contain light-emitting diodes which project patterns of light onto the eye instead of light being reflected on 'real' space-time objects, as with the cinema screen. In generalized experience, an architectural environment such as a shopping mall can be virtual when it comprehensively seals itself off from outside-references, becoming its own self-contained reality. The degree of comprehensiveness and self-referentiality of a given environment determines its quality as active or passive, as virtual or artificial.

Bandwidth (see Reality)

Biosociality

The distinction between biosociality and TECHNOSOCIALITY is a useful one in any discussion of CYBERSPACE and VIRTUAL REALITY. Biotechnologies are said to give rise to biosociality, Paul Rabinow's term for 'a new order for the production of life, nature and the body through biologically based technological interventions' (Escobar, 1994: 214).

Broadcast

Broadcast is an unequal relation between senders and receivers of messages, whereby the one (or the few) speaks to the many. In information societies, a distinction needs to be made between the form of this relationship and its various kinds of expression. For example, broadcast may be in real-time, as in a public address or elements of a news service, or in stored-time, as in the products of the culture industry generally. Broadcast nevertheless facilitates, as an agent of recognition, the objectivation (the making public) of a general will. While, at the technologically extended level, broadcast appears to be the means by which the one speaks to the many, it is also a means by which, culturally, the many speak to the many via the agent of a third party. The evening news or a game show might prescribe cultural values for audiences, but is also an agent for re-presenting the actually existing values which are adhered to by television audiences. Institutionally, political processes and practices have always centred themselves on broadcast as the dominant mode of integrating groups and reproducing norms. The mutual assembly of a mass, such as media consumers, a classroom or a readership, acts as an agent by which truth-claims are scrutinized by a speech community.

Cartesian space

'Cartesian space' is occasionally used to refer to the 'physical' or pre-virtual 'real' world. The fact that 'generalized space' has to be given a name is the first indication that it has been made problematic by the emergence of virtual or 'electronically reified' space. (See also REALITY, VIRTUAL SPACE.)

Commodification

The process whereby individuals and groups are separated from the means of satisfying their own subsistence or cultural needs. Presupposing a detailed division of labour, the satisfaction of these needs becomes increasingly tied to a market, in which the means of life or the means of acquiring a social identity are achieved by the purchase of commodities. In technologically extended societies two important forms of commodification are present – the selling of consciousness spans and the selling of abstract communication. BROADCAST commodification involves selling the concentration spans of audiences to advertisers. Here the individual consciousness of consumers, and the collective behaviour of a broadcast audience, becomes the commodity sold by television, radio or newspaper operators to advertisers. The broadcast form of commodification is only possible in so far as the mass audience is also atomized into individual consumers. The internet and other extended communicational forms enabling interaction exploit this atomization of compositional and geographic community by selling lost levels of social integration to consumers in the form of time-charging for human communication. So, while the economic analysis of the internet draws in issues of universal access, economic control and stratifications of information wealth and information poverty, its most significant feature can be found in the exploitation of a long-running historically produced human condition: the decline of less mediated and therefore less commodifiable forms of community.

Communication (conduit versus ritual view)

In writings about CYBERSPACE an emergent distinction is that between communication as information and communication as ritual. A ritual view of communication (see Jones, 1995: 12) argues that individuals exchange understandings not out of self-interest nor for the accumulation of information but from a need for communion, commonality and fraternity. In its technologically extended form, ritual communication does not need to draw its meaning from the face-to-face exchange that it partly emulates. When telecommuting becomes a primary mode of interaction, the communicational form (face-to-face) that it takes its reference from no longer remains the socialized norm. Virtual communities are ones which embrace these new forms of consumption based on very abstract but quite homogeneous and secure kinds of ritual. At the level of the personal, the individual's sense of place can be seen to achieve a new sense of security when control over 'simulated' environments becomes more attractive than negotiating inflexible institutional worlds.

Community

Technological changes to the possibilities of community in information societies have been accompanied by radical philosophical rethinking of the meaning of community and association (see Agamben, 1993; Nancy, 1991). The philosophical meaning of community has been traditionally dominated by the idea of communion and of association (as belonging). Ferdinand Tönnies (1887) distinguished between *Gemeinschaft*, relationships characterized by spontaneous intimacy and reciprocity, and *Gesellschaft*, social ties that are based on flecting impersonal contracts and the increased division of labour and individualization (Tönnies, 1974). In this century, theorizations of social integration have emphasized the consolidation of *Gesellschaft*. Such a conception can be found in theorizations of postmodernism such as that of Jean-François Lyotard, who suggests in *The Postmodern Condition* (1984) that 'Grand Narratives' which once held communities together have become difficult to sustain in computerized societies and have been replaced by the 'temporary contract' in 'professional, emotional, sexual, cultural, family and international domains, as well as in political affairs' (1984: 66). Recently, however, the work of Jean-Luc Nancy has suggested that community cannot be measured according to conformity or departure from communion or an essence. For Nancy, community is not made of or a relation of equivalence that could be constructed through a piece of technology, nor can it be consciously made by some collective realization that we are in danger of 'losing' it. The suggestion that the internet will save us from the loss of community is founded on a premise that community has to find an agent of commonality. This agent is usually transcendental and historically there have been many contenders for such a role: the Mind, God, the Fatherland, Leader, Internet . . . For Nancy, individual selves are unable to find community by looking to the glory of the infinite. Rather, it is in the realization of finitude that selves are able to experience being-in-common, an experience which is always negotiated and renegotiated in the neverending perception of difference between individual selves by which ethical responsibilities and forms of respect are arrived at. In this sense, according to Nancy, we can never lose community. (See also VIRTUAL COMMUNITY.)

Conscience collective

The nineteenth-century sociologist Émile Durkheim first used this term to denote the way in which a social group is bonded together via shared norms and values. Historically, Durkheim argues that social forms are typically evolving into weaker forms of integration, distinguished by an intense division of labour and a movement of 'individualization'. The emergence of CYBERSPACE results in a stronger form of social solidarity at a global level because of the connectivity that becomes possible, while at the same time there is a rapid disappearance of an easily discernible common culture. Cyberspace also presupposes highly individuated forms of social bonds, insofar as populations increasingly become atomized by workstation or homepage.

Cyberdemocracy

Cyberdemocracy refers to the possibility that the traditional AGORA, or political arena as expressed in CARTESIAN SPACE, can be extended and enhanced within CYBERSPACE (see Poster, Chapter 12, this volume). Poster asks whether or not the internet possesses enough stability for the ongoing recognition of members of internet communities and the stability of their own senses of self. In doing so, he partly echoes Steven Jones's concern in *CyberSociety* that '[i]n a near entirely ephemeral world, how does an individual, much less a community, maintain existence? (1995: 6). But also, for Poster the internet facilitates democratic forms of interaction insofar as it 'puts cultural acts, symbolizations in all forms, in the hands of all participants' and thus 'radically decentralizes the positions of speech, publishing, filmmaking, radio and television broadcasting, in short the apparatuses of cultural production' (Poster, this volume, p. 234).

Cyberspace

Sometimes used interchangeably with VIRTUAL REALITY, cyberspace specifically denotes the real and imagined space in which individuals meet in electronically mediated and simulated space. Unlike virtual reality, however, cyberspace does not rely on a deception of the senses to create the illusion of an integral realism as much as it requires the construction of computer-mediated worlds in which (predominantly text-based) communication can occur. Some commentators argue that 'the critical component of any definition of cyberspace is the element of community' because they maintain that a single person does not exist in cyberspace, but in virtual reality (see Benedikt, 1992).

Disembodied integration

Disembodied integration is the level at which the constraints of embodiment such as being in one place at one time can be overcome by means of technological EXTENSION: for example, by BROADCAST, computer networking or telphoning. This level is more abstract than the 'prior' levels of AGENCY-EXTENDED INTEGRATION or FACE-TO-FACE INTEGRATION. Each level of integration is implicated quite differently in the ways we live the relationship between nature and culture, and the ways we live our bodies and our 'presence' of others.

Extension

The concept of social extension provides a means of drawing attention to the different ways in which social interrelations can cross time and space. Radical social extension, for example through technologies such as electronic communication devices, involves the projection of the possibilities of human interchange far beyond the immediacy of face-to-face interaction. Technologies and techniques, from writing letters to setting up digitized computer banks, involve the storage of information far beyond the embodied time of a person's memory.

Face-to-face integration

Face-to-face integration is the level at which the modalities of being in the presence of others constitute the dominant ontological meaning of the relationship between people even when they are apart. The modalities of face-to-face integration include reciprocity, interdependence, long-term continuity of association, embodied mutuality and concrete otherness. Under such forms of interrelation, the absence of a significant other, even through death, does not annul his/her presence to us. Hence, it is important to emphasize here that integration is not used as a synonym for interaction. Just as it is possible for persons to be bound to each other at the level of face-to-face integration even when the self and the other are not engaged in immediate and embodied interaction, instances of interaction do not in themselves necessarily indicate anything about the dominant level of integration.

Individuation

The process whereby a population becomes atomized according to a technological network which privatizes participation in or access to a public realm. Taking the internet as a primary example, individuation may occur in public institutions, where a cellularization of information workers occurs according to the workstation; or in the domestic sphere, as a continuation of older forms of cellularization/nuclearization based on the telephone, the motor car or the urban household unit. Cellularization in the workplace is further intensified through surveillance and database technology. A key feature of both forms of relation is an attenuation of FACE-TO-FACE INTEGRATION and legal-rational forms of association. Individuation is most intense where a communication technology excludes embodied group participation. While television enables embodied as well as disembodied assembly, video games and computer-based technologies are consumed 'face-to-screen' according to a spatial scale which discourages embodied group interactions. (See also MONADIC INTERACTION.)

Interaction (see Face-to-face integration)

Information superhighway

The Information Superhighway is a metaphoric expression of the view that we are able to travel on the internet. The idea of the superhighway, as with the notion that CYBERSPACE is a space, can be contrasted with the view that it is actually a two-dimensional reality where electronic assemblies are programmed and conditioned by switching systems. The internet can thus be seen as a self-referential illusion of space and travel which has no frontier because its territory has always already been exhaustively mapped in advance. Each journey is a repetition, there is no undiscovered country, no exploration of discovering, only the recovering of what is already 'there', and no 'site' exists beyond its retrieval or invocational parameters (see Chesher, this volume).

Microworlds

The emergence of the technological management of physical (VR) and social (CYBERSPACE) perception encourages us to understand the 'phenomenological' frames of generalized experience. The way that virtual worlds transform everyday experience heightens an appreciation that different forms of consciousness are conditioned by goal-defined micro-worlds, where the perception of external reality is structured by the physical goals we try to achieve in it (see Cooper, this volume).

Monadic interaction

The term 'monad' has traditionally referred to the characteristic state whereby solitary individuals pursue their appetites and needs in complete isolation from one another (Leibniz). From the Greek *monas*, which prefixes 'monasticism' but is also closely related to 'monopoly' and 'mono-theism'. As Michael Heim states, the 'monad exists as an independent point of vital willpower, a surging drive to achieve its own goals according to its own internal dictates' (1993, 97). For the monad, the world does not extend beyond his/her own individual senses, immediate tastes and limited experiences. Characters stereotyped on the internet: the hacker, the net-surfer and the *flâneur*, are examples of monadic existence. The monad is seen from some standpoints to represent the antithesis of the societal condition. The presence of the monad in virtual environments affirms the continuing problems of defining the existence of virtual communities in such spaces.

Primitive virtual reality (proto-virtual reality)

Primitive virtual realities are technological environments which already presuppose a number of elements of VIRTUAL REALITY. Environments such as gymnasiums, freeways, shopping malls, flight simulators, and so on, are all instances of *sealed realities* which produce a standardization of experience and presuppose a very fixed relation between means and ends. Primitive virtual realities display a high degree of *instrumental control*, they are extremely good at instantly achieving narrowly defined ends (such as getting from A to B or shaping the body towards an ideal), but they generally tend to have little regard for aesthetic experience, for fostering face-to-face-interaction or for enabling utility outside of the ends for which they were constructed.

Reality

Very wide bandwidth. As Allucquere Rosanne Stone defines it, 'reality becomes redefined in the age of CYBERSPACE according to the amount of information that can be exchanged in unit time. "Reality" is wide bandwidth, because people who communicate face-to-face in real time use multiple modes simultaneously – speech, gestures, facial expression, and so on' (1992: 614–15). In defining reality this way, all other forms of information generation are placed on a hierarchical continuum, of approaching reality based on how closely their bandwidths approach that of reality. Email or computer conferencing is narrow bandwidth because it is confined to lines on a screen.

With the arrival of VIRTUAL REALITY, reality becomes redefined according to *scientific representation*. Typically a spectacular reversal or inversion occurs between History and Nature (as containers of technological development) and technological environments (as primary contexts for History and Nature). This means that ontologies taken for granted as unproblematic now must be renamed. Real time replaces time, because so much of our experience of time is mediated by information storage; and 'geographical location' replaces location, because we can now exist in cyberspace. The computer becomes our 'second self' because our first self is itself saturated by a digital anthropology. Perhaps the most outstanding example of the problematization of reality in the era of cyberspace is the case of Biosphere 2, the artificially constructed habitat near Oracle in the Arizona Desert. It is an enclosure which is laid out on three hectares of concrete slab and stainless steel to prevent any seepage to or from the earth and which supports five varieties of metal and glass domes called 'biomes'. These biomes, which are physically sealed but 'energetically and informationally open', support a tropical rainforest, savannah, marsh, marine and desert environments. Not only does this structure eminently qualify as a VIRTUAL SPACE in the way it physically displaces nature and culture, but its name is its most interesting feature. In naming itself Biosphere 2, the earth becomes Biosphere 1. The earth retains its identity as original biological environment, but is subordinated to Biosphere 2 insofar as it must now take its name from the latter.

Reciprocity (See Face-to-face integration)

Simulation (See Artificial Reality and Virtual Reality)

Space

An individual person's conception of space is defined from at least two related elements. The first element of spatial definition is frequently phenomenological – that is, readings derived from data collected by the senses and collated and analysed by the mind. However, in the process of collation and analysis the mind expands the broad spatial definition provided by the senses with culturally preconditioned data. This second aspect of spatial definition is related to the poetics of the space. It is formed by imagination and informed by previous experience and imperfect memory. Gaston Bachelard has suggested that whenever an individual experiences a space s/he combines the data derived from the senses (sight, smell, hearing, and so on) with his/her own expectations and memories of previous similar spaces. However, while the phenomenological reading of space will often have temporary precedence over the imaginary during the course of the experience, once it has passed the imaginary slowly begins to overwrite the phenomenological. In terms of virtuality, the phenomenological experience of space is directly proportional to the limits of bandwidth while the imaginary or abstracted experience of space initially acts as a bandwidth amplifier. After the direct stimulation of the senses has ceased the bandwidth amplifier continues to function, producing powerful and distorted echoes of the experience. This bandwidth amplifier is controlled by past experience. For this reason, the experience of virtual environments will necessarily always undergo bandwidth amplification of the magnitude of real-world experience, until such a time that a person may derive all his/her life's memories entirely from the experience of VIRTUAL SPACE. While space may be described by using geometry, a space that has been experienced transcends geometric description forever.

Subject

A subject is an identity within a communication process, or an identity subjected to a relation of power. In cultural and political theory as well as in CYBERSPACE, the subject is not the same as the individual. An individual is tied to the same body but may be many subjects at once, and in cyberspace this fact is made particularly salient. In cyberspace, as in pre-virtual social life, we take on many different 'subject-positions' whereby identity is tied to our location within a discourse, a communication process or an ideology. Some commentators on cyberspace argue that we do not merely change our intellectually mediated sense of identity in virtual worlds but also the way in which we experience our bodies, which is to change not only what it means to be a subject but what it means to be an individual as well.

Technosociality

Technosociality refers to 'the state in which technology and nature are the same thing, as when one inhabits a network as a social environment'

(Stone, 1992: 610). Technosociality is a more general state of being than BIOSOCIALITY, which refers to new ways of being human deriving from biologically based technological innovations. Technosociality is a term which seeks to overcome the problematic oppositions between individual, technology and 'society'. The way in which these terms are opposed to each other promotes the view that they are somehow complete and intransitive entities which interact. The concept of technosociality begins to reconceptualize the fact that ways of realizing identity are a priori mediated and individuality is formed simultaneously with the technosocial relationships which make it possible. To appreciate the concept of technosociality, extended communication technologies and agencies cannot be viewed as instruments serving pre-given bodies and communities; they are instead contexts which bring about new ways of being, new chains of values and new sensibilities about time, space and the events of culture. For this reason, the separations between the concepts of individual, technology and society are dissolved.

Virtual community

For Howard Rheingold, virtual communities 'are social aggregations that emerge from the Net when enough people' interact for 'long enough, with sufficient human feeling, to form webs of personal relationships in cyberspace' (1994: 5). Each and every discussion group is like a small country town; each collection of discussion groups is a city, with a highway or infobahn which 'opens onto the blooming, buzzing confusion of the Net, an entity with properties altogether different from the virtual villages of a few years ago' (1994: 10). Intriguingly, Rheingold continually associates his definition of virtual community with some form of interaction in the real world. For example, when describing his own virtual community, the WELL, he constantly reiterates the need for regular, real-world contact between members for baseball games, picnics and social gatherings. In all of Rheingold's writings on virtual communities he implicitly characterizes a virtual community as an extension of a more conventional community in the real world.

Avital Ronell in 'A Disappearance of Community' has suggested that too often the interactions which are occurring in VIRTUAL SPACE are simply extensions of models of interaction from the margins of conventional urban space. Virtual spaces are frequently simulations of 'real-world' office buildings, museums, shopping malls and theme parks, none of which is conducive to the formation of community. Such spaces encourage modes of interaction which are implicitly monadic (see MONADIC INTERACTION) and for this reason Ronell suggests that '[v]irtual reality, artificial reality, dataspace, or cyberspace are inscriptions of a desire whose principal symptom can be seen as the absence of community' (1996: 119). The concept of a virtual community, like the concept of utopia, is thereby seen as inherently flawed if it is based on existing modes of social interaction occurring in the margins of conventional urban space. Cameron Bailey contends that the vision of the internet as ideal democratic community in the mould of Parisian café society, the village green or the Greek AGORA 'contains its own ideological dead weight. . . . Like the democracy of the ancient Greeks, today's digital democracy is reserved for an elite with the means to enjoy it' (1996: 31).

Virtual convergence

Globally, the application of virtual mapping techniques, the standardization of architectural styles and the continuous wiring up of urban landscapes for internet, cable television and mobile telephone networks tend to flatten out the visual and cultural differences between the urban settings of information societies. The predictability that the individual experiences with personal information technologies increasingly becomes matched by the predictability of urban environments. Where our identity in CYBERSPACE can become equated with the cursor, our experience of self in urban space increasingly becomes programmed according to spatial logics which cross-reference each other and converge in physical, metaphorical and cultural ways.

Virtual reality

Often used interchangeably with CYBERSPACE, virtual reality is now more frequently confined to the technological management of the body's senses by way of cybernetic clothing or bioapparatuses. As Featherstone and Burrows define it, virtual reality is a 'computer-generated visual, audible and tactile multi-media experience' in which various bioapparatuses (headphones, eyephones, datagloves and datasuits) 'surround the human body with artificial sensorium of sight, sound and touch' (1995: 6).

Virtual space

Spaces which are both simulated and highly temporal may be referred to as virtual spaces. One of the essences of virtual spaces is that they are phenomenological – they are based on perception. If the senses are stimulated in such a way that the mind reads the collective experience as a distinct spatial entity, then that place is rendered phenomenologically present. If the senses have been manipulated by some device, technological or otherwise, to accept a simulation of spatial experience as commensurate to REALITY, then that space could be described as virtual. One of the differences between 'real space' and virtual space is the extent of the temporality of experience in each. The Cartesian experiential space of the 'real world' is temporal because it is limited to a particular time-frame. For example, a house may exist at a given moment in time, and may be experienced through direct sensorial perception, but if the house is demolished the spatial identity is erased. Therefore, 'real space' is temporal as it is based on a time-frame relative to the perceptions of the individual. However, virtual space exhibits a higher degree of temporal instability. The time-frame of experience in virtual space is not necessarily relative to the individual's. The perception of a distinct virtual spatial form is derived from secondary sensorial stimulation, which means that not only is the exact identity of the space dramatically different from one person to another, but the same virtual space may be perceived differently each time it is experienced. This is only partially true for 'real' or Cartesian space. For this reason virtual spaces are highly temporal simulations.

Virtual urban futures

The concept of virtual urban futures refers to the idea that the rise in virtual technologies is a natural extension of the way in which twentieth-century urban communal spaces have already developed. Office buildings, shopping malls and museums are often viewed as spaces which fill the margins of conventional urban, public space. Such marginal zones may be characterized by the way in which they encourage interaction which is technologically mediated. For example, the office building model of interaction is promulgated on the concept of individual, monadic segregation within a well-defined spatial hierarchy. Such a spatial structure encourages the individual to work with displaced notions of time and space (information technology, paper-work, voice-mail, electronic transactions, and so forth) until they start to operate in an environment which may only be described as virtual. The presence of these boundary spaces promotes the idea that the postmodern cityscape is already predicated more on systems of language than on architecture and more on technological mediation than on direct sensorial experience. This understanding leads to the realization that the marginal areas of 'real' urban space already constitute virtual environments, thereby suggesting a common future for urban space in the real and the virtual worlds.

Note

Thanks to Michael J. Ostwald and Paul James for assistance with this glossary.

References

Agamben, Georgio (1993) *The Coming Community* (trans. Michael Hardt). Minneapolis, MN: University of Minnesota Press.
Bailey, Cameron (1996) 'Virtual Skin: Articulating Race in Cyberspace', in Mary Anne Moser

and Douglas MacLeod (eds), *Immersed in Technology: Art and Virtual Environments*. Cambridge, MA: MIT Press. pp. 29–49.

Benedikt, Michael (ed.) (1992) *Cyberspace: First Steps*. Cambridge, MA: MIT Press.

Escobar, Arturo (1994) 'Welcome to Cyberia', *Current Anthropology*, 35(3): June: 211–31.

Featherstone, Mike and Burrows, Roger (1995) 'Cultures of Technological Embodiment: An Introduction', in Mike Featherstone and Roger Burrows (eds), *Cyberspace, Cyberbodies, Cyberpunk*. London: Sage. pp. 1–19.

Heim, Michael. (1993) *The Metaphysics of Virtual Reality*. Oxford: Oxford University Press.

James, Paul (1996) *Nation Formation: Towards a Theory of Abstract Community*. London: Sage.

Jones, Stephen G. (ed.) (1995) 'Introduction: From Where to Who Knows?', in Stephen G. Jones (ed.), *CyberSociety: Computer-Mediated Communication and Community*. London: Sage. pp. 1–9.

Lyotard, Jean-François (1984) *The Postmodern Condition: A Report on Knowledge* (trans. Geoff Bennington and Brian Massumi). Minneapolis, MN: University of Minnesota Press.

Nancy, Jean-Luc (1991) *The Inoperative Community* (ed. Peter Connor; trans. Peter Connor, Lisa Garbus, Michael Holland, Simona Sawhney). Minneapolis, MN: University of Minnesota Press.

Poster, Mark (1995) *The Second Media Age*. Cambridge: Polity.

Rheingold, Howard (1993) *The Virtual Community: Homesteading on the Electronic Frontier*. Reading, MA: Addison-Wesley.

Ronell, Avital. (1996) 'A Disappearance of Community', in Mary Anne Moser and Douglas MacLeod (eds), *Immersed in Technology: Art and Virtual Environments*. Cambridge, MA: MIT Press. pp. 119–27.

Sharp, Geoff (1985) 'Constitutive Abstraction and Social Practice', *Arena*, 70: 48–82.

Stone, Allucquere Rosanne (1992) 'Virtual Systems', in Jonathan Crary and Sanford Kwinter (eds), *Incorporations: Zone 6*. New York: Zone. pp. 609–21.

Tönnies, Ferdinand (1974) *Community and Association* (trans. Charles P. Loomis). London: Routledge and Kegan Paul.

INDEX